Disaster Mental Health Community Planning

A Manual for Trauma-Informed Collaboration

Robert W. Schmidt and Sharon L. Cohen

Routledge
Taylor & Francis Group

NEW YORK AND LONDON

First published 2020
by Routledge
52 Vanderbilt Avenue, New York, NY 10017

and by Routledge
2 Park Square, Milton Park, Abingdon, Oxon, OX14 4RN

Routledge is an imprint of the Taylor & Francis Group, an informa business

Library of Congress Cataloging-in-Publication Data
Names: Schmidt, Robert W. (Counselor), author.
Title: Disaster mental health community planning : a manual for trauma-
   informed collaboration / Robert W. Schmidt and Sharon L. Cohen.
Description: New York, NY : Routledge, 2020. | Includes bibliographical
   references and index.
Identifiers: LCCN 2019050367 (print) | LCCN 2019050368 (ebook) |
   ISBN 9780367247270 (hbk) | ISBN 9780367247263 (pbk) |
   ISBN 9780429285134 (ebk)
Subjects: LCSH: Disaster relief—Handbooks, manuals, etc. | Emergency
   management—Handbooks, manuals, etc. | Mental health—Handbooks,
   manuals, etc.
Classification: LCC HV553 .S36 2020 (print) | LCC HV553 (ebook) |
   DDC 362.2—dc23
LC record available at https://lccn.loc.gov/2019050367
LC ebook record available at https://lccn.loc.gov/2019050368

ISBN: 978-0-367-24727-0 (hbk)
ISBN: 978-0-367-24726-3 (pbk)
ISBN: 978-0-429-28513-4 (ebk)

Typeset in Palatino
by Apex CoVantage, LLC

"Mental health in the U.S. is unfortunately often overlooked or ignored in all aspects of our society. Case in point, many people who are traumatized from a disaster do not receive the treatment needed for long-term care. I hope that communities will use the information in this book to develop a plan specifically aimed to help the needs of these distraught survivors."

—**John T. Broderick, Jr.,** former chief justice, New Hampshire Supreme Court

"Collaboratives, such as those mentioned in this book and the one we established in California, provide an important way to provide immediate and long-term mental health needs to natural disaster survivors. We recommend such collaborations highly."

—**Debbie Mason, Past CEO**, Healthcare Foundation of Northern Sonoma County

"Congratulations to the authors for distilling the very complex topic of disaster mental health and providing all that is needed to develop a plan for effective preparedness and response after a serious incident."

—**Cindy Ehlers**, MS, LPC and executive vice president, clinical operations, Trillium Health Resources

Disaster Mental Health Community Planning

Disaster Mental Health Community Planning is a step-by-step guide to developing mental health disaster plans, assisting communities to act on long-term resilience and recovery.

As disasters continue to increase in severity and number, with 16% of survivors identified as potential PTSD victims if they don't promptly receive care, this book is a critical read. Chapters outline how to prepare, develop, and implement a trauma-informed collaborative process that prioritizes lasting emotional wellbeing along with survivors' short-term needs. The manual demonstrates how to form this partnership through effective communication, assess those individuals at greatest risk of distress, and deliver trauma-specific treatment. Readers will appreciate the book's practical, user-friendly approach, including case studies, checklists, and follow-up questions to better define goals. Cutting-edge treatment interventions are included, along with basic information on trauma's impact on the brain and the types and effects of human-caused and natural disasters to help readers make sound planning decisions.

Accessible to mental-health providers, community leaders, organizations, and individuals alike, *Disaster Mental Health Community Planning* is a Road Map for anyone interested in delivering a trauma-informed mental health supplement to their community's medical disaster preparedness and response plan.

Robert W. Schmidt, LPC, is a licensed professional counselor who lives and practices in Sandy Hook, Connecticut. He was given the ACA Samuel T. Gladding Unsung Hero Award for his work in Sandy Hook.

Sharon L. Cohen, MA Com, is a corporate/nonprofit communication and collaboration specialist with a background in the mental health field.

To all those who face the emotional trauma of
natural- and human-caused disasters

Contents

Foreword

As many people of my generation do, I clearly remember where I was and what I was doing when President John F. Kennedy was assassinated. The same thing happened on December 14, 2012, when a mentally ill man shot and killed his mother, then drove to Sandy Hook Elementary School to shoot and kill 20 first-grade children and six educators. I remember every detail of that day and what happened in the following days.

It was very personal for me and for my wife Josie. She was a substitute teacher at Sandy Hook Elementary before receiving a permanent position in another Newtown school. She was involved with the PTA when our daughter Lauren attended Sandy Hook School in the 1980s. I knew the school psychologist who lost her life that day, and Josie knew the principal.

Since then, I have learned that just about everyone in our town felt the same way as Josie and I did. Newtown includes about 27,500 residents. Geographically, the Sandy Hook section makes up about half of the town. The tragedy we refer to as 12/14 had a "ripple effect" in the community, and everyone was touched by this unimaginable event.

We all had connections to Sandy Hook Elementary School. Life would never be the same for the families who lost loved ones and for the families who had children who were in the room but managed to survive by hiding or running. Anyone closely connected to the children, the educators, or their families were devastated. The police officers, firefighters, emergency medical staff, and clergy were all deeply affected; bus drivers, neighbors, friends, coaches, and babysitters were emotionally overwhelmed. Sadly, the entire community was affected, and a great many were traumatized.

In Newtown, we learned a great deal about effective treatments for trauma and maintaining wellness, as well as that the sooner people's needs are recognized and care provided, the greater their ability to resume healthy lives. When a community does not have a plan on how to quickly and effectively provide psychological support, problems will be exacerbated and last much longer.

When our tragedy occurred, my first thought as a licensed professional counselor with a private practice in Sandy Hook was, "What can I do to help?" Not having any specific training in trauma, I asked my friend and work associate Deb Del Vecchio-Scully for advice. Deb is a trauma specialist who, at the time, was Connecticut Counseling Association Executive Director. She explained that unless therapists are trauma informed, they should not work with trauma victims: They can do more harm than good if unaware of how trauma affects people and if they have not mastered some trauma-specific treatments. I decided to learn as much as I could about trauma and the effective techniques that would help individuals. When the community received a grant to create the Newtown Recovery Center, Deb took the trauma specialist position. She now continues to help many other communities that have experienced tragedies and invited me to join her in Parkland, Florida, to teach the staff how to use Emotional Freedom Techniques (EFT)/Tapping for stress management.

Two days after the Sandy Hook tragedy, Ray Keegan, president of the Newtown Lions Club, called an emergency meeting to determine how the club could be of help. Knowing that many people would need counseling and insurance plans never cover the full cost of therapy, I proposed we start a fund to cover people's out-of-pocket counseling costs. The members all agreed, and we formed the Newtown Lions Sandy Hook Elementary Fund. But who would vet the claims? It would have to be someone who understood those forms, was in the mental health field, and could maintain confidentiality. The members looked at me, and I knew in a second this was how I could use my skills to really make a difference for people. Then they elected me chair of the committee.

I contacted the acting Sandy Hook Elementary School principal and emailed a flier to explain to teachers how they would be reimbursed for mental health needs. Fellow Lion George Arfaras and I went to the Sandy Hook Firehouse, the Newtown Police Department, the Newtown Volunteer Ambulance Corps and the Connecticut State Police barracks to provide similar information. Lion Walt Schweikert wrote letters to all Lions Clubs in the U.S. and asked for donations to the fund. In a few weeks, we had raised $250,000. The donations continued to pour in, and we reached over $400,000. Lion Ray Keegan wrote a personal thank you letter to every person or organization that donated. After I vetted a claim, Lion Kevin Corey wrote and mailed a reimbursement check. I was never more proud to be a member of the Lions Club.

I thought we would be set for a few years, but unfortunately, I learned that all the money the Lions raised was only a drop in the bucket. The need for mental health services has been overwhelming. That is one of the points of this manual: To help people understand the emotional impact of a tragic event. Too often, we either do not address mental health concerns or only look at short-term responses. Health insurance companies provide considerably more funding for medical needs than for mental health, yet any therapist will agree there is a link between mental health and physical health.

When Sharon L. Cohen approached me about partnering on this manual, I immediately said yes. Since the Sandy Hook tragedy, we have learned a great deal about how people are affected by a tragedy and how to meet their needs. We may have made some mistakes along the way, but we discovered that many people who were going through similar tragedies were willing to help us. So many good people came to our community to help: Frank DeAngelis, principal of Columbine High School, and several former students; a group of families from Nickels Mines, Pennsylvania, who experienced their own tragedy; and survivors of the Virginia Tech shooting. Specialist Bruce Perry, MD, taught us about how trauma affects the brain. I met Lori Leyden, PhD, an international trauma specialist, who was responsible for my becoming trained in the Emotional Freedom Techniques; this gave me the skills needed to treat trauma patients. Lori is an amazing person, and we remain close friends today. I also had the privilege of being trained in Brainspotting by its creator, David Grand, PhD. This book is my opportunity to pay it forward to all the people who helped me and my community.

This manual is a must read for any individual who holds a position in local government. It should also be an essential part of any master's-level course on trauma and an insightful guide for all therapists. It is critical for any community members who want to participate in a beneficial collaborative process. There are now so many valuable resources and organizations for mental health and wellness in Newtown. By sharing this knowledge with other communities and therapists "before" something happens, the information in this manual will be even more invaluable.

In addition to what has been learned through Sandy Hook, Sharon has spent countless hours researching other recent traumatic events and natural disasters and how each affected the emotional wellbeing of their communities. She understands their struggles, their experiences, and effective lessons learned.

I continually hope and pray tragedies like 12/14 will never happen again. Yet just about every time I turn on the news, I learn about another event that will dramatically affect the mental health of so many individuals and traumatize many others. All towns and cities must be prepared to provide for the emotional needs of their communities when the unspeakable happens.

By not preparing for a potential disaster, it will be much harder to manage once it occurs because many people will be traumatized and not function well. This manual will still be an excellent guidebook for a community after a tragic event, but why wait?

Robert W. Schmidt, MS, LPC

Preface

Mental health, particularly trauma, has long been a personal and professional concern of mine. After the Sandy Hook Elementary School shooting in my Newtown, Connecticut, community on December 14, 2012, I was compelled to act. I saw firsthand that our town was not prepared to handle the psychological impact of this event on so many residents of all ages and backgrounds. A pre-established disaster mental health intervention plan would have been extremely helpful and reduced much of the immediate emotional pain.

Newtown's trauma continues. Over six years later, numerous individuals are still seeing therapists, requesting mental health services for the first time, or continuing to struggle without seeking help. Like other communities, we recognize that certain people are more resilient after a disaster than others. Some individuals have initial problems and then return to their earlier lives. Other individuals suffer from trauma for months or years and/or face recurring symptoms: Several Columbine High School victims had nightmares after the Sandy Hook disaster, although their own shooting occurred in 1999.

I was working in my home office when the Sandy Hook shooting occurred. As I watched the TV coverage, it was extremely difficult to admit this was happening just 20 minutes away—a feeling people in New York City shared on 9/11. Both my sons previously attended summer programs at this elementary school, and I knew many residents whose family members were enrolled or worked there. After the Newtown tragedy, a large number of organizations were either created or expanded to provide needed services to the community. Several parents also formed supportive nonprofit organizations to honor their children. I spoke with many residents who sought therapy but did not know about available mental healthcare providers. To disseminate needed information as well as to support the Newtown Lions Club Fund for counseling services, I completed a reference manual on all pertinent organizations. This publication is now on its third printing and online through the Newtown Center for Support and Wellness. Communication after a catastrophe continues to be a vital service for our residents, especially since the community will be healing for many years to come.

A disaster like a shooting or earthquake lasts for a very short time, but the town changes forever. After our calamity, Newtown was bombarded by the media, phone calls, visitors, and a tidal wave of gifts and mementos. At first, residents rallied together, but as is the case in many such situations, this bonding dissolved over time. Unprepared for such a life-changing event, Newtown leaders called places such as Columbine High School and Virginia Polytechnic Institute for their input and responded to each challenge as best they could. Now, Newtown mental health professionals travel to other disaster areas to help these communities with their own challenges. All communities are vulnerable to a calamity of some kind. They need to be prepared to immediately help the traumatized. They also need to learn from their own experiences and those of other American towns and cities.

Bob Schmidt and I are publishing this community-based book for several reasons. First and foremost, it is due time that mental health assumes equal status with physical care and no longer plays a stepchild role. According to the National Alliance on Mental Illness (www.nami.org), one of five American adults experiences mental illness each year, and every catastrophic event increases this number to some extent. Second, communities must therefore develop plans that specifically focus on mental health needs. Nearly all American towns and cities have developed some form of disaster/emergency plan for medical care. Yet very few have a strategy in place for psychological interventions; they rely on state and/or federal agencies and nonprofit emergency response organizations. Or they gladly welcome nearby mental health providers to assist with their efforts. Many problems arise in such situations. For example, it may take several days for national organizations to reach the disaster area, leaving a community on its own and unprepared. Or volunteer therapists may mean well but may not have the necessary training and cause long-term harm. We want communities to collaborate and create an action plan that responds to their diverse population's mental health needs and long-term wellness. Mental health must be on equal footing with physical wellbeing.

Third, each type of disaster and the community in which it occurs creates different needs and challenges. The psychological support required immediately following a shooting varies from that after a hurricane; an urban area is impacted differently than a rural one. Every community also differs in the makeup of its vulnerable or at-risk population, whose needs must be clearly addressed or suffer the consequences. Lastly, neuroscientists are learning a great deal more about how the brain functions and the way this all-important part of the body is impacted by trauma. Although Trauma-Focused Cognitive Behavior Therapy (TF-CBT) has been the traditional means of treatment, other approaches of trauma-informed care are proving just as, if not more, successful. We must continually learn more about the traumatic impact of calamities since they often cause Post-Traumatic Stress Disorder (PTSD). Whether a community is hit with a natural disaster or human-caused act of violence or terrorism, most likely those closest to the event's center will suffer psychological trauma.

A community with many traumatized residents does not function well in the short or long term. Trauma impacts the residents' ability to work and provide for and relate to their families and friends. Those who do not receive proper help often try to self-medicate with alcohol or drugs. If those impacted can be identified and directed to areas where they can receive care in a timely manner, their chances for recovery are significantly better. Survivors must have what is called "trauma-informed care," which involves a broad understanding of common reactions to a stressful event by the brain and, in turn, the rest of the body. Only therapists who are trained in diagnosis and treatment of trauma and who continually acquire the latest information and insights into the best care possible should be on call.

No community wants to believe its residents may face a disaster or several duplicate disasters as those occurring in tornado-, forest fire–, and hurricane-prone areas. After Newtown, I felt compelled to create a Road Map that relies on the expertise and experience of mental health providers, social service organizations, academic researchers, emergency response teams, and valued residents for potential psychological intervention. For this manual, I turned in part to the guidance of the Society for Community Research and Action (SCRA), which published the report *How to Help Your Community Recover from Disaster: A Manual for Planning and Action* in 2010. The psychological knowledge and principles on disaster recovery by SCRA members presented a valuable springboard for my efforts.

I also spoke with and learned from research conducted by such psychological catastrophe trailblazers as Kai Erikson, PhD, and Dori Laub, MD. Erikson is William R. Kenan, Jr. Professor Emeritus of Sociology and American Studies at Yale University, author of the 1976 book *Everything in Its Path: Destruction of Community in the Buffalo Creek Flood*, and son of development psychologist Erik Erikson. Laub, who was Clinical Professor of Psychiatry at the Yale University School of Medicine and a psychoanalyst, authored numerous publications on victims of massive psychic trauma and their children. His experience as a holocaust survivor while a young boy led to a passion for helping others similarly impacted. In 1979, he interviewed four survivors and recognized the incredible impact of these stories on the interviewees and those listening to them. Laub then recorded and preserved thousands of witness testimonies.

I am very honored to have the expertise and guidance of co-author Bob Schmidt, a licensed professional counselor from Sandy Hook, Connecticut, with decades of experience in counseling, workshop training, presentations, and education in the counseling field. Schmidt is one of the first counselors trained in some of the new trauma-informed, brain-based endeavors. These have been very beneficial to his patients. In addition to counseling, Schmidt is two-time past president of the Connecticut Counseling Association and past president of the Connecticut Association for Counselor Education and Supervision. He received the American Counseling Association National Recognition Award and Samuel T. Gladding Unsung Hero Award. He was named Adjunct Professor of the Year in 2013 while at Fairfield University and was past chair of the North Atlantic Region of the American Counseling Association. He has been very much involved with the Newtown Lions Club's fund for communitywide mental health services and plays an integral role in the community's psychological wellbeing.

Jean Hill, SCRA executive director, and Brad Olson, associate professor of psychology at National Louis University, were critical assets. Hill, who significantly encouraged my work on this project, has focused her research efforts on displaced adolescents and school-based prevention and promotion programs and led a communitywide Communities That Care program. Olson is a passionate advocate for the psychologist's role as a promoter of human rights, founder of the Coalition for an Ethical Psychology, and recipient of the Outstanding Service Award from the American Psychological Association, Society for the Study of Peace, Conflict, and Violence Division.

My interviews with numerous mental health providers here in Newtown as well as others nationwide, who have experienced a wide range of disasters, have been personally rewarding and informative. These individuals clearly recognize the increasing need for disaster preparedness. I also personally empathize with the pain of the mentally ill and want to contribute to their healing process.

My heart aches and tears flow when I see the personal anguish of the victims of horrible devastation and terror, such as the teenagers in Parkland, Florida, who cried after scores died in their school; the Puerto Ricans who will never be the same after such hurricane destruction; the entire town of Paradise, California, that was destroyed; and the Tree of Life congregants, including a Holocaust survivor, who were slaughtered.

As I write this, other calamities are continually occurring, particularly with worsening climate change and mass shooting trends. By taking a preventative approach through trauma-informed collaborative planning, the harrowing aftereffects will hopefully be reduced, and people will be healed.

Sharon L. Cohen, MA Com

Acknowledgements

"Cheers" to all the editorial, design, and marketing people at Routledge/Taylor & Francis Group who aptly combined our suggestions with their recommendations. Our sincere gratitude to Anna Moore, whose advice and guidance shaped a difficult topic into a cohesive and useful form. A much heartfelt "Thank you" goes out to Ellie Duncan, who cheerfully held our hands and ably guided us through the book publishing process. The support from both of you was invaluable.

Bob & Sharon

I could not have done this project without the help of my amazing wife, Josie. Thank you for your editing, support, patience, and letting me off the hook from doing the dishes to work on the book. You are the best, and I am so blessed!

I am so lucky to have had the help and guidance of my good friend Deb Del Vecchio-Scully, LPC. You opened my eyes to the importance of becoming a trauma-informed counselor, and it literally changed my life.

My good friend and colleague: you are always there for me, whether it's to review the book or come to one of our gigs. Thank you, Pam Anderson!

I am so grateful to have had the pleasure of working with you, Jennifer Barahona. You gave so much of your time and your heart to help Newtown.

I want to thank Stephanie Cinque for all she did and continues to do to help our community heal. You are an inspiration to us all.

To Lori Leyden, PhD, who was my guru, my teacher, and my mentor. I am blessed to call you my friend.

Thank you to Leon Kamerman Schmidt for your excellent artwork.

Shannon Desilets, I appreciate your help with the book and all the time you spent working at the Resiliency Center to help the members of our community.

Bob

This manual truly went from concept to reality when I found the cutting-edge 2010 report "How to Help Your Community Recover from Disaster: A Manual for Planning and Action" from the Society of Community Research and Action (SCRA). Years before the increase in mass shootings and natural disasters from climate change, SCRA recognized the growing psychological impact of such events. I greatly appreciate Jean Hill, Brad Olson, and other SCRA members for the mini-grant that kicked off this project to update SCRA's initial project.

I was greatly motivated by conversations with sociologist Kai Erikson (son of the development psychologist), who in his late 80s has continued to lecture on the social consequences of catastrophes. He calls disasters like the BP oil spill a "new species of trouble" that "scare human beings in new special ways . . . and elicit an uncanny fear in us." Meeting Dori Laub (who recently passed away)— the first to interview victims of massive psychological trauma, as he was in the Holocaust—provided yet another indication of how long such traumatic events plague survivors and their children. I'm also inspired by John T. Broderick, Jr., former chief justice of the New Hampshire Supreme Court, who in his early 70s travels to schools throughout New England to encourage students to talk about mental health and not be afraid to seek needed help.

"Ditto" to Bob's "thank you" to Newtown professionals, who have done so much for our community since the Sandy Hook tragedy, as well as to Josie, with her keen proofreading eye and much-needed nourishment during all-day editorial sessions. Additional Newtown parties providing help and support include Jennifer Crane, Pat Llodra, Gene Rosen, Interfaith Association members, C.H. Booth Library staff, Dan Rosenthal, and many others involved with post-12/14 efforts. Personal Coach Millie Grenough and Social Communication Specialist Catherine Hogan showed me the possibility of starting new initiatives later in life; Jim Siemianowski, Connecticut Department of Mental Health and Addiction Services, provided valuable insights into disaster behavioral health initiatives; and Maria Mojica illustrated the power of collaboration.

I applaud the individuals noted in our manual's case studies for their tireless efforts on behalf of vulnerable populations, including the mentally ill. Their commitment offers another reminder of the goodness of humanity.

My hugs to dear friends and close family members, who continually ignore my book mantras and promise to buy hundreds of copies. An embrace also goes to my co-author, Bob, whose tranquility acts as the Zen of ocean waves.

Most important, love to my husband and best friend, Jean-Henry Mathurin, who always encourages the best in me and keeps my sights on the final goal.

Sharon

Glossary and Abbreviations

Acute Stress Disorder (ASD)   Trauma diagnosis for up to one month after a disaster. If the symptoms continue, in most cases the diagnosis is changed to Post-Traumatic Stress Disorder (PTSD).

Agenda   Formal list of items to be discussed or completed during a meeting or negotiation.

American Medical Association (AMA).

American Psychiatric Association (APA)   Largest psychiatric organization in the world. The association publishes the *Diagnostic and Statistical Manual of Mental Disorders (DSM)*.

American Psychological Association (APA)   Largest scientific and professional organization of psychologists in the United States, with over 118,000 members including scientists, educators, clinicians, consultants, and students. (In all cases in this guide, when the copy reads "APA approved," it refers to the American Psychological Association.)

Anecdotal research   Information based on personal experiences.

Anxiety   Mental state and intense emotional response characterized by a feeling of preoccupation and fear, more or less intense and enduring. It can be connected to a specific internal or external stimulus.

Aromatherapy   Using essential oils in order to help a person feel calm and relaxed. Oils may be inhaled, placed on the skin, or used in a diffuser.

At-Risk/Vulnerable Population   People who may be more susceptible to developing mental health issues after a traumatic incident.

BioLateral Sound Healing (BLS)   Music or nature sounds that move gently back and forth from the left side to the right side of headphones to bring both sides of the brain into synchronization. It was created by David Grand, PhD, to be used with Brainspotting, but can also be used alone for wellness and relaxation.

Brain-Based Treatment   Any newer trauma-specific interventions that calm the amygdala and the limbic system to reduce hypervigilance and intensity of traumatic memories (e.g., EFT, EMDR, and Brainspotting).

Brainspotting   Brain-based, trauma-specific intervention for treating trauma created by David Grand, PhD. It locates points near a person's visual field to access unprocessed trauma in the subcortical brain.

Cognitive Behavioral Therapy (CBT)   General term for a variety of counseling approaches. A form of talk therapy, it is a short-term therapy technique for changing thought patterns.

Continuous Improvement   Small, incremental, continuous steps by which an organization continuously improves its processes and procedures to meet or exceed customer requirements.

Center for Disease Control and Prevention (CDC)   Federal organization that evaluates conditions after a disaster to assess the level of danger to the public's health.

Community Emergency Response Team (CERT)   A FEMA program that educates volunteers about disaster preparedness, search, rescue, and basic medical operations.

Climate change   Long-term alteration of temperature and normal weather patterns, referring to a particular location or the planet as a whole, which may be impacting the frequency and severity of disasters. Climate change is currently occurring throughout the world as a result of global warming.

Code of ethics. Set of guidelines, standards, and rules that direct ethical behavior in a company, organization, or individual.

Cognitive Therapy   A broad term covering a wide range of counseling treatments, which primarily involve talking, or cognitive, interactions. It falls under the CBT umbrella.

Collaboration   When two or more people act in pursuit of shared high-level goals.

Community/Public Mental Health (Needs/Assets) Assessment   Used to determine the current strengths and gaps of a local mental health system and to help define the at-risk populations.

Compassion Fatigue   An occupational hazard for people in the helping professions characterized by lack of, or reduced, ability to empathize or sympathize with the people they serve.

Continuous Improvement   Small, incremental, continuous steps by which an organization continuously improves its processes and procedures.

Convener   Person who brings people together for a meeting or some public purpose, such as a collaboration.

Crisis Counseling Assistance and Training Program (CCP) FEMA-administered short-term disaster relief grant awarded after a presidential disaster declaration to support mental health services to survivors.

Culture System of shared behaviors, beliefs, customs, habits, knowledge, language, norms, perspectives, practices, rituals, and values setting one group of people apart from another.

Demographics Physical, social, and economic characteristics of populations, used to help determine a community's most vulnerable.

Department of Homeland Security (DHS) Department of the federal government, FEMA.

Depression Mental health diagnosis identified by lack of interest or pleasure in daily activities, sadness, and feelings of worthlessness or excessive guilt severe enough to interfere with working, sleeping, studying, eating, and enjoying life.

Diagnosis Clinical evaluation of the physical/medical or psychological diagnosis of an individual, conducted through tests, interviews, and checklists.

Diagnostic and Statistical Manual of Mental Disorders (DSM) Published by the American Psychiatric Association for mental health professionals to develop a diagnosis.

Disaster Defined by FEMA as an occurrence of a severity and magnitude normally resulting in deaths, injuries, and property damage that cannot be managed through routine procedures and resources of government. It requires immediate, coordinated, and effective response by multiple government and private-sector organizations to meet human needs and speed recovery.

Disaster Mental Health/Behavioral Response Teams (Crisis Response Teams) Through state counties, statewide, or private organizations, volunteers educated to assist survivors and first responders in mental healthcare, such as psychological first aid.

Efficacy Ability to produce a desired result.

Employee Assistance Program (EAP) Many insurance companies have an EAP to provide for mental health counseling for a specific number of sessions without pre-approval.

Empowerment Process of becoming more confident, especially in controlling one's life.

Emotional Freedom Techniques (EFT) (Tapping) Brain-based, trauma-specific intervention for treating anxiety, stress, and trauma involving tapping near the end points of "energy meridians" of the body.

Eye Movement Desensitization and Reprocessing (EMDR) Brain-based, trauma-specific intervention for treating anxiety, stress, and trauma, in which the patient attends to emotionally disturbing memories while simultaneously focusing on an external stimulus.

Emergency Medical Services (EMS) Also known as ambulance or paramedic services.

Emergency Medical Technician (EMT) Provide emergency medical care and transportation for critical patients.

Environmental Protection Agency (EPA) Independent federal agency to conduct and enforce assessments, research, and education.

Equine Therapy A horse trainer and a mental health clinician work together to provide emotionally therapeutic experiences.

Expressive Arts Therapy Master's degree–level clinician using a wide range of visual arts materials to facilitate expression and recognition of emotions and events.

Facilitation Collaboration process using a neutral third party to help a group reach goals or complete tasks acceptable to all participants.

Facilitator Individual acting as a neutral third party and leading a discussion or activity to extract feedback and information or reach agreement.

Federal Emergency Management Agency (FEMA) Lead federal agency in disaster response and recovery that provides funding for crisis counseling and grants to state mental health authorities following presidential-declared disasters.

First Responder Individuals first on the scene after a disaster, accident, or tragedy (e.g., police officer, firefighter, emergency medical technician, or clergy member).

Fracking A controversial method of drilling into the Earth using high-pressure liquid to create cracks in the underground shale to extract natural gas and petroleum.

Heart 9/11 Healing Emergency Aid Response Team of first responders—FDNY, NYPD, PAPD, and the NYC building trades—with the mission to respond immediately to natural- and human-caused disasters and rebuild community centers in hard-hit areas and community resiliency.

Health and Human Services Department (HHS) Federal department, also known as Health Department, with the goal of protecting the health of all Americans and providing essential human services.

Hypervigilant. An enhanced state of sensory sensitivity accompanied by an exaggerated intensity of behaviors with the purpose of detecting activity perceived as harmful. This is a common condition with individuals who have been seriously traumatized.

Intervention Action intended to help treat or cure a mental health condition, used after a disaster to target stress reactions.

Kickoff Meeting Used to acquaint collaboration team members and stakeholders with each other and an initial review of project scope and activities.

Licensed Clinical Social Worker (LCSW) Possesses a master's degree with supervised work experience.

Licensed Marriage and Family Therapist (LMFT) Completed master's degree or doctorate in this specialty.

Licensed Professional Counselor (LPC)/Licensed Mental Health Counselor (LMHC) Or Clinical Mental Health Counselors, they possess a master's degree with supervised work experience.

Meditation Mental process in which individual reaches increased self-knowledge and wellbeing through consciousness alteration.

Mental Health Awareness Training Grants (MHAT) SAMHSA funding to prepare and train community members and first responders on how to appropriately and safely respond to individuals with mental disorders.

Mental Health Provider State-licensed or certified therapist who possesses a master's degree or higher level of education.

Mental Health How people maintain successful mental activity, productive daily activities, and fulfilling relationships by the way they see themselves, evaluate challenges and problems, explore choices, and make decisions.

Mental Illness Refers to a wide range of clinically identifiable mental health diagnoses affecting thoughts, body, feelings, and behavior.

Mental Wellbeing State of mind in which individual feels comfortable, safe, and emotionally balanced.

Mindfulness Intentionally focusing on present moment in a nonjudgmental fashion.

Mission Statement Describes what the collaboration is going to do and why this is being done.

Mitigation Process or result of making something less severe, dangerous, painful, harsh, or damaging, as used in disaster mitigation.

Musgatova Neuro-Reflex Integration (MNRI) Nonverbal trauma-specific intervention for treating trauma, which supports the integration process of primary motor reflex patterns.

Memorandum of Understanding (MOU)/Agreement (MOA) Written agreement between organizations and/or individuals that establishes ground rules for working together.

Music Therapy Master's degree–level or higher mental health professional specializing in music for healing.

National Alliance on Mental Illness (NAMI) Nation's largest grassroots mental health organization.

National Institute of Mental Health (NIMH) Lead federal agency under HHS for research on mental disorders.

Needs Assessment Process of using tools such as questionnaires, surveys, interviews, and observation to identify the gap between what is known and needs to be learned.

Psychological First Aid (PFA) Assistance provided immediately post disaster through trained volunteers focusing on physical and emotional needs.

Play Therapy Type of mental health intervention using play (e.g., sand trays, games) for children and sometimes adults.

Post-Traumatic Stress Disorder (PTSD) Psychiatric disorder occurring in people who experienced or witnessed a traumatic event such as a natural disaster, serious accident, terrorist act, war/combat, rape, or other violent personal assault.

Preparedness Continuous cycle of planning, organizing, training, equipping, exercising, evaluating, and taking corrective action to ensure effective coordination during incident response.

Project AWARE State Education Agency Grants (Project AWARE-SEA) Through SAMHSA, provides funding for activities, services, and strategies to decrease youth violence and support healthy development of school-aged youth.

PsySTART Psychological Simple Triage and Rapid Treatment Developed by Merritt Schreiber, PhD, primarily for hospitals, clinics, and emergency medical services to link mental health to disaster system of care.

Recovery Processes in which people with mental illness begin to heal emotionally and no longer suffer from the symptoms of their disorder.

Resilience/Resiliency   Ability to recover emotionally after a stressful situation.

Response   Purposeful outreach to save lives, protect property or environment, and/or meet basic human needs after a disaster.

Risk Assessment   Identification, evaluation, and estimation of a situation's risk level as compared against benchmarks and acceptable level of risk.

Robert T. Stafford Disaster Relief and Emergency Assistance Act (Stafford Act)   Authorizes the president to issue a major disaster declaration for events overwhelming the combined capabilities of state and local government resources.

Substance Abuse and Mental Health Services Administration (SAMHSA)   Federal agency under HHS leading public health efforts to reduce impact of substance abuse and mental illness on America's communities.

Society for Community Research and Action (SCRA)   Division 27 of the American Psychological Association, serving disciplines focusing on community research and action.

Stakeholder   Person, group, or organization with interest or concern in an organization.

Stigma   Mark of shame, discredit, or a sign of social unacceptability. In mental health, stigma is thought to be widespread and often occurs as a result of ignorance and prejudice of fear of mental illnesses.

Stress   Feeling of tension, emotional and/or physical, common in those with/without mental illness and typically occurring in difficult or unmanageable situations.

Symptom   Subjective sign of a pathological condition, usually reported by the affected individual rather than observed by the examiner.

Tapping   (See Emotional Freedom Techniques.)

Trauma-Focused Cognitive Behavioral Therapy (TF-CBT)   Cognitive trauma-specific intervention for treating trauma.

Trauma   Emotional response to terrible event such as accident, rape, or natural disaster, with shock and denial immediately typical. Longer term reactions include unpredictable emotions, flashbacks, strained relationships, and physical symptoms like headaches or nausea.

Trauma-Informed   1. For collaboration members (in this manual): Having a general knowledge of trauma, the effects on the brain, and a variety of treatments; 2. For mental health practitioner: Having knowledge of trauma, its symptoms and how it affects the brain and having special training to administer trauma-specific interventions.

Trauma-Specific Interventions Techniques for trauma-informed mental health practitioners to treat trauma.

Vision Statement Formal declaration with inspiring language to define what a collaboration intends to accomplish.

Voluntary Organizations Active in Disaster (VOAD) Consists of large disaster relief organizations including the Red Cross and Salvation Army, plus many faith-based and small disaster relief organizations, which mitigate and alleviate the impact of disasters; provide a forum for promoting cooperation, communication, coordination, and collaboration; and foster more effective delivery of services to communities affected by disaster.

Victims of Crime Act (VOCA) Provides funding for individuals whose lives are lost or in grave danger because of a criminal or terrorist act. VOCA offers community grants to organizations providing victim support.

1

Introduction to Mental Health

Chapter 1 Preview
A. Increasing Extent of Disasters
B. Launch of Emergency Management
C. History of Disaster Mental Health
D. Statewide Disaster Mental Health
E. Parity of Disaster Mental Health Plans
F. Foundations of Community Psychology
G. Manual Overview

Events over the past several years have proved how both natural and human-caused disasters are on the rise, and American communities need to be prepared for potential calamites to come. That word, "preparation," is the main purpose of this manual: Most American towns and cities have developed disaster response plans or a set of action steps fire departments, police, and hospitals must take for response, reduction, and recovery for any catastrophic event from biological exposure to a mass shooting to an earthquake. Until recently, the ultimate goal of these plans has been solely the "physical" wellbeing of citizens. Mental health has not been a consideration, with long-term stress, anxiety, and trauma either ignored or treated as afterthoughts. This needs to change. Disaster mental health preparedness can no longer be overlooked if communities truly care about the effective long-term recovery and resiliency of their residents.

Disaster mental health planning is also not a one-size-fits-all process because of all the inherent differences:

1. Not all disasters impact the mental health of populations in the same way. This is especially true of natural versus human-caused disasters, where the latter lead to more severe trauma;

2. Although human-caused disasters can occur anywhere in the U.S., each geographical area is more prone to experiencing one type of event over another. Hurricanes are most common along the East Coast, for example;

3. Municipalities do not share the same ability to respond to a catastrophic event. Rural or low-populated areas, small communities, and urban localities face different challenges;

4. The demographics of each community differ along with those residents who are the most vulnerable. The socioeconomic makeup of the town or city, for example, impacts response effectiveness; and

5. Certain states are better prepared to respond to disasters than others. Some states, for example, have already developed statewide and/or regional mental health/behavioral plans and response teams.

By following the steps in this manual, you can determine the disaster mental health plan best for your community's unique parameters. Expect planning to be an ongoing learning process, in which improvements are made either post disaster and/or as information is acquired from other communities and newly published studies. Naturally, it is hoped your community will not need to implement your plan but only to keep it on hand to provide the best care possible whenever necessary.

A. Increasing Extent of Disasters

In the U.S. alone, by early October 2019, weather and climate disaster events, including storms, cyclones and flooding, had each led to losses exceeding $1 billion. In 2018, the U.S. was devastated by a multitude of extraordinary natural disasters, from the deadliest wildfires in California's history that destroyed the entire town of Paradise to the worst hurricanes on the East Coast since the late 1960s. The price tag of disasters is also quickly mounting with increased severity. Total costs of $306 billion in 2017 far surpassed the $214.8 billion in 2005, according to the National Oceanic and Atmospheric Administration (www.noaa.gov). Disasters cause significant economic impact to communities and the entire country for an undetermined time. Louisiana will never be the same after Hurricane Katrina in 2005, and scores of residents still struggle with the financial impact of Superstorm Sandy in 2012.

Human-caused catastrophes also broke records these past several years. According to the Gun Violence Archive (www.gunviolencearchive.org), which keeps track of gun-related injuries and deaths, 2017 topped the all-time record for mass shootings with a total of 345. This violence included two of the deadliest such events in American history within just 35 days of each other. In October, 64-year-old Stephen Paddock opened fire on 22,000 concertgoers in Las Vegas, leaving 58 people dead and over 500 injured. After an extensive federal study, Paddock's motive remains undetermined. Following this Las Vegas tragedy, one survivor of the 2016 Pulse nightclub shooting, which killed 49 and wounded 58 in Florida, said, "My heart is breaking all over again. . . . How much can we take?" (Santach, 2017).

Only a month after the Las Vegas shooting, 26-year-old Devin Patrick Kelly murdered 26 congregants during religious services at the First Baptist Church in Sutherland Springs, Texas. This catastrophe was even worse than the earlier Burnette Chapel Church of Christ shooting in Antioch, Tennessee, which killed one and injured seven. The number of mass shootings in 2018 was only a few lower than in 2017, but brutal all the same. These violent events included Marjory Stoneman Douglas High School in Parkland, Florida; the Tree of Life Synagogue in Pittsburgh, Pennsylvania; the *Capital Gazette* newspaper in Annapolis, Maryland; and the Borderline Bar and Grill in Thousand Oaks, California. As this book goes to press, continued shootings occur in schools and houses of worship.

In 2019, it seemed that every day brought a new shooting and that turned out to be true. There were more mass shootings than days in the calendar. It also appears that no location is safe, with gun violence in houses of worship, sports arenas, shopping malls, schools, theaters, and nightclubs. In addition, a new form of human-caused concern, cyberviolence, is growing steadily, and New Orleans was shut down after a cyberattack.

B. Launch of Emergency Management

Although disasters have battered the U.S. from its earliest history, the country reacted quite slowly in responding to the aftereffects. The first time the U.S. government took action on a local disaster was in 1803 when a congressional act provided financial assistance to Portsmouth, New Hampshire, which was destroyed by fire. Then, no great strides were made in emergency response until

Source: FEMA

the 1930s, when the Reconstruction Finance Corporation and the Bureau of Public Roads authorized disaster loans for public facility reconstruction. Congress also passed the Flood Control Act in 1934, which gave the U.S. Army Corps of Engineers greater authority to design and build flood-control projects. In the Cold War 1950s, numerous civil defense programs arose across the country.

A decade later, many natural disasters rocked the country. An earthquake in Montana, Hurricane Donna in Florida, and Hurricane Carla in Texas caused record damage. The 1962 Ash Wednesday storm destroyed over 620 miles of East Coast shoreline; the 1964 Alaskan earthquake measured 9.2 on the Richter scale and generated tsunamis that killed 123 people; and Hurricanes Betsy and Camille at the end of the decade were fast and furious, killing and injuring hundreds of people and causing hundreds of millions of dollars in damage—a considerable amount for the time.

The government was still acting in an ad-hoc fashion for disaster relief, with over 100 federal agencies offering some type of support after each event. With such a fragmentation of funding and no unified federal emergency management system, the state governors' frustration grew. They finally decided to act and launched the National Governors Association Subcommittee on Disaster Assistance (1979). Based on their concerns, President Jimmy Carter established a new Federal Emergency Management Agency (FEMA) in 1985 to make recommendations on how to prepare for and respond to national emergencies.

Now, most communities have developed emergency management plans to diminish the damage of disastrous events as well as Community Emergency Response Teams (CERTs) that are trained to immediately respond with medical, fire safety, and rescue efforts. FEMA (www.fema.gov) defines emergency preparedness as "pre-impact activities that establish a state of readiness to respond to extreme events that could affect the community."

The vast majority of emergency plans are focused on the community's environment, the physical wellbeing of the residents, and the effect on infrastructure. Information includes evacuation routes, emergency contacts, checklists, and critical operations. Preparedness is a step-by-step process, with an ongoing series of analyses, plan development, and education/training and skill development of participating individuals. Community emergency plans vary in their planning process; some have more formal and defined approaches, a specific planning budget, and clear outcomes, and others follow a more informal, less defined approach with a low budget or on a volunteer basis. The degree of formality of emergency plans often corresponds to community size and disaster history, such as a region regularly facing destruction by tornadoes.

Regardless of the type of emergency plan they develop, communities clearly recognize preparedness is essential in caring for the medical needs of their residents and the rebuilding of their homes and infrastructure. On the other hand, nearly all of these emergency plans lack a psychological component. Mental health typically takes a back seat in disaster response.

C. History of Disaster Mental Health

It was not until the late 1800s that psychologists Sigmund Freud and Pierre Janet began communicating about the impact of traumatic situations (Ringel & Brandell, 2012). Following World War I, and more so after World War II and the Vietnam War, studies depicted soldiers' traumatic reactions to their battle experiences. Research was also conducted on the effect of interpersonal violence, such as spousal abuse. Formal studies on the relationship between calamity and trauma go back at least 75 years. After Boston's Coconut Grove nightclub fire in 1944, Erich Lindemann (2006) published one of the first observations on the impact of disasters on mental health. For the first time, this study noted psychological upheaval, including symptoms of stress, anxiety, helplessness, and depression. After a year, these changes also led to an increase in mortality rates, a heightened frequency of physical ailments, and visits to physicians and hospitals. Social contacts were greatly reduced, and people were less satisfied with the quality of their lives and reported reduced participation in leisure activities.

Kai Erikson (1976) thoroughly covered the mental health impact of human-caused tragedies in his book about the deadly floods in Buffalo Creek, West Virginia. On February 26, 1972, 132 million gallons of muddy water broke through a temporary mining-company dam and immediately changed the town forever. Flood survivors, who had previously lived in a tightly knit community, were crowded into trailer homes with no concern for former neighborhoods. This disregard for living conditions resulted in a collective trauma, with tension and conflicts among the residents and a loss of personal connection, as well as disorientation, declining morality, a rise in crime, and outmigration.

In 1980, PTSD was added to the third edition of the American Psychiatric Association's *Diagnostic and Statistical Manual of Mental Disorders* (*DSM-III*), mostly due to the mental health concerns of returning Vietnam War veterans. This addition to the *DSM* led to increased research on the mental health impact of traumatic events, including disasters. At the same time, the International

Society of Traumatic Stress Studies was established to enhance the development of disaster planning and response strategies. As defined by the *DSM—Fourth Edition* (*DSM-IV*; APA, 1994), "The person experienced, witnessed, or was confronted with an event or events that involved actual or threatened death or serious injury, or a threat to the physical integrity of self or others."

More emphasis was then placed on establishing interventions to prevent or reduce high levels of stress and trauma after disasters, resulting in such approaches as Psychological First Aid (PFA) and Crisis Counseling Assistance and Training Program (CCP). Organizations like the World Health Organization (WHO) began to establish disaster planning and response guides, and more research was conducted on the impact of human-caused and natural disasters.

The September 11, 2001, terrorist attacks started a whole new chapter in disaster mental health as the country saw firsthand the horrendous psychological impact of such a calamitous event. FEMA began offering the Crisis Counseling Program in 2002, a grant to fund supplemental mental health assistance and training after the event occurred. In 2016, the Mental Health Reform Act was passed. This law included the most significant changes in federal mental healthcare policies since the 1960s, providing critical reforms to address the present lack of resources, enhance psychiatric and medical healthcare coordination, and develop meaningful solutions to improve outcomes for families dealing with mental illness. The Sandy Hook Elementary School shooting in 2012 acted as a major stimulus in getting this act passed (Szabo, 2016), since there was no established plan on how to handle the emotional impact on first responders, victims' family members, and the community as a whole.

Rise of Trauma-Informed Care

During this time, the word "trauma" was undergoing a change. Historically, the symptoms of traumatic stress experienced by returning veterans were seen as a character flaw. World War II military recruits were screened in attempt to identify those "who were afflicted with moral weakness," which would prevent them from entering military service, according to the Substance Abuse and Mental Health Services Administration (www.samhsa.gov). With time, traumatic stress began to be recognized in a more constructive manner. New approaches to trauma healing and recovery focused on interventions to address the PTSD symptoms, as well as the integration of trauma effects into ongoing life activities. More was learned about trauma and other forms of violence beyond war, such as natural disasters and terrorism, refugee and immigrant displacement, and emotional and sexual abuse.

Such issues and needs encouraged a second generation of approaches to trauma healing and recovery, where personal "fault" was decried. Research focused on finding ways to tap into self-healing and empowerment characteristics. These approaches were based on group and peer-support models providing both encouragement and education in how to manage trauma and its effects. These methods were not recommended as replacements for therapy, but rather as an additional supportive environment for further care.

The Meaning of Trauma

The word "trauma" can be confusing, so it needs to be clarified. Trauma, as a condition, is sometimes used incorrectly as referring to people who are suffering from PTSD. Trauma is a general term to describe a variety of symptoms experienced after an event in which an individual witnessed death or believed his/her life was in grave danger. The American Psychological Association's (www.apa.org) definition of trauma is quite broad: "**Trauma** is an emotional response to a terrible event like an accident, rape, or natural disaster."

People may loosely use the term "trauma" to describe a highly distressing event. For example, someone might say, "That situation was traumatic," when in fact it was a difficult or challenging situation but did not result in anyone actually becoming traumatized. For this manual, the authors will use the word "trauma" to refer to an event that actually traumatized people.

The Meaning of Trauma-Informed

This manual is based on the trauma-informed approach, which is recommended as part of your collaboration's plan for responding to mental health needs after a disaster. According to SAMHSA (www.samhsa.gov), a trauma-informed program, organization, or system follows the "Four R" guidelines:

1. Realizes the widespread impact of trauma and understands possible recovery paths;
2. Recognizes the signs and symptoms of trauma in a variety of situations and with varying populations;
3. Responds by fully integrating knowledge about trauma into policies, procedures, and practices; and
4. Works to actively resist re-traumatization.

With trauma-informed care, the knowledge of trauma is integrated into all aspects of service delivery. It is a general term that may include mental health services, such as trained volunteers providing crisis counseling or psychological first aid immediately following a disaster. Chapter 7 will discuss three types of crisis counseling. Disaster treatment may also include interventions by licensed clinicians.

"Trauma-informed" has become the new standard for establishing public mental health and human services, recognizing that the essential support, education, and empowerment can only take hold and offer emotional help in "trauma-informed" organizations. The question for mental health professionals changed from "What is wrong with you?" to "What has happened to you?" Trauma-informed care recognizes that all people seeking help are trauma survivors who need to design their own path to healing with the guidance and experience of the service provider. For organizations, such as your collaboration, this means establishing proactive approaches, which include all possible programs and processes that support expedient healing.

Trauma-Specific Interventions or Treatments

Trauma-specific treatment is another term that has become a major component of trauma evolution. Trauma-informed mental health licensed professionals understand and incorporate the "Four R's" into their practice. They have also received training in "trauma-specific" interventions and can competently use these techniques to help traumatized individuals. Trauma-specific treatment is a best-practice approach used to directly address the impact of trauma on an individual's life and facilitate trauma recovery (www.samhsa.gov). All trauma-specific treatments should be delivered in a safe and empowering environment. These interventions will be explained in greater detail in Chapter 7.

D. Statewide Disaster Mental Health

After 9/11, FEMA asked states to have a mental health plan for survivors and responders because it was so critical to disaster response. According to the U.S. Department of Health and Human Services (HHS, www.hhs.gov), however, 64% of the state emergency response plans do not adequately plan for emotional needs. Having these statewide plans is enormously beneficial, especially when no other emergency mental health plans exist. Times may arise when your community must rely on the state's emergency support for a major human-caused or natural disaster. The state's plan can also provide valuable input for your collaboration's planning efforts. However, for several reasons, the authors of this manual recommend that local municipalities also develop their own disaster mental health action plans:

1. First, even smaller communities can handle certain mass emergencies on their own without regional or state backup. By having your own disaster mental health plan, your community can instantly respond to psychological needs that arise;
2. Second, depending on the type of disaster, such as floods or chemical spills, it may be difficult for state emergency response teams to reach

those most in need because of closed roads, extensive structural damage and debris, or ongoing disaster incidents. Your local community must follow its own plan until outside help arrives;

3. Third, the more a response and recovery team knows about community variables, such as geography, demographics, and the most vulnerable populations, the better. For example, it is important to know a town's economic makeup since a poorer community will react differently to disasters than a more affluent one. Research (Fothergill & Peek, 2004) found poorer residents were less prepared for a serious incident because they could not afford earthquake insurance. Also, people who live a more stressful life because of economic issues suffer more from depression and are at greater risk of trauma from disasters (Tracy, Norris, & Galea, 2011). A local plan can better respond to such specific population needs; and

4. Lastly, your community's mental health action plan will include valuable information such as the names of individuals in charge of disaster response and their roles and responsibilities, the community's resources, and the best place to set up mental health crisis centers and shelters, such as in schools, certain town offices, and business locations.

E. Parity of Disaster Mental Health Plans

This manual stresses that a mental health disaster component should be considered with equal value and weight to emergency medical preparedness in every community. Mental health must be a priority because:

1. Catastrophic events are a serious risk factor for psychological wellbeing: Numerous people suffer from some level of trauma after a disaster;

2. Mental illness can easily worsen after a disaster if counseling and required medicines are not received. This places additional strain not only on the individuals but also on relationships throughout the entire community;

3. Emotional wellbeing is furthered through community support. Such support is considered one of the most important aspects of resiliency;

4. The sooner the traumatized receive appropriate care, the more effective their treatment. The opposite is true as well: The longer treatment is put off, the worse the condition may become;

5. The mental health of survivors is positively or negatively impacted by the manner in which they receive such basics as shelter, food and water, and sanitation. Cultural and ethnic awareness is critical in the support of survivors;

6. The most marginalized people require special response and recovery measures. Unfortunately, they are the ones who normally are overlooked or ignored;

7. Future resiliency can be enhanced when disaster victims can recall positive experiences. People want to remember the better memories and ways they were helped rather than dwelling on the negative;

8. Mental and physical health greatly impact each other; both need to be simultaneously addressed. It is only recently through neuro-research that an emphasis is being placed on how the whole body works together to heal.

9. Local communities need to be able to respond on their own or in tandem with regional, state, and national agencies and organizations. Your municipality knows the residents' needs best and acts as a reliable source and liaison when disasters occur;

10. Communities wrongly assume a state- and/or federal-level response will come immediately following a disaster. With sufficient forewarning of a major catastrophe, enough time may exist for the mobilization of such support. However, a community cannot rely on such a response: Most disasters take place with little or no warning; the most effective mental healthcare is provided by community members who best understand their residents' needs;

11. Most post-disaster funding, including that from the federal government, is for short- rather than long-term recovery projects. Nearly all communities nationwide receive federal community development funds, but most use the money to revitalize troubled neighborhoods and meet the current resident needs. All federal grants for mental healthcare are provided after a disaster has occurred;

12. To help those with emotional issues, most communities rely on mental health services of existing organizations that may not be trained to help traumatized individuals or even know how people are impacted by major catastrophes; and

13. Disaster-impacted communities are overwhelmed with immediate needs and cannot focus on long-range planning; Emphasis also needs to be placed on building healthier, more resilient communities for the long term.

The Complexity of Mental Health

The complexity of mental health, particularly of trauma, is another critical reason for having a psychological disaster plan. Variability, in fact, is one of the most challenging aspects of disaster mental health, with degree of personal resiliency, type of disaster, geography or rural/urban location, population demograph-ics, gender and age, level of risk, and distance from the disaster's ground zero all impacting the degree of trauma experienced. It is recognized, for example, that trauma is more prevalent in women than men, according to the Veterans Administration (www.va.gov).

The type of disaster also leads to different responses. The National Center for PTSD (www.ptsd.va.gov) found a higher percentage of people who experi-ence a shooting develop post-traumatic stress over a longer time than those who experience a natural disaster. Further, trauma can come and go with triggers or reminders. After the Sandy Hook Elementary School violence, some Columbine High School shooting survivors had nightmares for the first time in many years.

People with the greatest proximity to the event are considered at most risk of severe trauma, and then a ripple effect moves outward to the entire popula-tion. The role delineation model (Taylor & Fraser, 1982) may be helpful when considering the allocation and distribution of mental health resources in terms of the individuals impacted. The authors produced a classification of disaster victims using the imagery of a ripple effect of events based on factors such as proximity to the impact zone and psychological consequences of the disaster experience. Potential victims include those directly emotionally and physically injured, those bereaved, and those who may be involved either as witnesses or responders. This stresses how the line between victims and non-victims is not black and white but includes a wide variety of "hidden" victims:

1. Primary victims: people directly exposed to the elements of the disaster;
2. Secondary victims: people with close family and personal ties to primary victims;
3. Tertiary victims: people whose occupations require them to respond to the disaster; and
4. Quaternary victims: concerned and caring members of communities beyond the impact area.

Therefore, first responders, the very people who offer the most hands-on care, may be most at risk of psychological harm. A recent report (Ruderman Fam-ily Foundation, 2018) examined several factors contributing to mental health concerns and high suicide rates of first responders. PTSD and depression rates among firefighters and police officers are as much as five times higher than those of civilians. Another report by SAMHSA (www.samhsa.gov) added that by being at the forefront of each disaster incident, first responders are at great danger of being exposed to traumatic situations and for PTSD, depression, sub-stance abuse, and suicide.

Yet, inconsistencies exist even with disaster proximity due to other factors, such as personal vulnerability; for example, someone living miles from ground zero but having experienced childhood trauma may be at greater risk for PTSD. The Inter-Agency Standing Committee, including both U.N. and non-U.N. humanitarian organizations, published "Guidelines on Mental Health and Psychosocial Support in Emergency Settings" (2007), which noted how mental health was impacted most in those people who had:

1. Pre-existing social problems, such as those who are impoverished or marginalized through discrimination;
2. Emergency-induced social problems, including family dynamic breakdown, social network disruption, infrastructure and home damage and displacement, and lack of resources;
3. Event-induced distress and mental disorders, such as high levels of stress, anxiety, and grief;
4. Post-traumatic stress and/or depression and personality changes;
5. Humanitarian aid–induced social problems, including undermining of community structures or traditional support structures;
6. Community/humanitarian aid–induced psychological problems, such as lack of food and water, loss of home, and major miscommunication; and
7. Pre-existing mental health and/or substance abuse problems.

In one of the most recognized studies (Felitti, 2002), the experiences of 17,000 children were compared to the quality of their life as adults. Those adults who had Adverse Childhood Experiences (ACEs) or chronic, unpredictable, and stress-inducing events as children, such as living in an alcoholic family, losing a parent, or being sexually/physically abused, had a greater chance of future illnesses such as cancer and depression as well as a shorter life span. Clearly, this extensive study showed how traumatic experiences can impact a person both psychologically and physically for the long term. It also demonstrated that mental and physical wellbeing go hand in hand. Yet, ask anyone to name a body organ, and the most immediate answer is heart or lung. Very few people name the brain, which is the most complex of all 78 organs and controls the entire body.

Mental Health Inequality

It is not surprising that mental health takes a backseat role in disaster preparedness planning. Despite passage of the Mental Health Reform Act, significant barriers continue to exist in accessing mental health treatment and support. Obstacles include insurance company denials, short-shrift or high out-of-pocket costs for mental healthcare, difficulties accessing psychiatric medications, and finding trained and compassionate psychiatrists and other providers in health networks.

In 2017, the National Alliance on Mental Illness (NAMI) published the results of its third nationwide survey to explore the relationship between health coverage and access to mental healthcare, finding how people with mental illness continue to experience significant barriers to finding affordable, accessible treatment. Such challenges occur regardless of whether someone is covered by private insurance or a public plan such as Medicaid. Results showed that 28% of responders who received psychotherapy relied on an out-of-network provider versus 7% who used an out-of-network medical specialist. Over a third (34%) of those taking the survey said it was difficult to find any mental health provider to accept their insurance, compared to other types of medical specialists (13%) or primary care providers (9%). Finding a new provider was a major hurdle because over half of psychiatrists and 45% of therapists did not accept new patients, and 56% of psychiatrists and 11% of counselors did not accept their health plan. The U.S. has made headway, but abuse and discrimination continue to be serious problems, with one in five Americans having a diagnosable mental health disorder.

The stigmatization of mental illness is still an important societal problem. The general population is largely ignorant about this problem, and fear of the mentally ill remains prevalent (Rossler, 2016). The word "stigma" is easily attached to mental illness, but how did this tendency come about? In her book, Marjorie Baldwin (2006) suggested five causes of persistent and institutionalized problems of stigma:

1. Responsibility: Frequently, the mentally ill are held accountable for their condition as if they were purposely choosing this painful life. If mentally ill individuals are thought to have a choice and to be able to control their circumstances, they are blamed and receive little or no sympathy;
2. Uncertainty: When people have an uncertain condition, not knowing if or when it can be improved, they are more likely to be stigmatized and ignored. Helpless situations are difficult to support;
3. Unpredictability: Similarly, people do not feel comfortable when they face change and lack of stability. Mentally ill individuals may act differently from day to day;
4. Incompetence: People also want life to be rational and objective, although it rarely is. They view the mentally ill as incapable of making rational decisions, so why should they have any decision-making power? and
5. Danger: Unpredictability and irrationality may go hand in hand with harm to others, which enhances fear and lack of care.

"It's Way Past Time"

Editorial: John Broderick, Jr.—Former Chief Justice of the New Hampshire Supreme Court

Many people know very little about mental illness and often gain their knowledge and views from unreliable sources. Until actually confronted with a personal situation at home, with friends, or at work, they continue to be uncaring and uninvolved.

For the last three years, John Broderick, the former Chief Justice of the New Hampshire Supreme Court, has devoted much of his energy speaking over 400 times to high schools, middle schools, and community gatherings in northern New England, trying to begin a new conversation around mental illness. "For too many generations, mental illness in America has been treated as a character flaw or a personal weakness," Broderick stated. "That's the result of fear and ignorance and an unwillingness to open our hearts and our minds to learn about mental illness, accept it as the health problem it is, and recognize that treatment is possible," he added.

Over the last three years, Broderick's eyes have been opened. "In my childhood and for much of my adult life, nobody talked about mental illness," he said. "That helped no one." When a very public mental health tragedy struck his own family 15 years ago, Broderick was forced to see what he never had. "But I never did anything about it because I came from the baby-boomer bubble where nobody talked about it." When learning of the national Campaign to Change Direction, which stressed the five signs of mental illness, he became involved and began his ongoing efforts to engage young people to help change the culture and discussion around mental illness.

Broderick described it as the most important work of his professional life. "I love this generation," he said, "because they are the least judgmental generation in the U.S. history. These kids want to change the conversation and eliminate the stigma, the shame, and the shadows around mental illness."

He concluded, "It's way past time because the way we have treated mental illness since the Earth was considered flat is not morally right nor medically sound. I see it now, and I am impatient for change."

F. Foundations of Community Psychology

Many of the ideas presented to you throughout this manual are founded on the field of community psychology, which is guided by the following principles emphasized by the Society of Community Research and Action (SCRA, 2010), which closely align with the trauma-informed approach:

1. Solid research promotes effective decisions in the real world, and vice versa. Scientific research and practical action are of equal value when trying to bring about positive forms of change. The relationship between research and action is cyclical. Community psychologists obtain information from a variety of sources, consolidate it and make plans, become involved, and finally use that information in real-world actions. Things do not always work out perfectly, but community psychologists analyze and rethink results, gather more information, and start again. This manual encourages creative thought, capacity building, and the acquisition of knowledge to provide needed support.

2. The most important advice for this manual is not to take the information at face value but to be flexible based on your community's makeup and needs. Community psychologists always try to acknowledge and encourage varying contexts. In any calamity, despite the seemingly random nature of events, there are varying themes, generalities, and theories that drive action.

   Other forms of experience and common sense are as important as research. No two disasters yield the same set of challenges. Every community is different, and the ways in which people react to a catastrophe—even the same type of catastrophe, such as a tornado hitting a community twice in a year—are different. To make effective decisions, it is essential to pay attention to the changing situations and remain open minded. It is essential to accept change, since disasters always result in new circumstances: Plan for the unexpected and never become too attached to any one idea or approach when a particular strategy does not seem to be working.

3. Social justice is always at risk in any community under duress. During and following disasters, inequality is likely to arise and should always be a major source of concern. Certain subgroups—people struggling financially or with certain disabilities as well as children—tend to be most affected and often have the least political clout to protect their rights. Your role as planner is to give a community the skills to recover, restore a greater sense of wellbeing for all, and maintain fundamental rights for everyone.

   Certain steps can appear to be the only strategic ones in the short term, but if they ever seem to infringe on the rights of members of specific groups, other paths should be considered. Participatory approaches, or those seeking input from all involved, help ensure the rights and perspectives of all community members are fully valued. Collaborative approaches make good sense. They build trust that often leads to better collective decision-making, greater community cohesion, and mutual benefits for all.

4. Knowledge is valuable for the public, not merely for specialized, private groups. Helpful community practitioners eagerly give away knowledge or expertise. This philosophy will hopefully provide fruitful guidelines for helping a community establish a long-term disaster response.

5. Actions should emphasize strengths and solutions, not simply challenges and deficits. It is tempting to simply list typical problems encountered during a disaster and then describe the various resources communities use to lessen these problems. The combination of research and experience can reveal both challenges and assets, such as the contribution of supportive social networks that increase a person's wellbeing.

What assets exist in a town? How can a sense of community and social support better develop? How does the community build on the unique strengths of different stakeholders? How is it possible to positively deal with more or less well-intentioned figures who show up from outside the community? How can more specific roles be established for

Source: Wikimedia Commons

all participants so the community can benefit from their contributions? How can planning groups leverage the strengths of existing organizations and mobilize new volunteers? Many sections of this manual provide strategic advice on these key issues.

6. There is one more important point about emphasizing the community psychology approach: Frequently, people are concerned that actions and interventions can do more harm than good. Such a possibility deserves attention even if it delays action. The solution is simple: If you want to help your community, especially those who are most vulnerable; if your goal is to enhance the lives of others outside of the immediate family; if your focus is on strengths; and if you take a participatory approach, any risks from taking action are greatly reduced. If your heart is in the right place and centered on the positive, mistakes will be made, but recovery will be greatly facilitated.

G. Manual Overview

Readership and Goals

This manual is specially written for a variety of groups and individuals who believe their community is not doing all it can to ensure long-term mental health wellness, particularly in the area of disaster response. These parties include:

1. Public and private social service and public healthcare delivery organizations and agencies;
2. Emergency management and strategic planning officials;
3. Mental health practitioners and organizations;
4. Neighborhood-based and interfaith community support individuals and organizations;
5. Public and private educational systems and organizations;
6. Businesses and other private-sector stakeholders;
7. Empowered and caring community members; and
8. Undergraduate and graduate students and coursework in such areas as emergency management, community development, disaster/behavioral mental health, disaster preparedness, trauma, socioeconomics, climate change, public health, and sustainability.

The desired outcomes of using this manual include:

1. Forming a new community collaboration with the purpose of developing a mental health disaster action plan, which integrates with the existing emergency medical response;

2. Updating and/or expanding an existing mental health plan; and/or

3. Strengthening collaboration with local, state, and national partners and gaining insights on services available from external organizations for mental health disaster strategy.

It is thus emphasized how the following should be incorporated into all mental health disaster plans:

1. A communitywide assessment that determines vulnerabilities and gaps existing between the present and desired status of different populations and develops goals, priorities, and strategies based on this information;

2. A unified vision where recovery is recognized as the opportunity to further a healthier and more resilient and sustainable community;

3. Decisions based on the potential extensive and broad-based mental health impacts of disasters; and

4. Integration of the latest and most effective trauma-based assessments and treatments.

Communities, as noted in Chapter 3, can be defined in different ways. This manual should also be considered helpful for diverse communities. For example, with increased mass shooting incidents in colleges and universities, it is essential for these institutions to develop their own disaster mental health plans. They need to immediately set up a crisis center or provide psychological first aid to the students and to provide them with options for trauma-informed treatment for the long term. They also need to prepare students in advance for a potential shooting incident. This goes well beyond the particulars of the campus lockdown procedures. Students should know the possible psychological impacts of such an event. What symptoms might they experience, and where do they go for help? What are the consequences of ignoring these issues? What support groups will be available if a crisis occurs?

Similarly, even municipal centers, government vendors, and military facilities need to be prepared for what to do in case of violence or natural-caused disasters. Since 2013, a number of shootings have occurred at military instillations, including two at Fort Hood in Chattanooga, Tennessee.

Structure

The second chapter starts with an overview of the four main principles or components necessary for any mental health planning group. Chapter 3 then provides a step-by-step approach on how to form a collaboration and design a mental health action plan. In subsequent chapters, information is provided on community assessment, the types of disasters and their impact, forms of trauma-informed therapeutic treatment, lessons learned from previous events, and resiliency. A Road Map and checklist are also included to expedite your process. Sources are located at the end of each chapter, and the Appendix includes additional materials to read. Based on this information, your collaboration can make sound decisions, fine-tune its action plan, and delineate the response team's essential roles and responsibilities. The material provided comes from a number of different sources, including academic research, professional training manuals, anecdotal evidence, case studies, online articles, and government publications.

It is recommended that your core group and facilitator become familiar with the manual before the first meeting or orientation to promote better understanding. Before each meeting, collaboration members should be encouraged to read a specific section, take notes in the provided area, and respond to the "To-Do" list of questions and activities that encourage further thought and discussions. Appreciate all input, since each member has a unique knowledge base and valuable personal experience.

Due to the complexity of mental health, this guide includes a synopsis of the literature on the topic. You can use the sources throughout the book, the lessons learned, and the list in the Appendix for further information. In fact, it is suggested that planners attend disaster preparedness conferences and seminars and share information with towns and cities facing similar challenges. Reinventing the wheel can be a misuse of valuable resources, whereas sharing best practices hastens and increases the effectiveness of the rebuilding and recovery process.

When forming a collaboration, you will naturally find that members have different areas of expertise and/or interests. There is no need to cover the entire manual as a group; committee members may break into topic-based subgroups and focus on specific issues. These can be reviewed with everyone when the entire group convenes. The bottom line: Acting now in any capacity is better than acting after the fact. When it comes to mental health issues, prevention is highly recommended.

Understanding the reasons for developing a mental health action plan and integrating it into the existing emergency medical response strategy is only your first step. Following through to the next steps is more difficult. Many reasons can be, and are, given for not developing a disaster mental health plan: Time and financial concerns, no private or public body acting as a motivating force, denial ("not in our community"), mental health's secondary standing, misplaced dependency on state and national assistance, and organizations feeling threatened by collaboration.

As with anything of importance, the most essential step is committing to a high-quality plan that will be completed by a certain date. This manual provides you with an interactive, user-friendly overview of disaster mental health and recommendations on how to form a community collaboration to plan for long-term, trauma-informed response and recovery. It gives your planning group specific procedures that can respond to the unthinkable—a serious natural or human-caused disaster. The goal is to determine which community members are major stakeholders in mental health improvement, from organizational CEOs to neighborhood parents, and give them the opportunity to come together and gain new information, share ideas, and determine a thoroughly thought-out plan to meet the varied needs of your unique community.

TO DO

1. What do you and your planning group hope to achieve through the use of this manual?
2. What is the desired time line for accomplishing these goals?
3. What are some of the challenges or barriers you may confront in the planning process? What strengths does the community offer that will help in the process?
4. Generally, who will be participating in this effort?

References

American Psychiatric Association. (1980). *Diagnostic and statistical manual of mental disorders* (3rd ed.). Washington, DC: Author.

American Psychiatric Association. (1994). *Diagnostic and statistical manual of mental disorders* (4th ed.). Washington, DC: Author.

Baldwin, M. (2006). *Living and working with schizophrenia*. Lanham, MD: Rowen & Littlefield.

Erikson, K. T. (1976). *Everything in its path: Destruction of community in the Buffalo Creek flood*. New York, NY: Simon and Schuster.

Felitti, V. (2002). *The relation between adverse childhood experiences and adult health: Turning gold into lead*. Retrieved from www.ncbi.nlm.nih.gov/pmc/articles/PMC6220625/

Fothergill, A., & Peek, L. A. (2004). Poverty and disasters in the United States: A review of recent sociological findings. *Natural Hazards, 32*(1), 89/110.

Inter-Agency Standing Committee. (2007). *Guidelines on mental health and psychosocial support in emergency settings*. Retrieved from www.who.int/mental_health/emergencies/guidelines_iasc_mental_health_psychosocial_june_2007.pdf?ua=1

Lindemann, E. (2006, April 1). Symptomatology and management of acute grief. *American Journal of Psychiatry*. Retrieved from https://ajp.psychiatryonline.org/doi/abs/10.1176/ajp.101.2.141

National Alliance on Mental Illness. (2017). *The doctor is out: Continuing disparities in access to mental and physical health care*. Retrieved from www.nami.org/About-NAMI/Publications-Reports/Public-Policy-Reports/The-Doctor-is-Out/DoctorIs Out.pdf

National Governors' Association. (1979, July 8–10). *Seventy-first annual meeting Louisville, Kentucky*. Retrieved from https://classic.nga.org/files/live/sites/NGA/files/pdf/1979NGAAnnualMeeting.pdf

Ringel, S., & Brandell, J. (Eds.). (2012). *Trauma: Contemporary directions in theory, practice, and research*. London: Sage Books.

Rossler, W. (2016). The stigma of mental disorders: A millennia-long history of social exclusion and prejudice. *EMBO Reports*, *17*(9), 1250–1253.

Ruderman Family Foundation. (2018). *White paper: Mental health and suicide of first responders*. Retrieved from https://rudermanfoundation.org/white_papers/police-officers-and-firefighters-are-more-likely-to-die-by-suicide-than-in-line-of-duty/

Santach, K. (2017, October 2). Las Vegas shooting brings fresh pain for Pulse survivors. *Orlando Sentinel*. Retrieved from www.orlandosentinel.com/news/os-las-vegas-shooting-reopens-pulse-trauma-20171002-story.html

Society of Community Research and Action (SCRA). (2010). *How to help your community recover from disaster: A manual for planning and action*. Retrieved from https://www.scra27.org/files/2114/0605/7122/SCRA_Disaster_Recovery_Manual.pdf

Szabo, L. (2016, December 7). Senate approves landmark mental health bill as part of 21st Century Cures Act. *Kaiser Health News*. Retrieved from http://khn.org/news/senate-approves-landmark-mental-health-bill-as-part-of-21st-century-cures-act/

Taylor, A. J. W., & Fraser, A. G. (1982). The stress of post-disaster body handling and victim identification work. *Journal of Human Stress*, *8*, 4–12.

Tracy, M., Norris, F. H., & Galea, S. (2011). Differences in the determinants of posttraumatic stress disorder and depression after a mass traumatic event. *Depress Anxiety*, *28*(8), 666–675.

Reader's Notes

2

Four Principles of Disaster Mental Health

Chapter 2 Preview
A. Collaboration of Community Partners
B. Communication and Relationship Building
C. Vulnerability of Community Populations
D. Understanding Trauma

Sometimes it pays to throw all plans out the window and assume a haphazard approach to life's events in order to enhance creativity and enjoy new and fresh outcomes. In such cases, much can be learned. Many people follow this live-and-let-live approach when they go on a vacation. They let the outcome of one experience move them toward another. Such results can bring much enjoyment and different ways of perceiving the norm.

This cavalier approach is inexcusable when lack of planning can actually scar people's lives forever. Such is the case with disaster mental health planning. Not following a specific strategy to prepare for and respond to a horrendous disaster can lead to much suffering by hundreds if not thousands of people. Lack of planning can actually be worse in such circumstances because many of the individuals who are doing their best to help others may also be traumatized. First responders are often impacted the most, for example, because they are at the center of the event. These people need to follow a strict, practiced routine.

Disaster mental health planning is a method allowing those concerned about the psychological wellbeing of their community members to identify their residents' needs and the resources required to determine the optimum solution in a disastrous situation. Successful planning:

1. Equally engages all participants in the decision-making process;
2. Supports collaboration and a dialogue between the planning members as well as community residents;
3. Gives collaboration members the information they need to make effective decisions;
4. Encourages the entire community to weigh in on and learn from decisions made;
5. Enables the sharing of resources and filling in needed gaps in service;
6. Discourages expensive redundancies and encourages spending on items most needed;
7. Provides a means for assessing and caring for those at greatest risk;
8. Offers an approach specifically focused on the local conditions and priorities;
9. Encourages give-and-take among people with different interests, life goals, and knowledge;
10. Educates citizens in how to prepare for potential adversity;
11. Builds resilience and personal strength to better cope with the next disaster; and
12. Establishes a way to make continuous improvements over time.

This manual stresses four principles required for successful community planning: Collaboration, constructive and unbiased communication, assessment of the most vulnerable populations, and trauma-informed treatment.

A. Collaboration of Community Partners

In the strictest definition, words such as "collaboration," "teamwork," "coalition," "partnership," and "network" have individual meanings based on who is participating and how long the members meet to reach their goals and objectives. As in this manual, these terms are often used interchangeably, particularly by communities working together for joint purposes. In general, collaboration means just that—more than two groups and/or individuals working together for a shared goal.

Collaborating divides a larger goal into more easily doable tasks. As problems become more complex and comprehensive, and solutions are required for larger numbers of people, collaboration acts as a powerful tool for mobilizing individuals. By working together and integrating personal abilities, experience, knowledge, and services in your disaster mental health collaboration, you can tap excellent resources and refrain from duplicating efforts.

Humans have been collaborating since prehistoric times when they joined forces to drive bison off a cliff. Now decisions are much more complex, and people recognize increasing the value of meeting and sharing with one another to reach an intended goal. This does not make collaboration an effortless process. Given the complexity of the goals as well as the varying personalities and agendas of those collaborating, it is anything but easy. The old joke goes, "What do you get when you put ten economists (or any other occupation) in a room? Eleven different opinions."

Collaborations may be loose associations in which members work for a short time to achieve a specific goal and then disband. They may also become organizations in themselves, with governing bodies, particular community responsibilities, funding, and permanence. Regardless of their size and structure, they exist to create and/or support efforts to reach a particular set of goals based on their vision and mission. The collaboration's goals are as varied as the structures themselves, but often contain elements of one or more of the following:

1. Influencing or developing public policy, usually around a specific issue;
2. Changing people's behavior, such as reducing smoking or drug use;
3. Building a healthier community;
4. Addressing an urgent situation;
5. Empowering certain elements of the municipality, or the community as a whole, to take control of its future, such as addressing the needs of senior citizens or determining how youth may be used as community resources;
6. Obtaining or offering services, such as funding for a needed intervention;
7. Offering more effective and efficient programming, in which organizations enhance cohesiveness and coordinate responsibilities so more participants have access to a greater variety of services.
8. Pooling services and resources of several organizations to accomplish a task that cannot be done alone;
9. Increasing communication among groups in which there was previously little contact in order to break down barriers and stereotypes and create alliances that learn from each other, establish trust, and face common goals;
10. Invigorating the depleting energies of group members who are trying to accomplish too much alone by focusing efforts around an issue through heightened hope and renewed strength;

11. Planning and launching large communitywide initiatives on a variety of issues for long-term campaigns in areas that were previously considered impossible or very difficult to achieve;

12. Combining the collaborative influence of once separate groups to advocate more change; and

13. Accelerating positive community change by combining the strengths of several groups to jointly solve problems and make decisions on important issues fulfilling community needs.

To effectively respond to mental health needs when a disaster occurs, it takes the diversity of know-how, ideas, experience, and interests of a collaboration. The hard work is well worth the end result: With each disaster, it becomes more apparent that joining forces is required to best help those in need.

B. Communication and Relationship Building

No one can say enough about the importance of constructive communication in the collaborative process. This includes ethical and objective give-and-take between the sender and receiver. One person closely listens to what is being said by the other, accepts this message, and acknowledges it is heard with or without additional information required. Communication is a critical component in all aspects of planning and implementation.

Trust is critical to relationship building. Collaboration members have a wide variety of backgrounds, experiences, and opinions, and it can be difficult to bring these people together without effective communication that allows them to better understand one another. If individuals want to make the most productive use of their knowledge, they need to trust and be trusted. They must know people are carefully listening to what they have to say, without bias or suspicion. A strong correlation exists between the amount of trust people have for one another and their ability to make worthwhile decisions.

Misinformation breaks down communication and leads to faulty or lack of positive actions. When people carefully listen to one another, misinterpretations and misunderstandings are greatly reduced. Further information and clarification can be conveyed by asking questions and confirming that a message has been effectively sent and received.

Situations are continually changing in these complex times. Effective communication also allows your collaboration to readily share updated information needed to alter future actions. Similarly, in today's environment, every minute is important. Positive communication encourages fewer disagreements and faster decision-making. Likewise, collaboration requires motivated members.

Why would anyone want to spend valuable time on a process when this input does not matter? If their ideas count, people will become more involved in planning. They will also go out of their way to volunteer additional time to future responsibilities.

Having effective communication greatly relies on the facilitator or person(s) leading the planning process. However, that person also needs to remind all members they must take responsibility for their own personal interactions. Everyone at the collaborative table assumes an equal role in the outcome.

C. Vulnerability of Community Populations

According to the World Health Organization (WHO, www.who.int), vulnerability is the degree to which a population, individual, or organization is unable to anticipate, cope with, resist, and recover from the impacts of disasters. The populations at greatest risk before a disaster, including the mentally ill, are the ones most shunned or ignored when the event actually occurs. Later in this manual, you will read more about those at most risk when catastrophes hit and how your planning group can define its own disenfranchised population through assessment.

The increasing frequency and severity of disasters is having more of an impact on these vulnerable populations. When normalcy is shattered in a mass shooting or structures are destroyed in natural catastrophes, it becomes very difficult to support those who previously had difficulty acting on their own. Response takes longer, and more risks arise for these individuals.

When arriving at a disaster site, state and national first responders may not prioritize those at greatest risk. This is not due to lack of caring, but rather because they are not familiar with the specific community and who requires the most support. Your collaboration, through assessment of local residents' needs, can direct responders to high-risk facilities or neighborhoods. You can also work closely with the medical teams, since vulnerable populations often require more supportive physical care.

Persons with mild to moderate mental health disorders often suffer from additional emotional problems in calamitous situations. It is not unusual to see displaced individuals wandering alone by their damaged homes or terrified and emotionally distraught in shelters. Mental illness also goes hand in hand with other types of vulnerabilities, such as aging, physical disabilities, and impoverishment. These individuals may have been coping relatively well before the disastrous event but now feel additionally burdened by changing circumstances. Those with more severe mental disorders may not search for help at all, being constrained by such barriers as isolation, stigma, fear of rejection, lack of knowledge, and limited or nonexistent access to services. In many cases, they may have been abandoned by their families or displaced from their homes. If your community does not have a plan to help the mentally ill, these vulnerable individuals could become even more cut off from support services and quickly deteriorate.

D. Understanding Trauma

Immediately after a disaster, the people most emotionally affected should be offered a form of care through the Crisis Counseling and Training Program (CCP) or Psychological First Aid (PFA) because many will experience anxiety or mild depression. Depending on how close they were to the epicenter of the disaster and what they saw and experienced, from 6% to 33% of the people exposed to a disaster will develop Acute Stress Disorder (ASD). In general, survivors of acts of violence such as mass shootings have shown higher rates of ASD than people who survived natural disasters (U.S. Department of Veterans Affairs, 2019).

ASD can occur during the first month after a disaster, and the symptoms are very similar to PTSD. The diagnosis of ASD is applicable from three days up to

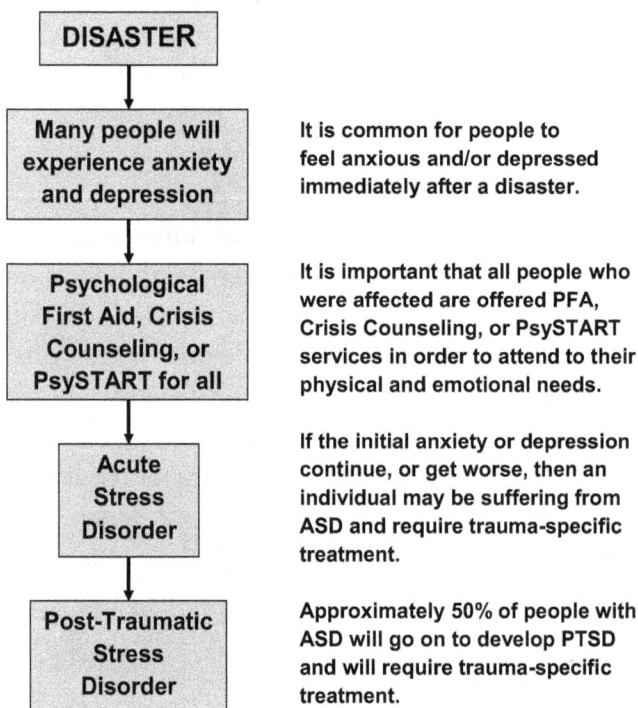

FIGURE 2.1   From a disaster to PTSD

a month following the initial trauma. If symptoms continue after a month, then it is diagnosed as PTSD. Approximately half of all people with ASD will go on to develop PTSD (*Psychology Today*, 2019). Individuals who are still experiencing stress and anxiety but do not have a diagnosis of ASD or PTSD can still benefit from wellness activities to deal with the stress of their experiences. (See Chapter 7 for examples.)

Trauma Symptoms

If people are showing several of the following symptoms, they may be suffering from some level of trauma and not realize it (Timberline Knolls Residential Treatment Center, 2019). This can happen to anyone after a disaster, even the therapist treating the victims.

Physical Signs of Trauma:

Unexplained sensations including pain;
Sleep and eating disturbances;
Low energy; and
Increased arousal (hyper-arousal).

Emotional Symptoms:

Depression and fear;
Anxiety and panic;
Numbness, irritability, and anger;
Feeling out of control; and
Avoidance.

Cognitive Changes:

Distraction;
Decrease in concentration;
Memory lapse; and
Difficulty with decisions.

Behavioral Signs and Effects:

Compulsion;
Substance abuse;
Eating disorders;
Impulsive, self-destructive behavior;
Dissociation/changes in interpersonal relationships;
Isolation, avoidance, and social withdrawal;
Sexual disruption; and
Feeling threatened, hostile, and argumentative.

Re-experiencing the Trauma:

Flashbacks;
Nightmares;
Intrusive thoughts; and
Sudden emotional and/or physical flooding of co-occurring disorders.

In the best-case scenario, anyone who struggles with some abnormal symptoms after a disaster should be encouraged to get treatment and not worry about any stigma attached to seeking help from a mental health professional. Also, many people do not have visible signs of physical injury after a tragedy but are nonetheless experiencing great emotional turmoil. In addition to offering immediate psychological support such as CCP and/or PFA, part of your collaboration's plan should be to ensure trauma-informed therapists are also available and readily accessible at post-disaster sites to encourage further help if necessary. Remember, the longer the trauma symptoms remain, particularly after a month, the greater chance PTSD is present, and the symptoms will not go away on their own—and will perhaps even become worse.

Trauma's Impact on the Brain

This manual also stresses the importance of recent changes in trauma treatment that are an outgrowth of better understanding of the brain. When people experience a horrific event or live through a highly stressful and life-threatening situation, they can become traumatized. As a result, they may become highly anxious and depressed, sleep poorly with nightmares, and lose weight from loss of appetite. Over the past decade, neuroscientists have learned considerably more about changes occurring in these individuals' brains that lead to trauma symptoms, although these researchers have much further to go.

Brain scans literally shed a lot of light on what happens when someone has PTSD. A traumatized brain does not function efficiently or effectively. The lower part of the brain contains the amygdala, a small almond-shaped organ. When sensing danger, the amygdala tells the body to fight back or run away. This is known as the "fight-or-flight response." Sometimes people cannot run or fight, so they just freeze and keep all these powerful emotions inside (Huey, 2018).

PTSD sufferers display hyperactivity in the amygdala when responding to stimuli that in some way resemble the original traumatic event or events. The amygdala tries to protect the individual by being on constant alert and ready to react. This condition is called "hypervigilance." If the amygdala senses danger, it overpowers the frontal lobe, or the cognitive part of the brain, where reasoning and logic occur and makes the person react as if the threat is real and present.

For example, when some combat soldiers return home and hear a car backfire, they dive for cover. They are "triggered" by the sound because it resembles gunfire. People without PTSD react differently when hearing this same loud sound. They can immediately evaluate the situation and determine that nothing is threatening their safety because the amygdala is not overpowering the frontal lobe. Similarly, PTSD sufferers who have lost their homes or family members in a horrendous hurricane may react to strong winds and rain by shaking, sweating, or trying to seek shelter. Sleeping also becomes difficult because the brain is never completely resting; it is in an ever-vigilant protection mode. Prolonged lack of sleep only worsens the trauma symptoms.

Memories Formed Under Stress

The brain of someone with PTSD also handles memories differently. According to neuro-researchers, memories formed under the influence of intense emotion, such as a traumatic event, are difficult to forget, unlike those from a routine day. Memories are stored in the part of the brain called the hippocampus. When perceiving an event is a serious threat, the amygdala tells the hippocampus to "flag this because it is important." The hippocampus may not recall some aspects of the event but can hyper focus on strong details of the incident such as sounds and smells (Huey, 2018). The amygdala, the hippocampus, and the hypothalamus lie very close to each other. The hypothalamus works with the pituitary gland, which sends hormones to the body so it is safe from a perceived danger (Johnson, 2018).

When people have PTSD from a traumatic event, such as those who were very close to the disaster's epicenter, their negative memories will not go away

Frontal Lobe

Thalamus

Hypothalamus

Hippocampus

Amygdala

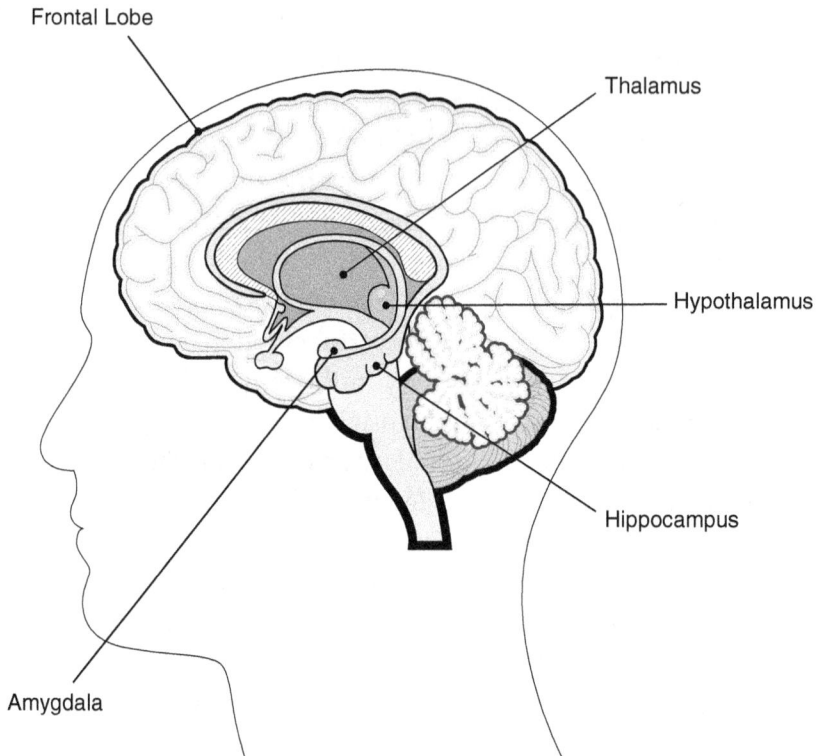

FIGURE 2.2   Parts of the brain affected by trauma

Source: Illustration by Leon Kamerman Schmidt

on their own. As a result, these individuals constantly feel as if the traumatic incident just happened. It is thus critical that these persons get treatment as soon as possible. Unfortunately, many first responders to a disaster mistakenly think their training will keep them from being severely affected by a traumatic event. They ignore any ongoing symptoms and do not seek help. Many of them will try to self-medicate with alcohol or drugs, which only worsens the problem. Police officers, firefighters, medical professionals, and clergy members, who are usually the first on the scene, should be encouraged by their employers and community leaders to seek a mental health evaluation to determine if they have PTSD. Suffering from trauma is not a sign of weakness; it is a normal reaction to a very abnormal event.

Changes in PTSD Treatment

Cognitive approaches such as Trauma-Focused Cognitive Behavioral Therapy (TF-CBT), which focus on the top of the brain, or the frontal lobe, have been the accepted treatment for PTSD. However, recent studies now suggest another approach using techniques that work to calm the brain and release traumatic memories. For example, several studies with veterans have shown a substantial reduction in PTSD symptoms in just six hours of treatment with Emotional Freedom Techniques (EFT), a somatic approach that uses the body's acupressure points (Church, Geronilla, & Dinter, 2009; Geronilla, 2016).

Psychiatrist and noted trauma specialist Bruce D. Perry, MD, PhD, prefers to help PTSD patients "from the bottom up" rather than "from the top down" (Lyons, 2017). Instead of working with the cognitive functions of logic and reasoning found in the frontal lobe at the top of the brain, Perry focuses lower down on the amygdala and hippocampus. This bottom-up approach is necessary because the amygdala can easily be triggered in a traumatized person. It is unable to reason and designed for protection and will overpower the frontal lobe and take action. When treating people with PTSD, it is important to calm their amygdala and reassure them there is no present threat. This is the only way to release the traumatic memories imbedded in the lower brain and once again allow the self-regulation of emotions. As Perry (2014) puts it, "Regulate, relate, reason." Bottom-up treatments include Eye Movement Desensitization and Reprocessing (EMDR), EFT or tapping, and Brainspotting. These mind/body techniques calm the amygdala, allow access to the traumatic memories, and gently release those that are "stuck." (See Chapter 7 for more information on these trauma therapies.)

TO DO

1. Think about the business and personal groups of which you have been a member. How did the communication and collaboration between and among members strengthen or hinder the group's progress? As your community forms a disaster mental health collaboration, what will help the group form stronger bonds and get more accomplished? What may stand in the way of furthering communication and progress? For example, if many of the members are from similar types of organizations, they may be fearful of sharing data with one another.

2. Whom do you consider the most vulnerable populations in your community? How would/did these individuals fare in a disaster? Are they presently receiving the support needed to prepare them for major impact and change?

3. How familiar are you with PTSD through your employment or personal life? Do you think mental illness is increasing in the U.S., or has it historically been of major concern but now more recognized?

4. This chapter suggests that collaboration, communication, recognizing vulnerable populations, and trauma-informed care are the four principles to best help your disaster mental health intervention process. Do you have any other suggestions on how to more effectively respond to mental health needs following a community disaster?

Resources

Church, D., Geronilla, L., & Dinter, I. (2009). Psychological symptom change in veterans after six sessions of EFT: An observational study. *International Journal of Healing and Caring, 9*(1), 1–13.

Geronilla, L. (2016). EFT remediates PTSD and psychological symptoms in veterans: A randomized controlled replication trial. *Energy Psychology: Theory, Research and Treatment, 8*(2), 29–41.

Huey, E. D. (2018, September 26). The science of memory. *CBS Morning News*. Retrieved from www.cbsnews.com/news/why-we-remember-traumatic-events-better/

Johnson, J. (2018, August 22). What does the hypothalamus do? *Medical News Today*. Retrieved from www.medicalnewstoday.com/articles/312628.php

Lyons, S. (2017, July 26). *The repair of early trauma: A bottom-up approach*. Retrieved from https://beaconhouse.org.uk/developmental-trauma/the-repair-of-early-trauma-a-bottom-up-approach/the-repair-of-early-trauma-a-bottom-up-approach

Perry, B. (2014, April 1). *Regulate, relate, reason*. Retrieved from www.thinkkids.org/regulate-relate-reason/

Psychology Today. (2019, February 7). Acute stress disorder. Retrieved from www.psychologytoday.com/us/conditions/acute-stress-disorder

Timberline Knolls Residential Treatment Center. (2019). *Trauma and PTSD; signs and symptoms*. Retrieved from www.timberlineknolls.com/trauma/signs-effects/

U.S. Department of Veterans Affairs. (2019, October 17). *How common is ASD?* Retrieved from https://www.ptsd.va.gov/understand/related/acute.stress.asp

Reader's Notes

3

Action Planning Through Collaboration

Chapter 3 Preview
A. The Importance of Collaboration
B. Action Plan Overview
C. Beginning the Collaborative Process
D. Organizational Structure
E. The Action Plan's Ultimate Purpose
F. Membership Agreements
G. Assembling Pertinent Information
H. Establishing Goals and Objectives
I. Final Action Plan Organizational Roles
J. Additional Collaboration Resources

Forty-five years have passed since the U.S. governors requested a nationwide emergency management system for medical care, which was created through FEMA. It is surely past time for the same emphasis to be placed on disaster mental health planning. The intended goal of this manual is to help your community develop an action plan that specifically meets your residents' needs when calamity strikes. The reason: Regardless of the type of disaster, some people in your town or city will be psychologically impacted. The "fortunate" ones will steadily improve in a few months; the less fortunate may seek treatment and take much longer to feel better or, at worst, ignore their emotional state and try to cope with the deepening mental illness. The more you know about your community's needs, and the more quickly you respond to them when a disaster occurs, the better the long-term results for everyone's wellbeing.

This chapter provides you with a step-by-step guide on how to establish your action plan through community collaboration: It clearly defines how to develop and implement the mental health processes and procedures to effectively prepare for, respond to, and recover from a disaster. The steps provide flexibility because of the variation in communities and the resources and tools available. For example, larger communities may have more financial latitude as well as a greater number of resources to help in the planning process. Yet these more populous areas grapple with their own public health issues. Smaller towns have their own challenges, such as limited budgets and personnel, access to healthcare, low population density, and communication issues. Some remote rural areas lack public health departments and hospitals and instead must rely on nearby cities or statewide services; however, they may not be as mired in red tape and so can progress more quickly in the planning process.

Your collaboration will need to determine the scope of its disaster preparedness, recovery, and response efforts. What roles and responsibilities will your planning group's members assume in the protocols and procedures when a disaster is declared, and which will they share or delegate to other parties? This chapter includes some options your collaboration can consider for external support. You may want to partner with other communities and form a coalition or receive help from county or state resources, for example. The bottom line: Disaster preparedness is far, far better than trying to pinch hit when a disaster occurs.

Regardless of your collaboration's capacity, the following are the fundamentals required for creating a mental health plan as cited by the Centers for Disease Control (CDC, www.cdc.gov) and this manual's authors:

PREPAREDNESS/PLANNING

Assess

1. Be familiar with your community's cultural and religious composition, ethnicity, shared values, social resources, healthcare access, education levels, at-risk populations, spoken languages, and nongovernmental and community-based organizations;

2. Build relationships with public health officials, community mental health stakeholders, spiritual leaders, private and public medical providers, and school officials;
3. Identify policy and resources for staff support; and
4. Determine pertinent legal issues involved with disaster mental health intervention.

Establish

1. Designate specific roles in mental health services before, during, and after a disaster;
2. Identify and train mental health professionals and response staff to provide counseling, triage, outreach, and education (as well as the types of therapy utilized and when);
3. Arrange for interpreter and translation services and neighborhood liaisons;
4. Train providers in the mental health consequences of natural and human-caused disasters (and the types of disasters and their varying impacts);
5. Develop a risk communication plan and templates for dissemination to both the residents and the media;
6. Determine a triage system to connect victims with additional mental health services when needed; and
7. Contact the state counseling association, state social workers' association, state marriage and family therapists' association, and psychologists' and psychiatrists' organizations and request a list of licensed trauma-informed therapists who practice in the area.

RESPONSE

1. First and foremost, meet basic safety and security needs of the predetermined populations;
2. Provide PFA (or other early intervention for disaster survivors) at established response sites;
3. Use crisis and emergency risk communication principles in all messaging;
4. Monitor the mental health needs of survivors;
5. Provide access to counselors in all appropriate languages;
6. Distribute appropriate educational information;
7. Deploy volunteer licensed trauma-informed therapists to shelters to help survivors in acute distress; and

8. Rely on pre-established relationships with mental health partners (and only allow pre-approved individuals to interact with survivors).

RECOVERY

1. Continue to monitor and respond to mental health needs in the impacted population;
2. Train social and community leaders on how to help their groups cope;
3. Give the community opportunities to come together;
4. Promote availability of coping resources; and
5. Anticipate and plan ways to deal with trauma reminders, such as anniversary dates.

EVALUATION

1. Monitor for long-term mental stress in the community and for PTSD;
2. Identify and address gaps in the mental health preparedness plan; and
3. Update the action plan.

A. The Importance of Collaboration

The development and implementation of comprehensive plans require purposeful collaboration among public and private agencies and organizations. As noted in the University of Kansas "Community Tool Box" (2018), community problems or issues are often too complex and overwhelming for any one entity to tackle on its own. In simplest terms, a collaboration is a group of individuals and/or organizations with a common interest that agrees to work together toward defined goals. A goal can be as narrow as obtaining funding for a specific intervention or as broad as trying to permanently improve the overall quality of life and wellbeing for all community members.

The collaboration might be drawn from a narrow area of interest or include representatives of nearly every segment of the community, depending on the breadth of the issue. Regardless, successful partnerships require connecting parties that want to significantly improve an area of concern, nurture healthy relationships among diverse communities of individuals, promote mutual respect and trust, and ensure that everyone is on equal footing. Community psychologists stress how human behavior is frequently based on external conditions. Individuals exist within a very complex interconnected social and environmental framework. To determine the best response to an issue that greatly impacts human behavior, it is necessary to leverage the collaborative process and allow individuals and organizations in a common geographical area to work collectively and bring about positive community change. A formal and considerate decision-making process empowers a collaboration and strengthens its efforts.

The collaboration of individuals with a variety of interests and backgrounds leads to greater resource availability, responsibility sharing, expertise and skills, and consistency of information and communication. Cooperation can also reduce, if not eliminate, service duplication and implementation time. In addition, planning and preparedness activities enhance the response capabilities needed to effectively handle any arising emergencies. Through collaboration, a community is ready to face the major consequences of a catastrophe even before it hits. This collaborative group establishes a mission and vision, goals and objectives, ongoing assessment, resiliency development, and a means for continuous improvement. All members involved in the planning process assume specific roles and responsibilities and are trained as necessary. They also incorporate what they have learned into their own organization's structure to develop a continuum of services supporting individuals with immediate- to long-term care and place an emphasis on the most vulnerable and disadvantaged individuals.

Collaborative integration has the potential to:

1. Promote compliance with health and wellbeing directives;
2. Enhance individual and community resilience;
3. Expand prevention through education;
4. Facilitate rapid identification of those in need of immediate care;
5. Improve accuracy in diagnosis and treatment;
6. Reduce long-term mental health problems;
7. Help with adjustment to loss and coping with adverse situations;
8. Further cost-effective and seamless care;
9. Identify and lower potential barriers to treatment compliance;
10. Hasten resources for at-risk and special needs groups;
11. Support culturally informed services;
12. Promote confidence and trust in government;
13. Empower individuals to care for themselves more effectively; and
14. Further a community's timely return to normal.

Assembling resources for disaster recovery and response can be compared to the creation of a patchwork quilt (Thomas & Bowen, 2009): Community leaders symbolize the quilters, who must initiate the creation and realization of a new vision; the quilt's pattern represents the intervention plan, which is developed with information from previous plans, data, and specialists; and the quilt's materials are developed from a collection of programs offering funding and/or services to realize the vision. The quilt is developed through the collaborative input of the entire community—all sewing the pieces together into a united whole.

Establishing and implementing the responsibilities of a collaborative planning process can be challenging but also very rewarding to the individuals involved, those impacted by a disastrous incident, and the community as a whole. The object is to not get lost in the minutiae—and sometimes politics— but keep focused on the end result of best serving your community.

B. Action Plan Overview

Planning is the process of defining what needs to be done, when, and by whom to reach desired results. Your collaboration's action plan will include a detailed Road Map with the goals and objectives, time lines, and personal accountability required for the four stages of mental health disaster management: Preparedness/ Planning, Response, Recovery, and Evaluation. The ultimate purpose is to increase your community's ability to effectively develop meaningful mental health outcomes for its residents for the long term. Action planning will help your collaboration:

1. Determine an understanding of both your community's issues and their potential solutions;
2. Create a strategy that effectively addresses these issues;
3. Ensure your proposed strategy is feasible and/or realistic based on the community's unique needs and assets;
4. Coordinate all strategic steps without duplication of efforts and with as much consistency as possible;
5. Assign pertinent roles and responsibilities across all community sectors, making the best possible use of available resources, including volunteer activities and time;
6. Ensure all collaboration participants follow through with their obligations on the prescribed time line;
7. Confirm that all pertinent details are included and sustainable for the long term, which may be months or even years;
8. Provide all required training and exercises so the strategy can be immediately and effectively carried out if/when necessary;
9. Determine measurable activities for tracking and assessment; and
10. Make any necessary changes and updates and ensure all is in place for the next implementation.

As you establish your action plan, it will be necessary to refer to subsequent chapters in this manual for additional information. For example, one of the collaboration's first steps is conducting a community assessment, which is covered in depth in Chapter 5.

C. Beginning the Collaborative Process

Designate the Convener

The first step in the planning process is for one person, typically a representative of an organization, to act as the convener for the collaboration. In this case, the convener wants to create a disaster mental health plan because issues have been raised concerning future "what-ifs," or a human-caused or natural disaster has already occurred and demonstrated the vital need for preparedness. Since the factors involved with disasters are so diverse, it is better to have a convener with a broader and more general knowledge base of the different populations being served and of trauma-informed mental healthcare. This may be someone, for example, from one of the municipality's public or mental health departments or a nonprofit mental health organization.

Your community's office of emergency/disaster management may be a possible convener, since your collaboration should be working hand in hand with this agency. Keep in mind, however, many emergency personnel do not have knowledge of or experience with mental health and may not even understand its importance when responding to a crisis. Based on this directive, it has been their department's responsibility to focus on the medical and safety needs of impacted individuals.

Conveners should have no formal authority over the group and its members, its direction, or the results to be achieved. They should have no hidden agenda. Rather, they act as motivators who see how the vital need must be addressed by the entire community and encourage others with the right expertise and interest to participate. Conveners must have strong influence and persuasion skills, a sincere belief in the need for planning, and a great deal of patience. They need to project the mission and its importance to professionals who are hesitant to be involved with another project. Too many individuals are willing to put off disaster preparedness because the chances of such an event happening are significantly less than other community issues.

Choose the Core Group and Full Collaboration

The convener then asks for the help of several individuals who act as a small core group. They clarify the final composition of the collaboration, making sure it corresponds to the community's demographics. One of your planning group's first efforts will be to conduct a community assessment; the collaboration's makeup needs to reflect the findings of this analysis. Which individuals best represent the community and have the interest and abilities to execute an effective disaster mental health response and recovery effort? Who will be committed to fulfilling the mission, rather than simply feeling obliged? How can this group be encouraged to work together most productively? The collaboration needs to include participants from multidisciplinary areas who are greatly interested in disaster mental health and have a pertinent background or experience. However, their involvement cannot be to anyone's exclusion: All members must have the opportunity to voice their ideas and participate in the planning process. A well-functioning collaboration finds an appropriate role and responsibility for each participant: Some people are planners and see the larger picture; some are leaders and want to oversee a committee; and some are valuable doers who ably accomplish the tasks they are given.

At the same time, the group cannot become too large and unwieldy. You can divide into committees and subcommittees, where the chair of each group reports on recommendations and attends the major meetings. Topic-specific task groups or subcommittees can address such general areas as recruitment and training, operational and deployment protocols, special incidents planning, intervention stages, communication, and pre- and post-disaster assessment. Some members, such as the fire chief, may only attend one or two meetings to provide input and determine how your collaboration will work with emergency services.

Importance of Flexibility

Each collaboration will have its own specific member makeup. Some groups may form through a local trauma-informed nonprofit youth and family services organization that recognizes the community needs to prepare for a potential disaster. This group plans on teaming with similar organizations and utilizing the combined strengths of their administrators and mental health teams to meet the psychological needs of survivors. A different collaboration may form through the municipality's department of mental health. For support, it convenes other community members who have a sincere interest or experience in mental health.

Similarly, a city's emergency management department may undertake this project because it understands the importance of adding a mental health component to its medical response plan. Or, in a rural area, several small towns may join ranks to develop a plan. They expect to rely on one of the state's regional disaster mental health response teams, which responds to critical incidents when local resources are depleted or overwhelmed. This rural group may also plan to rely on the services of a local Red Cross chapter. In many cases, a community may have already experienced a catastrophe firsthand and wants to be prepared for the next eventuality.

The group's resources as well as the type and extent of the event will influence whether a collaboration can proceed on its own or needs to call in state and federal backup. In Connecticut, for example, the Department of Mental Health and Addiction Services may be called on to lend team support of disaster mental health services if a catastrophe occurs. In the worst-case scenario, the state will refer to the Robert T. Stafford Disaster Relief and Emergency Assistance Act. The governor and FEMA conduct a preliminary damage assessment to demonstrate the disaster is of such severity and magnitude that effective response is beyond the state's capabilities. A request is made to the U.S. president to declare that a major disaster exists, and federal programs will assist in the effort.

The collaboration members will develop their own action plan. Some of the members will focus on planning; others will be involved with planning as well as fill a vital role at the disaster site. Based on the authors' suggested action plan design and implementation (see end of this chapter and Road Map), the collaborative's primary members could assume the following titles and responsibilities:

- ◆ Assessment Specialist—Developing a community mental health assessment;
- ◆ Call Center Coordinator—Handling all telecommunications and contacting volunteers;
- ◆ Communications/Media Coordinator—Playing a key role in all disaster communication;
- ◆ Emergency Management Director—Assuming responsibility for disaster medical response;
- ◆ Facilitator—Leading the collaboration team efforts;
- ◆ Fire Chief—Providing input on issues relating to safety and mental health;
- ◆ Grantsperson—Researching and applying for grants;
- ◆ Local Municipal Leader—Liaison between the town/city and the collaboration;
- ◆ Medical Professional—Offering support with medical issues related to mental health;
- ◆ Mental Health Response Leader—Interfacing with the Emergency Management Director and overseeing the disaster mental health plan's implementation;
- ◆ Psychological Services Center Coordinator—Being responsible for setting up the free psychological services centers and working with the Call Center Coordinator;

- ◆ Police Chief—Providing input on safety and mental health;
- ◆ Resiliency Specialist—Determining ways to build community strengths;
- ◆ Social Services Manager—Representing diverse community populations; and
- ◆ Volunteer Center Coordinator—Creating a list of trained volunteer crisis counselors/PFA volunteers in the area.

You can recruit collaboration members from the following groups and individuals.

- ◆ Adult independent-living communities;
- ◆ American Red Cross chapter;
- ◆ Attorneys;
- ◆ Chamber of Commerce;
- ◆ Community mental health–related nonprofits;
- ◆ Disaster recovery organizations;
- ◆ Educational community—schools, universities, and childcare providers;
- ◆ Emergency response team members;
- ◆ Faith-based organizations;
- ◆ Geriatric support groups and organizations;
- ◆ Grant writers;
- ◆ Health and wellness centers;
- ◆ Healthcare coalitions;
- ◆ Homeless service providers;
- ◆ Local and state government agencies;
- ◆ Local medical and mental healthcare provider associations;
- ◆ Media and social media specialists;
- ◆ Medical center mental health personnel;
- ◆ Military associations and veterans;
- ◆ Neighborhood organizations;
- ◆ Parent organizations;
- ◆ Prevention programs;
- ◆ Private companies and businesses;
- ◆ Public health clinics;
- ◆ Public and/or mental health municipal departments;

- ◆ Service organizations (Lions, Rotary);
- ◆ State behavioral response teams;
- ◆ Substance abuse treatment service organizations;
- ◆ Tribal organizations;
- ◆ Youth services municipal departments; and
- ◆ Volunteer groups.

Collaboration Members' Personal Traits

Energetic: Demonstrates the ability to stay actively involved in stressful situations.

Open Minded: Remains objective to different opinions and appreciates ethnic and cultural variation.

Self-Esteem: Values one's own abilities and can accept positive criticism.

Flexibility: Demonstrates the ability to accept situations where change is critical.

Attentive: Listens carefully to what others are saying and provides valuable input in return.

Practical: Looks for new and more effective ways to find and utilize limited resources.

Team Player: Enjoys combining areas of expertise to accomplish greater ends.

Dependable: Stands by commitments made regardless of changing circumstances.

Positive: Continues to see the glass half full, even when circumstances are at their most severe.

Sensitive: Cares about the needs of others and wants to help in any way possible.

Self-Controlled: Keeps level headed and in control during stressful situations.

Name the Collaboration Facilitator

The convener or a core group member may become the facilitator and oversee the entire collaborative process. If funds are available, you may instead hire a professional facilitator. This leader needs excellent communication, organization, time management, and diplomacy skills, as well as the ability to recognize diverse opinions. The facilitator may also work hand in hand with a planning coordinator, who helps with logistics.

Specifically, the facilitator assumes the following responsibilities:

1. Establishes the meetings' ground rules, such as strictly adhering to the agenda, starting and ending on time, providing everyone with the opportunity for input, ensuring members complete their expected tasks, and treating all opinions with respect.

2. Determines the meeting dates and agenda, based on the goals, tasks, and time line. The agenda includes the topics to be discussed and by whom, as well as the time allotted for providing information and group discussion. In some cases, a formal or informal vote will follow a presentation. The agenda is provided to all members in advance of the meeting, either through email or online. The facilitator also determines which members are to attend meetings based on the collaboration's structure.

3. Helps members determine the vision and mission for short-term goals and long-term interests. This includes establishing a Road Map with specific objectives designed to ensure successful completion.

4. Clarifies each person's roles and responsibilities, recruits additional support if needed, and reminds individuals of upcoming deadlines and collaboration presentations. All participants will be expected to prepare for the meeting's topics and to attend training sessions, exercises, and drills to fulfill their roles. Since all members are accountable for their commitments, the facilitator ensures no one promises more than can be personally achieved; likewise, no members are to be significantly less involved than others.

5. Makes sure all members have input (including those who are more hesitant to express themselves) and equal time to ask questions and voice concerns at each meeting. The facilitator keeps anyone from monopolizing the discussions and cutting others off. Meetings can easily stray away from the agenda when disagreements arise. Facilitation maintains order and curtails side conversations. At the same time, the facilitator encourages give-and-take and productive discussions.

6. Summarizes all key points after the speaker completes a presentation to assure everyone understands and agrees with the information. Sometimes visuals or handouts are needed to better display more complex items or those to be altered with members' input. The most important points made in the meeting can be restated before adjournment.

7. Ensures and reviews minutes sent to all members before each meeting and their acceptance with changes, if necessary.

8. Regularly reviews goals, objectives, and timetable to ensure they are being appropriately followed.

D. Organizational Structure

Before the collaboration meets for the first time, the core group should discuss the collaboration's structure, or how meetings are organized, decisions made, and members held accountable. The core group's suggestions are to be brought up to the entire collaboration for review, comments, and adoption. The sooner members can agree on a structure, the sooner they will be able to develop and implement effective responses to the situation at hand. Furthermore, when everyone agrees the structure is fair, opinions will be more openly voiced, and better decisions and more effective actions are likely to occur.

You can choose from several different organizational structures, which determine the utilization of committees and subcommittees, the degree of community input, and the communication exchange and decision-making process for end goals. Whatever approach is used, Thomas Wolff, PhD (https://www.tomwolff.com/), a coalition-building specialist, stresses the importance of "collaboration for equity and justice." He lists six key components of collaborative structure: engage a broad spectrum of the community; encourage true collaboration as the form of exchange; practice democracy and promote active citizenship and empowerment; employ an ecological approach that builds on community strengths; take action by addressing issues of social change and power; and align the goals with the process.

The most effective structure is:

1. Responsive to the needs of the situation and to the collaboration;
2. A catalyst for effective decision-making;
3. Acceptable to all group members;
4. Accountable to the larger community it represents;
5. Flexible enough that it can adjust according to varying circumstances;
6. Inclusive, allowing everyone who wants to participate to do so in a way that builds on personal skills and interests; and
7. Assessed, when possible, to determine how well it works, then adjusted as necessary.

Disaster-related planning creates additional circumstances to be taken into account:

1. Making quick decisions, since the consequences of undue delay can sometimes be serious;

2. Deciding on the basis of incomplete information; and

3. Communicating decisions rapidly and efficiently to the community at large.

Based on these factors, a disaster mental health action plan structure may have these distinct characteristics:

1. As much participation and deliberation as circumstances allow, but where leadership must act swiftly when needed;

2. The ability to clearly and swiftly communicate decisions to members; and

3. A well-defined, easy-to-use means for providing feedback to decision makers.

Orientation/Kickoff Meeting

The collaboration's first full meeting can act as an orientation and provide an overview of community planning; determine community readiness; review the reason for the collaboration; define roles and responsibilities; and explain benefits, challenges, and expected key outcomes. The orientation presents an estimated overview of the project. The length of time needed to complete the planning process is typically based on the size and skills of the team, resources available, and stage of readiness, as well as the complexity of what is to be accomplished. Members need to agree to the schedule of meetings and time line.

At this orientation, the facilitator assists members with defining a code of ethics. Ethical guidelines are clearly established for all participants and depend on the specific situation. The standards for creating an ethical code are based on the balance of three important factors: What is good, what is right, and what is best for whom in which situation. Ethical considerations must include the demographics of the entire population being served, with a focus on equal support for all individuals. The importance is looking at socioeconomic differences, race, language, age, gender, physical disabilities, mental illness, substance abuse, and homelessness. Specific input may be necessary from typical at-risk groups. If your community has not yet conducted a mental health assessment, this should be placed on the "to-do" list at this time. Many of your decisions for disaster preparedness, response, and recovery will be based on this assessment. You can learn more about assessments in Chapter 5.

Attendees may want to draft an initial vision and mission statement or at least begin to formulate thoughts and discussion points to be voted on at the first formal meeting. Since many of the people in the collaboration may not have an understanding of disaster mental health intervention, the facilitator can provide:

1. A general overview of what needs to be accomplished;
2. Some examples of mental healthcare issues following a disaster for the short, intermediate, and long term; and
3. Copies of this manual and other reading materials.

E. The Action Plan's Ultimate Purpose

Vision Statement

Your vision statement communicates what your collaboration believes are the ideal conditions for the health and wellbeing of your community: What would be the ultimate goal if your most important issue was perfectly addressed? This aspiration is generally described by one or more phrases, statements, or brief proclamations conveying the community's future expectations. By developing a vision statement, your collaboration makes its beliefs and governing principles clear to all members and the greater community.

There are certain characteristics most vision statements have in common. In general, vision statements should be:

1. Understood and shared by members of the community;
2. Broad enough to encompass a variety of local perspectives;
3. Inspiring and uplifting to everyone involved in your effort; and
4. Easy to communicate with a few words.

Mission Statement

A mission statement, which follows in the action planning process, describes what your collaboration is going to do and why this is being done. A mission statement is similar to but more concrete and "action-oriented" than a vision. Without going into too much detail, it begins to relate how your collaboration may proceed in order to reach the vision. Mission statements are generally:

1. Concise. Although not as short a phrase as the vision statement, a mission should still make its point in one sentence;
2. Outcome oriented. Mission statements explain the overarching outcomes your collaboration is working to achieve; and
3. Inclusive. While a mission specifically describes your group's overarching goals, it is very important that it does so very broadly.

The following vision and mission statements are examples meeting these criteria:

Vision: "To build a resilient community prepared to rapidly respond to and recover from natural and human-caused disasters that adversely affect the public's mental health."

Mission: "To use the knowledge, experience, and interests of a diversified community-based collaboration to develop a disaster mental health action plan that provides specific roles, responsibilities, and steps for the stages of assessment, preparedness, response, and recovery that are required before, during, and after a disaster."

F. Membership Agreements

Memoranda of Understanding/Agreement (MOU/MOA)

It is important that all collaboration members understand and agree to their roles and responsibilities. Sometimes a Memorandum of Understanding (MOU) is written as an agreement between organizations and/or individuals to establish ground rules for working together. The MOU outlines what each party will contribute and the expected time line. Fawcett, Francisco, Andrews-Payne and Schultz (2000) provide this example:

The collaboration members agree to work toward community change and improvement in the following ways:

1. Community partnership: Consistent with the community's vision and goals, the community partnership, including local people and community-based organizations, will select a modest number of broad goals;

2. Support organizations: These groups will assist the community partnership in establishing a broad-based vision and mission for community health and development, focusing on specific locally determined issues or concerns and framing objectives as challenging community-developed goals; and

3. Grantmaker(s): Grantmakers will lay the groundwork for multi-year grant application(s) to be submitted to relevant funders. The grant(s) will outline coordinated investments in a long-term, comprehensive, and community-determined development process. The expected length of time of the collaboration's work should be included.

Legal Considerations

Until recently, the emergency preparedness legal environment has been largely based on the swift and effective response to physical harm from disasters. Federal and state emergency responders ensure personnel and supplies are readily accessible to address physical injuries. With mental health, the difficulty lies in even longer-lasting health concerns and the legal environment. Also, regulations can vary from state to state. It is recommended that your collaboration speak with an attorney to determine how laws might be interpreted, amended, or created to address immediate and long-term mental health impact.

G. Assembling Pertinent Information

Now that your collaboration is up and running, it can begin to put together the pieces for your disaster mental health plan. You need additional information on some of the major topics. One of the most essential areas is learning more about your community's population, particularly who are the most vulnerable, at-risk residents. Socioeconomic, cultural, and institutional factors can greatly increase someone's susceptibility to major change. It is clearly understood that disaster risk depends on much more than the severity of the event; it also is based on the level of susceptibility.

Knowing a disaster's negative impact on mental health alters the emphasis from post- to pre-disaster, from response to preparedness (Bada Math, Nirmata, Moirangthem, & Kumar, 2015). Assessing populations prior to a calamity is critical in knowing where mental health services are most needed to be integrated into your plan. You can find more information on assessments in Chapter 5.

You also need to know if your entire community is more at risk for one type of disaster than another. If you have experienced numerous tornadoes in the past, that provides a good clue. However, some locations are just experiencing climate change effects for the first time. Just as critically, all communities are unfortunately at risk of human-caused tragedies. When writing your disaster mental health plan, you need to take prior events into consideration. From a positive standpoint, you have experienced the impact firsthand, which provides helpful knowledge for future events. What lessons have you learned? What actions proved beneficial, and which need to change for better results? Chapter 6 provides an overview of disasters and their varying impacts on mental health.

Hopefully, increased knowledge about post-disaster mental health treatment will reduce the number of survivors with both short- and long-term serious illness, particularly PTSD. The information in Chapter 7 can help you determine the roles and responsibilities of mental health response teams and other organizations and individuals involved with crisis intervention. It also offers specific information on the most effective types of trauma-informed treatment and wellness. Chapter 8 provides insights into ways to enhance pre- and post-disaster resiliency. The takeaways from the lessons learned in Chapter 9, as well as case studies in the other chapters, give you valuable assistance for making decisions. Finally, look at the Road Map at the end of the manual to review the most important steps in the action planning process. No need to reinvent the wheel for positive actions or to repeat mistakes made.

H. Establishing Goals and Objectives

What needs to be done, when, and by whom? The answers will be addressed through your collaboration's goals and objectives that respond to the mission statement. Goals are the specific results or purposes expected from your collaborative efforts. They specify what will be accomplished over the entire project period and directly relate to the mission. Each goal is achieved through the project objectives or specific steps being taken. These objectives are to be specific, measurable, achievable, relevant, and time bound (SMART). According to SAMHSA (www.samhsa.gov), they help transform overarching ideas into action steps that move you forward, provide accountability, adhere to timing criteria, and allow your plan to be effectively implemented.

Specific—The objective is clearly stated, so anyone who reads it understands what will be done, when, and by whom;

Measurable—How this objective will be measured to ensure it is being carried out as planned;

Achievable—The objective needs to be realistic based on the community's limitations. Setting reasonable objectives helps set the project up for success;

Relevant—An objective must fit the makeup and structure of the community collaboration and address the vision and mission; and

Time bound—Every objective has a specific time line for completion.

I. Final Action Plan Organizational Roles

As noted at the beginning of this chapter, the authors suggest specific individuals who are on the collaborative and participate in the disaster mental health intervention. In this section, as well as in the Road Map, you can find specifics on the activities involved in every phase of collaboration formation and disaster preparedness, response, and recovery. These listings can act as an informative guide for all activities that must be taken. In addition, the Appendix includes sources for other mental health and behavioral plans.

Pre-Disaster Responsibilities

The Volunteer Center Coordinator ensures that the necessary number of volunteers are trained to respond to mental health needs when a disaster occurs. Possible training includes PFA, which typically takes place during the first hours and days of a disaster or crisis event, and CCP, an early intervention intended for days, weeks, and perhaps months after the event to address early-stage disaster distress reactions. Some nonprofit, private, and public entities offer a PFA certification covering competencies and attitudes necessary to provide appropriate mental health services to survivors. FEMA provides CCP training. (See Chapter 7 for more information.) The Volunteer Center Coordinator regularly offers updated courses for trainee information retention and ongoing updates. Training also includes disaster drills or exercises with the goal of evaluating the operational aspects of the mental health action plan, in addition to solidifying relationships with collaboration members and community participants.

The Psychological Services Center Coordinator compiles a list of trauma-informed practitioners from the local area who are to provide therapy through the psychological services centers and shelters at the disaster site. This list is continually updated and checked for appropriate trauma-trained adherence.

Disaster Responsibilities

The Mental Health Response Leader oversees the implementation of the disaster mental health intervention plan and works in tandem with the town/city's Emergency Management Director (and police, fire, emergency response teams, etc.). These individuals are the first to be notified when a disaster occurs (or is expected to occur). They confer with the Volunteer Center Coordinator and Psychological Services Center Coordinator and, based on the extent of the disaster, determine the number of mental health providers needed and whether additional support will be requested from other mental health responders. Some states have trained units who are available on call, such as the Connecticut Disaster Behavioral Health Response Network (DBHRN). Or, services such as the American Psychological Association Disaster Response Network may be contacted. The team leaders will also make decisions on the need for and location of general and specialized shelters.

The Call Center Coordinator is responsible for contacting and deploying the required number of volunteers and other mental health providers. Updated lists of volunteers are supplied by the Volunteer Center Coordinator and Psychological Services Center Coordinator. Depending on the extent of the event, calls may come from throughout the world and concern a myriad of topics from fearful family members to the media and to volunteers/donors. The call center also fields any calls to/from psychological/medical contacts regarding a survivor's mental health needs, medication, or possible hospitalization. Since the call center is the central communication hub, it is staffed 24/7 well beyond the end of the disaster.

The Volunteer Center Coordinator oversees the volunteer center and registration of all mental health volunteers, such as those for PFA and CCP. The interfaith representative on the collaboration team also works closely with the volunteer center, and all clergy should sign in when arriving. Everyone's identification and training certification are confirmed and badges supplied; names and arrival times are noted on sign-up sheets. Volunteers receive information on the type of disaster; its extent; expected personal, property, and structural impact/damage; and where they will be located. They are to check in on a regular basis and will receive protocols on how this communication is to take place depending on the state of utilities/technology. This Volunteer Center Coordinator also acts as the primary contact for any external mental health services and providers (VOADs), such as the American Red Cross and the Salvation Army. These outside services are typically not familiar with the community's geographical layout or the population demographics. They need to be informed on the best way to proceed. A more secluded part of the volunteer center acts as a respite location for volunteers and first responders. In mass casualty events, emergency disaster responders may need to work for long periods in rescue-and-recovery operations.

The Psychological Services Center Coordinator is responsible for confirming the credentials of licensed trauma-informed mental health therapists who report to free psychological services centers at the disaster site. During and after the disaster, these services centers are located at central locations, such as schools or municipal offices, or in the shelters. This coordinator ensures services centers are staffed and prepared with the necessary number of therapists and intake coordinators. The shelters and services centers may remain open for a week or two, or longer, after the worst part of the disaster. The Psychological Services

Center Coordinator also recommends ways to educate the public on the need for seeking mental health services. This individual interfaces with the <u>Mental Health Response Leader.</u>

<u>The Communications/Media Coordinator</u>, who liaises with the community/ state's public information officer, is the only person who provides information to the media and community on local disaster mental health issues. All relevant external requests need to go through him or her (or another designated individual). This coordinator is also responsible for the dissemination of all print and digital public mental health materials (e.g., fact sheets and list of mental health providers) to survivors, the general public, and the media. He or she identifies any external (possibly most at-risk) populations that may need special information (e.g., non-English speakers and the hard of hearing). The Communications/Media Coordinator has a list of mental health experts and resources who can provide additional information to outside sources as needed. This individual may also interface with the call center regarding media requests for information. Different technology forms must be considered for communication because of knowledge/experience base, geography (e.g., dead zones for cell phones), and utility issues.

Post-Disaster Responsibilities

- ◆ Collaboration-designated representatives should focus on at-risk populations or neighborhoods who may require specialized care in order to stem high rates of PTSD and suicide. Outreach efforts must be implemented in a timely manner so a better understanding of long-term mental health needs can be evaluated and trauma-informed providers contacted.
- ◆ Depending on the extent of the disaster, the collaboration's grant writer may request FEMA CCP funding and any other financial support available.
- ◆ A community may receive financial contributions from donors worldwide. In such cases, an organization must be created to decide on the equitable distribution of the funds with long-term mental health considerations. This organization should apply for 501(3)(c) status.
- ◆ Several weeks after the disaster, collaboration members need to reassess the action plan and encourage public input. Holding an appreciation event for all volunteers and first responders is recommended.

J. Additional Collaboration Resources

As noted, collaborations may turn to state and federal government and private organizations for added support to prepare for or respond to mental health needs in a disaster. These include:

Pre-Disaster/Disaster Support

In 2018, SAMHSA (www.samhsa.gov) announced two pre-disaster funding opportunities for a total of nearly $60 million to support nonprofit organizations and state and tribal educational agencies wanting to provide PFA training. The Mental Health Awareness Training Grants (MHAT) and Project AWARE State Education Agency Grants (Project AWARE-SEA) are designed to increase awareness of mental health and emotional disturbance illnesses, especially serious ones. Training helps such parties as school and emergency services personnel, veterans, law enforcement, and firefighters identify people with mental disorders and respond to crisis situations, connect individuals and their families who need school and community services for treatment and recovery support, and educate individuals about community resources for mental health or substance abuse challenges. In 2019, SAMHSA announced grants for nearly $16 million for training purposes.

The federal program Emergency System for Advance Registration of Volunteer Health Professionals (ESAR-VHP, www.phe.gov) was created to support states and territories in establishing standardized volunteer registration programs for disasters and public health and medical emergencies. Administered on the state level, ESAR-VHP confirms identities, licenses, credentials, accreditations, and hospital privileges in advance, saving valuable time in emergency situations.

Citizen Corps (www.citizencorps.gov), through FEMA, was created to help coordinate volunteer activities to make communities safer, stronger, and better prepared to respond to hazardous situations. Based on its mission to "harness the power of every individual through education and outreach, training, and volunteer service," Citizen Corps provides participation with a range of opportunities to make families, homes, and communities safer from the threats of crime, terrorism, public health emergencies, and hazards of all types. Citizen Corps is a vital part of USA Freedom Corps, and both help communities prevent, prepare for, and respond to crime, terrorist attacks, and other emergencies.

Many nonprofit and professional organizations have agreements with the American Red Cross to be mental health volunteers. The disaster mental health team responds to the immediate emotional needs of disaster survivors, supplements mental health resources during these events, and supports the community through resilience building. In San Diego, for example, a team of YMCA Youth and Family Service Social Workers and Marriage and Family Therapists (www.

ymca.org) were trained to assist during Red Cross disaster and mass casualty response efforts. Numerous national, state, and local organizations offer PFA training in person or online, free or at cost, and for varying numbers of sessions and amounts of time. Before making a decision, compare the pros and cons of different options and speak with other groups that have been trained.

National Voluntary Organizations Active in Disaster (VOAD) (www.voad. org) consists of large disaster relief organizations including the Red Cross and the Salvation Army, plus many faith-based and small disaster relief organizations, which mitigate and alleviate the impact of disasters; provide a forum for promoting cooperation, communication, coordination, and collaboration; and foster more effective delivery of services to communities affected by disaster.

Most states and/or counties have disaster behavioral health response teams, trained groups of volunteers who can mobilize resources to provide post-disaster mental health services. Nonprofit groups and organizations also provide licensed mental health volunteers to work within affected communities.

Post-Disaster Funding

You may apply for post-disaster-related grants through state and federal funding if an event is beyond combined response capabilities of state and local governments. The Robert T. Stafford Disaster Relief and Emergency Act of 1988, an amended version of the Disaster Relief Act of 1974, authorized the delivery of federal technical, financial, and logistical assistance to states and localities during declared major disasters or emergencies. FEMA (www.fema.gov) coordinates the administration of disaster relief resources and assistance to states. The act includes funding for training and services to alleviate mental health problems caused or exacerbated by a presidential-declared major disaster.

The Crisis Counseling Assistance and Training Program (CCP, www.fema. gov) provides immediate and regular program funding. The "immediate" services program provides screening, diagnostic, and counseling techniques, as well as outreach services such as public information and community networking, to help meet mental health needs immediately following a disaster up to 60 days from date of the declaration. The "regular" services program offers funding for crisis counseling, community outreach, and consultation and education services to assist people affected by the disaster for up to nine months.

Post-disaster mental health funding is available from some national and local companies. For example, after the California wildfires in 2018, the Google Foundation gave a $1 million grant to the First Responder Support Network, a peer-based organization in San Rafael (Newman, 2018). It is recommended that collaborations utilize the services of a grant writer to find financial opportunities for resiliency, preparedness, and disaster mental health planning.

Other Mental Health Collaborations

A number of American states have developed a statewide disaster mental health/behavioral plan. In addition, a few region- and county-based planning groups have created mental health action plans linking to emergency medical response systems. These collaborations, which differ in their structure and members, are often connected to local universities, medical centers, and foundations. However, the establishment of such groups is slow going. It appears communities are more prone to develop such plans after a disaster occurs. Only through their experiences are they motivated toward preparedness. As the number of natural and human-caused catastrophes continues to rise, and the number of long-term trauma survivors likewise grows, this motivation for pre-disaster planning could become greater as well.

CASE STUDY: Monroe County, New York, Disaster Mental Health Response Team

After 9/11, the federal government encouraged states, regions, and counties to create disaster behavioral health response teams as an integral part of the overall public health and medical response to any emergency event. The need was to address the psychological, emotional, cognitive, developmental, and social impact disasters have on survivors and responders. Behavioral health response teams provide an organized response to individual victims, first responders, family members, survivors, and other community members affected by critical incidents or disasters.

A prime example is the Monroe County Disaster Mental Health Response Team, a collaboration of the Monroe County Office of Mental Health (MCOMH), Public Health Department, and Office of Public Health Preparedness in western New York State, which responds to major health and safety emergencies and to disaster/crisis situations in a variety of settings around the county. Monroe County faced a disastrous shooting incident at the end of 2012. In the early morning of December 24, firefighters responded to a fire in West Webster, New York, a Rochester suburb, and were ambushed by a perpetrator believed to have deliberately set the fire. Two firefighters, one also a police officer, were lost, and two others were injured. The shooter then shot and killed himself. Six other houses burned to the ground, and two more were considered uninhabitable. This incident once again demonstrated the need for the Disaster Mental Health Response Team and other post-disaster intervention efforts to provide crisis support.

Monroe County's Disaster Mental Health Response Team consists of approx-imately 165 "master" prepared or licensed mental health professionals trained to provide crisis intervention and assistance. In addition, support is provided to other organizations such as schools, mental health facilities, the Monroe County Office of Emergency Management, Public Health, and other county staff and leadership as requested. The team also works closely with the American Red Cross Greater Rochester Chapter in coordinating a community response to mental health needs during emergencies. Presently, 165 local volunteers have had training in Disaster Mental Health Preparedness and PFA and are on call to respond to area disasters. The Monroe County Office of Mental Health has also implemented the multi-agency Consortium for Trauma, Illness & Grief in Schools (TIG) to prepare school districts for mental health support during inci-dents of trauma, violence, illness, and death. TIG assists schools in response to the needs of children, parents, teachers, and other school personnel in times of crisis.

David L. Putney, former director of community services for the Monroe County Office of Mental Health, and Sarah Moravan, mental hygiene program analyst, shared several lessons learned in the area of disaster recovery and response:

1. When a community develops any form of disaster mental health pro-gram or plan, it should always ensure the local government has a seat at the table. Most likely, the government can provide some form of train-ing or other support to the effort. The government is also knowledge-able and up to date on issues of liability, which can prove to be helpful during an event.

2. The collaboration needs to set a minimum set of training requirements for its members and offer these classes at least once a year. Some of these members may have received more advanced training, which pro-vides two tiers of responders, but all should be required to take the set minimum for consistency sake. Be sure there is a pool of volunteers at all times who are trained and ready to respond quickly, and skills do not become rusty when the team is not called for some time. Continue out-reach efforts with local university graduates, for example, to keep this pool filled. Having too many trained and vetted volunteers before an event occurs is the ideal problem to have. There will always be reasons a portion of the team cannot respond to the event (for example, maybe they were victims of the event). Make sure the list of volunteers is up to

date: People still live in the area, remain interested, and can still respond if they have other responsibilities. Annual exercises and online surveys, for example, can be helpful to collect updated information and poll volunteers. MCOMH recommends all volunteers have a conversation about disaster response with their employers before committing to the team. Some employers may count the hours volunteered as time worked.

3. It is essential to keep abreast of the training and goals of other emergency groups in surrounding counties and states, as well as resources available from other mental health–related national organizations such as the Red Cross, even in other areas such as suicide coalitions. These individuals should meet for idea sharing. This builds the credibility of your group and also creates awareness by others in the area. Awareness before a disaster can foster relationships and lead to additional educational opportunities. For example, when the local airport advertised it was conducting a training program, it was not aware of the breadth and scope of the Monroe County Disaster Mental Health Response Team. MCOMH contacted the airport, explained the situation, and MCOMH internal staff and Disaster Mental Health Response Team volunteers were asked to participate in the training. Additional training helps volunteers improve their skill level.

4. Funding for training and other resources has dwindled and become more difficult in the area of disaster mental health preparedness, which makes coalition building more challenging. Place an ongoing effort on finding grant money and other sources of support. Collecting data around the team, including any outcome measures that can be captured, is incredibly helpful when applying for potential financial opportunities.

5. Responding volunteers must be reimbursed for their expenses, if at all possible, particularly if they need to remain in an area away from home for a few days. Collaboration with the local government may assist in determining the appropriate processes for reimbursement.

CASE STUDY: C-LEARN and Resilient Baton Rouge

Certain areas of the U.S. are hit repeatedly by one natural disaster after another, which encourages them to build community resilience in preparation for the next onslaught. Louisiana not only faces repeated destructive storms, but also has several highly vulnerable populations. Another record-breaking hurricane season in 2017 clearly illustrated the ongoing need for a coordinated participatory disaster response team, which would rely on lessons learned to determine what was most needed by Baton Rouge and other parts of the state. The National Academies of Sciences–awarded Community Resilience Learning Collaborative and Research Network (C-LEARN, www.c-learn.org) was developed to help other communities plan for and respond to post-disaster mental health needs and recovery.

Resilient Baton Rouge (RBR, www.resilientbatonrouge.org) provides funding, training, tools, and a workspace for collaborators to focus on disaster-related complications through a partnership of residents, health services providers, community organizations, government, and academic participants that encourage and support improved mental health services for disaster-impacted communities. RBR builds upon successful models implemented in such areas as South Louisiana post-Katrina and Los Angeles and is supported by community-based and academic stakeholders, including representatives from the national Community and Patient Powered Research Network, a collaboration with over a decade of implementing community-engaged, culturally tailored interventions focused on improving mental health.

RBR's first goal was to improve post–mental health issues, beginning with adult depression. It hired a new staff that provided direct services and trained providers on evidence-based models of care. It also developed a training portfolio to support mental health practitioners, primary care providers, and community health workers. In addition, RBR developed partnerships to promote community resilience and created a national community resilience learning collaboration for experts to share resources and best practices.

CASE STUDY: Healthcare Foundation of Northern Sonoma County

When the California wildfires started taking hold in 2017 as the worst in the state's history, the Healthcare Foundation of Northern Sonoma County was already looking at ways to enhance the residents' mental healthcare needs. "Our foundation's mission is to bring together our community by engaging donors in the support of creating a healthier region through healthcare access, mental health, and early childhood development," stated past CEO Debbie Mason. "We realized our efforts had to immediately focus on the needs of the wildfire survivors." Mason had earlier lived in Florida and experienced firsthand the trauma natural disasters could cause. "I knew many in our community would require counseling services once the fires ended and for a long time thereafter."

Mason quickly formed the Wildfire Mental Health Collaborative—a "think tank" of local mental health experts to determine the steps needed to reduce expected high stress levels and promote self-help. The collaborative conducted research to find evidence-based strategies on the efficacy of possible interventions. It established relationships with national disaster recovery mental health professionals and agencies to learn best practices from such events as 9/11, Hurricane Katrina, and the Colorado wildfires. Members knew the need for these interventions would ebb and flow for at least the next five years—if anything, the region would face future fires, which would aggravate existing mental health conditions.

The collaboration's goal was to ensure Sonoma County residents learned to recognize the signs of mental health distress and had access to free, bilingual resources and services for personal recovery and long-term healing and resiliency skill building. Treatment was guided by principles of stepped care, such as community conversations, group counseling, individual counseling, trauma-informed yoga and meditation, and web-based and mobile technological tools. Specifically, the group leveraged FEMA grant money with private-sector wraparound free mental health services.

As a result, the collaborative trained over 400 licensed therapists using Skills for Psychological Recovery (SPR), a psycho-education procedure developed by The National Child Traumatic Stress Network. For fire survivors, it now offers cost-free bilingual outreach sessions by SPR-trained therapists; yoga/meditation classes; individual counseling; self-guided residence assistance through the Sonoma Rises free app; and mysonomastrong.com, which is a wildfire mental health recovery website. Individuals who may benefit from a deeper level of care are referred to a resource base maintained by the local National Alliance on Mental Illness (NAMI) chapter for clinics and nonprofits offering free bilingual group individual counseling by SPR-trained professionals.

Mason said any U.S. communities following the lead of Northern Sonoma County should contact their state government right after disaster hits. "Find the name of your state/regional FEMA contact and see what resources are available to negate duplication of services." Also, be proactive and develop an emergency warning system before any possible catastrophe arises. Do not take for granted that the government will take care of this.

CASE STUDY: Forming a Collaboration after a Disaster in Newtown, Connecticut

Donation Management

What does a community do when it receives a significant amount of donations after a disaster or tragedy? How are funds distributed fairly? What is the best way to form a committee to determine how the funds will be used? This was only one of the many challenges Newtown, Connecticut, faced after its 12/14 tragedy.

Source: Illustration by Jay Roeder

Immediately after the Sandy Hook Elementary School shooting on the morning of December 14, 2012, donations began pouring into Newtown. Because of its name, Newtown Savings Bank (NSB) became one of the primary places where donors sent their contributions. The bank immediately established a special account for the donations. Due to the overwhelming generosity of people worldwide, NSB quickly realized these funds needed to be placed in a secure tax-free 501(c)(3) account. It turned to the United Way of Western Connecticut (UWWC) for help, and by the end of that same day, the Sandy Hook School Support Fund was established by NSB and UWWC.

With the help of two local attorneys, NSB and UWWC created a transition team including town government leaders, local medical professionals, and

Newtown business leaders. In February 2013, just two months after the tragedy, Newtown Sandy Hook Community Foundation Inc. (NSHCF) was established. It consisted of a board of directors with expertise in business, law, spiritual support, mental health, and finance. They established the first distribution committee, which was tasked with developing a victim compensation model to provide financial support for the families of children and staff who lost their lives, the two injured staff members, and the families of the 12 surviving eyewitness students. While funds are typically given exclusively to families of the deceased and survivors with physical injuries, this distribution committee also recognized the severe psychological trauma endured by the eyewitness students and provided them with a small percentage of the donations. The emotional toll on survivors is devastating, and their mental health needs should be carefully considered in any plan.

In September of 2013, NSHCF hired Jennifer Barahona, a licensed clinical social worker with nonprofit management experience, as the executive director. One of her first challenges was to create a second distribution committee with members of the community who would represent the most deeply impacted groups. This committee's role was to solicit input from the stakeholder groups it represented and create guidelines for fair and equitable funding for mental health services. The original committee consisted of a:

- Parent who lost a child in the tragedy;
- Mental health professional representing the surviving eyewitness families;
- Physician and Sandy Hook parent;
- Sandy Hook Elementary School teacher;
- Sandy Hook school bus driver;
- Representative from the Board of Fire Commissioners;
- Clergy member;
- Police officer;
- Social worker and Newtown parent;
- Grants specialist; and
- Financial advisor.

The author of this manual, Bob Schmidt, was one of the original members and currently serves as committee chair.

This second distribution committee set reimbursement rates to assist impacted individuals with the cost of therapy related to trauma from the shooting. To preserve resources, the foundation required individuals to use their insurance, and then the fund covered remaining out-of-pocket expenses up to reasonable and customary limits. Recognizing that trauma recovery is not a one-size-fits-all approach but rather comes in many forms, the foundation also set up guidelines for reimbursement for wellness activities such as yoga, therapeutic massage, acupuncture, Masgutova Neurosensorimotor Integration Method (MNRI), physical fitness programs, and social-emotional support for children. As with any tragedy, this committee also knew there were certain individuals who would not fit within the established criteria but who required and deserved mental health services. NSHCF therefore created a three-member review committee to evaluate requests for mental health services falling outside specific criteria and guidelines.

In addition, NSHCF established a Collaborative Recovery Fund that streamlined several of the smaller funds created for the same purpose of supporting mental health needs. This model helped foster collaboration and communication while providing streamlined services for impacted individuals, offering clarity and avoiding duplication of efforts.

NSHCF set a date to "sunset" and close its doors in 2025 when the children who were in kindergarten at the time of the tragedy would graduate from high school. Each year, the board of directors reviews the remaining funds and allots a specific amount to the distribution committee with the goal of supporting the community and those most impacted by the tragedy.

Barahona has been invited to many American communities to share what was learned in Newtown. In her discussions, she has emphasized how the board quickly recognized there would be a need for both short-term and long-term mental health funding. Rightly so: Many unpredicted funding requests have come in since the foundation was created. It is thus essential to keep a reserve of funds for the unforeseeable. She also recommended right from the beginning a foundation should clearly define who will be helped by the funds. This is also important to the individuals, community service organizations, and corporations wishing to make donations.

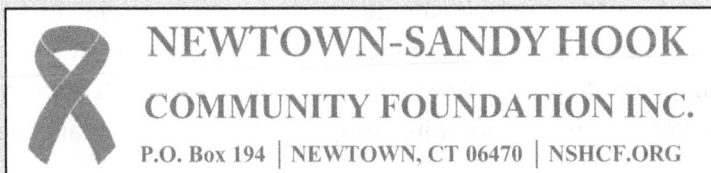

NEWTOWN-SANDY HOOK

COMMUNITY FOUNDATION INC.

P.O. Box 194 | NEWTOWN, CT 06470 | NSHCF.ORG

Source: NSHCF

Newtown Lions Club Foundation

Newtown Memorial Fund

Collaborative
Recovery
Fund

Newtown Rotary Club

Sandy Hook School Support
Fund (NSHCF)

Other Potential Funds

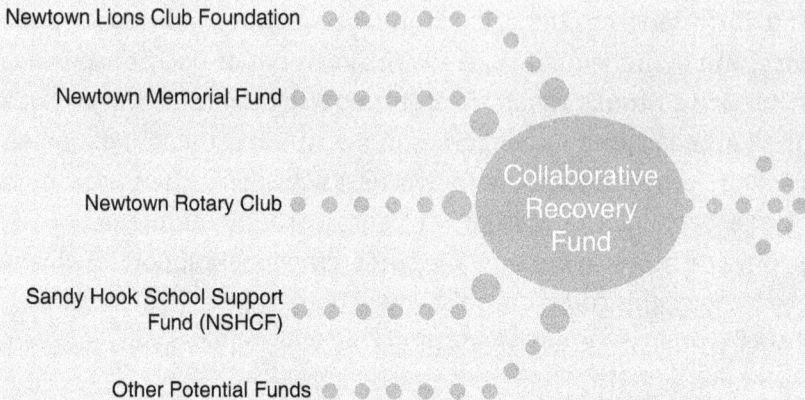

FIGURE 3.1 Organizations that worked with and contributed to the NSHCF

So that services are not duplicated, Barahona further advised that a foundation must be made aware of the function and goals of other organizations volunteering to help. For example, the Funeral Directors Association in Newtown covered the funeral expenses for many of the children's families. Federal and state organizations such as the Office of Victim Services also have funds available for specific groups.

Public input is very important as well. The disbursement committee was set up as a diverse group of members for obtaining input from all stakeholders. Although this group was very helpful, NSHCF annually sought additional input from town residents to form a broader understanding of community needs. Using online surveys, NSHCF was able to create an annual budget based on where community funds were most needed. The school system, the town, and the local newspaper, the *Newtown Bee*, spread the word about the surveys and the need for input.

A Collaborative Team

The first Newtown collaboration formed after the tragedy was organized by General Electric Company employee Elizabeth Rallo. Collaborative members covered the counseling costs for people affected by the tragedy as well as sponsoring other financial hardships the incident caused. Shortly after NSHCF was formed, it became apparent there was also considerable need for a collaborative team to coordinate with all other community groups for the town's mutual benefit. Since the foundation had developed relationships with all community organizations, it became the central collaborative team. In this role, it provided leadership, training, workshops, and grants for community groups to help the town heal.

NSHCF invited experts and individuals from other communities who had suffered similar tragedies to meet with those most impacted by 12/14. Walnut Hill Community Church opened its doors to members of the Newtown Sandy Hook community to talk with survivors of Virginia Polytechnic Institute, Columbine High School, and the Amish of Nichols Mine, Pennsylvania. The foundation also supported the Newtown Recovery Center's workshops to enhance counselor wellness and brought in trauma experts such as Bruce Perry, MD, who met with parents and therapists. In its role as the central collaborative team, NSHCF worked with Newtown officials, the superintendent of schools, the Resiliency Center of Newtown, Newtown Youth and Family Services, and the clergy, as well as community charities started by families who experienced a loss from the tragedy.

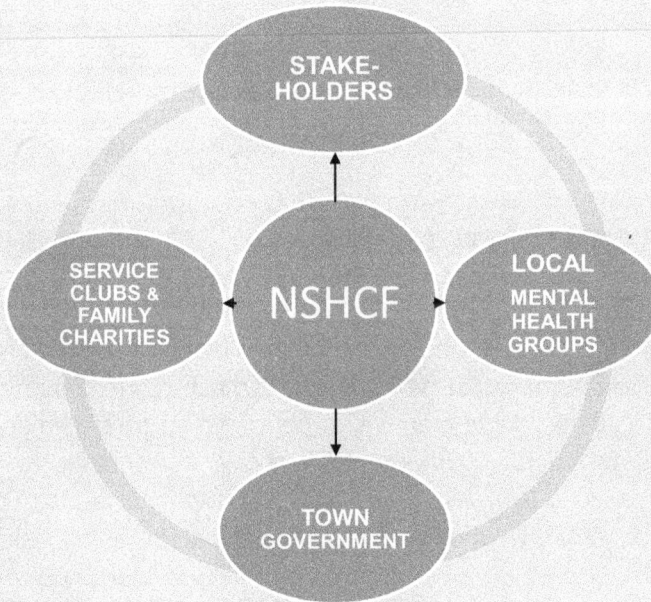

FIGURE 3.2 The collaborative model of the Newtown Sandy Hook Community Foundation

TO DO

1. Research your community to see if any collaborations already exist that may provide general assistance or more specifics, such as a potential list of members and their affiliations.

2. Talk with the town/city emergency management director or similar officials to determine if existing expertise can be utilized. Perhaps some thought has already been given to mental health planning integration and addition to present safety and medical ones.

3. Look at local organizations with the mission to help individuals with mental health needs to determine if they could take on the convener/facilitator role.

4. Ensure that all individuals asked to be on the action planning collaboration know their responsibilities and are willing to make the needed commitment for the time allotted.

References

Bada Math, S. B., Nirmata, M. C., Moirangthem, S., & Kumar, N. C. (2015). Disaster management: Mental health perspective. *Indian Journal of Psychological Medicine*, *37*(3), 261–271.

Community Tool Box. (2018). *Center for community health and development University of Kansas*. Retrieved from https://ctb.ku.edu/en

Fawcett, B. S., Francisco, T. V., Andrews-Payne, A., & Schultz, A. J. (2000). A model memorandum of collaboration. *Public Health Reports*, *115*, 174–179.

Newman, K. (2018, October 26). Google grant aids to help first responders. *U.S. News*. Retrieved from www.usnews.com/news/healthiest-communities/articles/2018-10-26/google-grant-will-support-first-responders-mental-health

Thomas, E. A., & Bowen, S. K. (2009). *The patchwork quilt: A creative strategy for safe, sustainable and long-term development and post-disaster rebuilding*. Retrieved from www.gafloods.org/%5C/pdf/2009/Patchwork_Paper.pdf

Reader's Notes

4

Collaboration Outreach and Education

Chapter 4 Preview
A. Relationships With External Groups
B. Action Plan Public Information
C. Disaster Communication Plan
D. Media Relations Recommendations

Communication is an essential part of the collaboration process, and, given the personal nature of mental healthcare, effective communication is critical to the wellbeing of everyone communitywide. This communication includes interactions with individuals and organizations outside your collaboration that can help reach out to the public. Who will be able to help you most when a disaster arises? Utilize the information from your community assessment to know which groups are most in need of certain announcements and special services when disasters strike.

Media communication—from TV news to social media—is another area that should be important to your collaboration. The media rarely cover issues concerning disaster mental health, nor do they understand the impact of their catastrophe coverage on viewers—particularly the most vulnerable. You need to designate a Communications/Media Coordinator who is the only person speaking to the press. Many problems arise when various individuals provide information, which could be misleading, misinformed, or incorrect. This only leads to higher stress levels. You should keep templates of communication materials—fliers, information sheets, and press releases—on hand, so they can quickly be completed in relevant languages. Also have a list of critical communication contact phone numbers and emails. You may never know for sure what type of disaster may hit, if any; yet, depending on location, some are more prevalent than others. Ideally, you will write copy based on the most likely disasters listed when preparing your disaster action plan. Instead of writing materials for every foreseeable event, create a few to be used for different audiences and at different times.

If disaster mental health is in its infancy, disaster mental health communication is even younger. Each event serves as a learning opportunity for how to communicate better in the next disaster. Reviewing recent studies with lessons learned will be helpful, since most communities are facing the same issues. Gaps in a communication plan can result in target populations not receiving necessary information. Having your municipality's emergency management director involved with your collaboration will be a big plus. Your communications coordinator can work closely with this director in distributing information critical for both physical and psychological response and recovery.

A. Relationships With External Groups

Your collaboration will need input from other community groups in order to achieve its goals and objectives. Avoid being completely overwhelmed by assuming too many responsibilities and instead tap into the capacities and skills of other community members. The committee responsible for disaster crisis centers, for example, may request help from other organizations or individuals who have knowledge in this area.

Establishing relationships with those who are closer to the scene and in a position to help on a street-by-street and moment-to-moment level can be of considerable benefit. You may request help from designated neighborhood representatives who can help identify needs and acquire resources. For example, they can help obtain a survivor's medicine left at home or find a lost service animal. Essential sources of community mental health support may come from:

Adult independent-living communities;
The American Red Cross chapter;
A children and youth task force;
Child welfare organizations;
Community-based health-related organizations;
Criminal justice system representatives and organizations;
Disaster recovery organizations;
Domestic violence prevention and services agencies;
Elected officials;
Faith-based organizations;
Geriatric support groups and organizations;
Healthcare coalitions;
Local and state government agencies;
Individual and family therapists trained in trauma;
Media and social media groups;
Medical and mental healthcare provider associations;
Medical Reserve Corps;
Military installations;
Neighborhood clubs;
Nonprofit organizations working on mental healthcare issues and/or disaster
    work;
Peer-to-peer support groups;
Prevention groups;
Private companies and businesses;
Senior citizen centers and nursing homes;
Schools, childcare providers, universities, and homeschool organizations;
Service organizations;
Service providers for individuals and families experiencing homelessness;
Substance abuse treatment services organizations;
Tribal organizations; and
Veterans' associations.

The needs of your residents can be better understood by visiting local institutions and meeting some of the members. Similarly, by making an effort to establish bonds with leaders of various religious organizations and ethnic minorities, you can further communication efforts. This includes meeting with representatives from the smaller, lesser-known organizations, not just those from the more established ones.

Focusing energy on a few trusted community leaders can be an effective way to gain support from a group that is not well known. For example, in schools, liaisons may be administrative staff or trusted teachers, as well as student leaders and members of the parent-teacher organizations. However, keep in mind ethnic differences. When you become aware of local customs, there is less of a chance of being disrespectful of the community's practices and values. For example, in some Native American groups, it is respectful for outsiders to first make an effort to establish bonds with the local elders or tribal leaders.

By reaching out to typically uninvolved groups, close relationships can be established and maintained between and among different parts of the community, by both function and location. Local needs are more easily identified and met, and resources are more readily located and delivered. Each community has particular characteristics of size, history, social or cultural patterns, existing organizations, and resources that create a different relationship structure. As with your collaboration, one entity does not fit all. Regardless of what partnerships and liaisons are formed, it is critical to communicate about them to the community at large. It is essential not only to have an efficient relationship structure but also for the entire community to know more about this relationship and how it is accessed and utilized. Clear, efficient, ongoing, and multi-directional communication makes this system work properly.

B. Action Plan Public Information

Your collaboration's communication committee will interface with both the general public and the media. When the first draft of your disaster mental health action plan is completed, it needs to be explained to the public and made available for input. Hold information sessions during the day and night and on a weekday and weekend to ensure time flexibility. Disseminate information and fliers about the meetings through the local media, bulletin boards, public locations such as the town hall and library, community businesses, schools, and nonprofits, as well as on social media to ensure the word gets out. A copy of the communication plan draft can be uploaded online with an e-mail address for comments, which allows for input from those who cannot attend meetings.

It is always helpful to request information from individuals and organizations not active in your collaboration. Your planning group can encourage these other parties to appoint a representative to attend a meeting and act as a liaison to their members. Some of these groups may want to hold their own public meetings with a collaboration representative to get suggestions from attendees. For example, the Rotary Club programming committee may want to devote a bi-weekly meeting to this topic. Constructive remarks, as well as praise, should be seen as desirable; in a disaster recovery effort, it is almost inevitable that improvements can be made. Positive comments are always gratifying to hear, but productive criticism can provide an opportunity for helpful ideas about new directions. Then, after your disaster mental health plan is finalized, copies need to be available communitywide, to the media, and online. Input should always be welcomed.

All collaborations should have a website dedicated to mental health services in a disaster so both the mentally ill and their families know what to expect. The community needs to find ways to ensure residents are aware of the website and feel comfortable following up with the services listed. Who helps survivors with their immediate emotional distress? Where will these individuals be located? What about needed medications? How will counselors partner with spiritual advisors? Who will be able to provide mental health services in the coming weeks and months? The site can be easily updated when additional support services become available; it can also be accessed through the website of one of the collaboration's members.

This website should include a list of trauma-informed therapists who are specifically trained to treat survivors and other community members, as well as offer available wellness activities and programs. It should also include information on the varying levels of stress and trauma following a disaster and age-specific warning signs; trauma-informed treatment; substance abuse and trauma; trauma's impact on family dynamics; recommendations for self-care; and contact information on communitywide nonprofit and public mental health organizations and institutions such as schools, religious organizations, and local businesses.

"All Collaborations Should Have a Website"

C. Disaster Communication Plan

Develop a communication plan to be easily implemented during a large-scale disaster or even when a threat exists. At this time, many people and organizations are going to be working to get the word out to community members. You will need to interface with them to ensure information gets out in a timely manner.

Communication Checklist Sample

Pre- and During Disaster

1. Designate the Communications/Media Coordinator and members of the communication committee, their roles and responsibilities, and how they will interact with other disaster contacts, such as crisis centers;
2. Identify policies and procedures for the dissemination of mental health information; continually stress that all communication goes through the disaster chair or other designated spokesperson. Remember, have only one spokesperson for all public and media communication;
3. Stipulate external populations that may need special warnings and procedures for implementing them, such as the deaf and elderly;
4. Establish a relationship with the local public health and/or emergency management agency communication director; collaborate on communication efforts with state and federal medical and mental health organizations;
5. Determine the public information materials required for multiple languages, such as emergency statements, fliers, fact sheets, information guides, and press releases;
6. Identify a process for distributing educational and informational materials to mental health service sites;

The Indiana Department of Mental Health (www.in.gov) includes the following as important for communicating with the public:

1. Do no harm. Remember, your words have consequences, so select them carefully.
2. Use empathy and care and focus on informing rather than on impressing.
3. Utilize everyday language.
4. Do not over-reassure. Present the facts as they are.
5. Say only those things comfortable for reading on the front page/breaking news.
6. Do not use "No comment," which appears something is being hidden.
7. Acknowledge people's fears.
8. Do not speculate, guess, or assume. If something is not known, say so.
9. Advise survivors on media interaction.
10. Reinforce that everything possible is being done to improve the situation as quickly as possible.

---

7. Designate experts and resources outside your collaboration who may be utilized as extra hands during times of disaster;

8. Establish a "pressroom" location and phone number from which information will be disseminated, and press inquiries will be answered. Have a comprehensive list of all media contacts and a means for uploading website information. Be honest and transparent. Do not respond to questions that are still uncertain. Provide regular updates;

9. Have a list of collaboration members and external contacts who are providing input; and

10. Identify communication channels and establish a backup plan for communication if technology lines go down.

Post-Disaster Communication

Post-disaster is a very stressful time, and overloaded, damaged, or nonexistent phone networks make matters worse. Being connected to other people is essential for mental health wellbeing. When conducting your assessments, talk with different community groups on how they can help with personal communication after a disaster. Can they hold smaller gatherings at local establishments? These meetings can also be held in shelters if many people are relocated. Translators for non-English languages spoken in your community as well as communication for the hard of hearing are essential. Ethnic considerations are also important.

Your communication committee should also have a list of possible public education presentations for open meetings. Mental health issues are only considered following the accessibility of other primary needs such as safety, housing, and employment, so when these meetings are held and for how long will depend on the disaster type and extent. Especially in widespread catastrophes such as wildfires and hurricanes when utilities are down, these meetings will be delayed. Some community members may not seek help immediately after a disaster or even in the long term. Other people may simply give up because they lack confidence in the community's ability to or interest in providing them with necessary assistance or are concerned about existing discrimination. Previous relationships developed with varying community groups can be helpful at this point.

Rarely does a disaster impact all members of a community or sectors of a society equally. Typically, certain groups disproportionately bear the brunt of the suffering and loss, magnifying these inequities. Community members with greater access to resources and services before the disaster frequently have greater authority when the disaster occurs. Inequality can lead to a sense of competition for limited resources between groups or distrust of government authority or responders. Working collaboratively with a variety of constituencies across ethnic, religious, economic, and political lines can be very constructive. Establishing trust among underrepresented groups requires an understanding and acceptance of past and present injustices, clear communication, and honest efforts to avoid continuing those inequities.

Sometimes individuals may be members of an underrepresented group; other times they will not be. Regardless of status, they should always be encouraged to provide input. You can enhance your communication outreach by speaking to people from diverse cultures and better understand the purpose of their beliefs and practices. This will make it easier to relate to them and additionally gain their trust. It is a way to discover common ground for discussion in the early stages of developing trust.

D. Media Relations Recommendations

Communication during the various stages of a disaster is greatly enhanced by developing a relationship with the community's media, including the public TV station, radio, and newspapers. The media can provide valuable warnings before a pending event, interview respected authorities about actions residents should take, and provide information on shelter and mental health locations and emergency numbers. For example, before category 4 Hurricane Florence hit North Carolina, Governor Roy Cooper warned viewers in evacuation zones that staying in their homes would be a grave mistake, and they had "to get out now."

In many cases, the media are not familiar with the impact their programming will have on viewers. The news media have an obligation and a right to report these dangerous events, but they also have a responsibility not to enhance fear and emotional stress. How the media covers a catastrophic event can make all the difference in the impact on local residents. Studies looking at the impact of televised trauma on the emotional wellbeing of viewers have suggested how the general public is at risk of developing distress and even PTSD from secondary exposure via mass media.

Research found more than six hours of exposure to media coverage of the Boston Marathon bombings in the four weeks after the attack led to greater stress than actually being at the event. The *DSM-V* (APA, 2013) also reported that PTSD can occur when viewing graphic imagery. Facebook content moderators experienced severe mental health symptoms when continually looking at graphic images of violence (Newton, 2019). A study (Hall et al., 2019) found people who viewed repeated television broadcasts of a China typhoon with violent images, such as a man almost drowning, significant home damage, and people being injured was associated with the onset of PTSD.

A 2015 Israeli study of the Gaza War media coverage (Bodas, Siman-Tov, Peleg, & Solomon, 2015) revealed that viewers who watched constant newscasts for a longer period of time were nearly twice as likely (or more) to report having one or more anxiety symptoms, such as sleeping problems and fearful thoughts, than those watching at their usual frequency or less. Additional reports need to be conducted to determine more specific cause-and-effect factors and to study the variance of viewers; not everyone will be traumatized because of differences in risk factors.

In addition, research (Pae, 2014) has shown how suicide coverage can inspire at-risk individuals to make their own suicide attempts, or "the copycat effect." Some media outlets only announce suicides with extraordinary news value. The American Foundation for Suicide Prevention and the World Health Organization (Resnick, 2019) advise publications to limit information related to the method of suicide, rather than giving these stories premium placement, and to provide suicide prevention resources along with the news.

In the meantime, the following are recommendations to the media based on to-date experience and common sense:

For all events:

1. Do not interview survivors immediately after a traumatic event. It can re-traumatize them.
2. Be respectful of the families who have suffered a loss, and do not try to interview them. They may be re-traumatized. The same thing applies to children who just witnessed a horrible event.
3. Respect the culture and customs of the population affected. Understand when it is time to pull back and leave the interviewees alone.
4. Limit the disturbing or violent videos to later in the evening when young children are asleep. A study (Heir, Hussain, & Weisaeth, 2008) revealed that young children who repeatedly saw the same footage of an event believed each replay was another new disaster, which greatly added to their stress levels.
5. Do not report information that is unconfirmed. Reports immediately after the Sandy Hook Elementary School tragedy incorrectly said the perpetrator's mother taught at the school or was a school aide. The media also wrongly named the perpetrator's brother as the shooter, only because the shooter was carrying his brother's library card in his pocket.
6. Do not dwell on the story. Cover the essential facts and then move on to other stories.

For acts of violence:

It is important the media do not glorify the perpetrator of violent acts by doing the following:

1. Use words like "cowardly act" when describing the perpetrator's actions. Refer to the perpetrator as "emotionally disturbed." This may deter a potential shooter from acting.

2. Do not show the perpetrator's photograph. Do not use the name in a headline. Limit the name to one mention per story. Media coverage tends to glorify the shooter in the eyes of other unstable individuals.

3. Do not give a shooter notoriety. Emotionally disturbed people often seek attention by committing these unthinkable acts. Just like a little child who cannot get positive attention, they will settle for negative attention. Also, coverage can lead to "copycat" acts. Emphasize the "how" of the attack and motivation, rather than the "who."

An Interview With *Dallas Morning News* and Roxane Cohen Silver

In a 2016 *Dallas Morning News* article, Roxane Cohen Silver, PhD, wrote about the impact of television and radio news of "eye witness" accounts following the shooting and murder of six police officers. She said how it reminded her of the much earlier violent events of the Kennedy assassination, when emotion was also front and center on the screen. However, unlike in the 1960s, most people in Dallas now carried a camera in their hands and pockets and could capture the mayhem of the events themselves or quickly learn about it on social media. The tragedy was tweeted, shared on Facebook and Instagram, and posted to YouTube and Reddit. Even people who were not there were "there," and the violence occurred over and over again worldwide.

After the 9/11 terrorist attacks, news editors quickly made the decision not to show people jumping out of the World Trade Center windows, but those decisions are no longer made by media professionals. "News sites lure unsuspecting eyeballs to click on links. Most annoyingly, many videos now start when one opens a URL, often without anyone clicking on any link at all."

Many argue, added Silver, about the importance of seeing graphic pictures to spur action against social and racial injustice. Yet, as a psychologist, she would leave that decision to social commentators. While the political pros and cons might be debatable, the pros and cons of the psychological impact are not. She stated there is no psychological benefit to repeated exposure to graphic pictures of horror. Instead, evidence has mounted about how media can serve as a powerful means of spreading the trauma of a community tragedy.

For example, following the Boston Marathon bombings, people reported greater numbers of psychological stress symptoms as the number of hours of exposure to traditional and social media about the bombings increased. In fact, repeated exposure to the bombings was more strongly associated with an acute stress response than knowing someone who was at the site of the marathon or even having been there oneself. Evidence by psychologists has mounted over recent years how both live and video images of traumatic events can trigger flashbacks and may promote fear conditioning. When graphic images are continually repeated, they may be playing into a similar process. Repetitive media exposure may turn an acute event into a chronic stressor, with the potential of long-term physical health problems.

Silver therefore has advocated turning off the TV, avoiding gruesome pictures, and resisting any inclination to search for online images. Delete rather than watching graphic tweets. Although some have said graphic images and sounds should not be censored, too few people recognize their potential for harm. Falling prey to the images of violence may prolong distress and anger and interfere with the ability to repair damaged relations. "Focusing on the future rather than reliving gruesome images of the tragedy may prevent, or at least minimize, the likelihood of another community trauma."

TO DO

1. Compile information your community already uses for communication in emergency response. Determine what additional materials may be needed.
2. Make a list of individuals, neighborhood groups, and organizations with emergency response materials, training and/or specific persons designated for response responsibilities. Look for gaps to be filled in community education and areas of overlap that can better be eliminated.
3. Do you believe the media should have specific guidelines on what should and should not be shown or covered on air? What are the pros and cons of such a decision?
4. Talk with other communities to determine lessons learned on public education and what is suggested for most effective results.

References

American Psychiatric Association. (2013). *Diagnostic and statistical manual of mental disorders* (5th ed.). Arlington, VA: Author.

Bodas, M., Siman-Tov, M., Peleg, K., & Solomon, Z. (2015). Anxiety-inducing media: The effect of constant news broadcasting on the well-being of Israeli television viewers. *Psychiatry, 78*(3), 265–276.

Hall, B. J., Xiong, Y. X., Yip, P. S. Y., Lao, C. K., Shi, W., & Elvo, K. L. (2019). The association between disaster exposure and media use on post-traumatic stress disorder following Typhoon Hato in Macao, China. *European Journal of Psychotraumatology, 10*(1), 1558709.

Heir, T., Hussain, A., & Weisaeth, L. (2008). Managing the after-effects of disaster trauma—The essentials of early intervention. *Touch Briefings*. Retrieved from www.researchgate.net/profile/Trond_Heir/publication/256605332_Managing_the_after-effects_of_disaster_trauma_-_the_essentials_of_early_intervention/links/00b49523774095f9b1000000/Managing-the-after-effects-of-disaster-trauma-the-essentials-of-early-intervention.pdf

Newton, C. (2019). Moderating content doesn't have to be traumatic. *The Verge*. Retrieved from www.theverge.com/2019/2/27/18243359/content-moderation-mental-health-ptsd-psychology-science-facebook

Pae, C. U. (2014). Influence of media on suicide: Proper coverage of media on suicide. *Journal of Korean Medical Science, 29*(11), 1583–1585.

Resnick, B. (2019). Teen girls are now poisoning themselves at alarming rates: There are ways to help. *Vox*. Retrieved from www.vox.com/science-and-health/2019/5/1/18523881/teen-suicide-poisoning-how-to-help

Silver, R. C. (2016, July). *Repeated viewing of police ambush videos can cause trauma*. Retrieved from www.dallasnews.com/opinion/commentary/2016/07/16/roxane-cohen-silver-repeated-viewing-police-ambush-videos-can-cause-trauma

Reader's Notes

5

Assessing Mental Health Needs
and Assets

Chapter 5 Preview
A. Definition of Community
B. Meeting Diverse Population Needs
C. Community Resources
D. Impact on the General Population
E. Conducting the Assessment
F. Post-Disaster Re-assessment
G. Ethical Considerations

Before serving people with special needs in a community, one must know whom to serve. To ensure residents receive the mental health services they require post-disaster, it is necessary to have a baseline understanding of demographics of both the general public and, particularly, the most vulnerable populations. These are the individuals most at risk of being traumatized for the long term in a disaster. You can define your population specifics by conducting a mental health assessment or a systematic examination of the status for a given population that identifies key community problems and assets (Rosenbaum, 2013). These assessments recognize how disasters and their impact are unique to a given community.

Community assessments rely on such principles as:

1. Cross-population collaboration sharing a desire for community improvement;
2. Proactive, extensive, and multi-sectored participation to enhance results;
3. Communitywide measurements focusing on population vulnerabilities;
4. Enhanced communication to promote community engagement, understanding, and accountability;
5. Out-of-the-box approaches with refined measurement and evaluation;
6. Evaluations stressing continuous improvement; and
7. Results shared with all cross-community public and private sources.

Your community may already have conducted an assessment when developing its emergency medical plan or other communitywide endeavor. If the population has not changed significantly since this assessment was completed, it may provide a valuable starting point for your collaboration's plan. Confirm the purpose of the two assessments and that the demographics acquired align and obtain additional information as needed.

Assessment is a very important part of pre- and post-disaster mental health intervention planning. Overall, such assessments can help your collaboration make the best decisions right from the start of its action planning efforts rather than waiting for the event to occur. In the wake of a disaster, the pressure to act can be overwhelming, and many mistakes and neglect can occur. Spending valuable time and resources in gathering information before a potential calamity may seem like a waste of effort, especially if you do not believe a catastrophic event may be on its way. Sadly, any community hit by an unexpected tragedy can say differently.

If possible, a community assessment should be conducted prior to or immediately upon the beginning of the planning process, since so much depends on the population being served not only in "any" disaster but, more specifically, in "select" types of events. It is also important to delineate the entire community and its subgroups to ensure their specific needs are met. This definitely includes those who are the most vulnerable or at risk. The challenge is to find a balance between responding to the special needs of at-risk populations and promoting the resiliency of others in the greater affected communities. When you conduct your pre-disaster assessment, it is important to determine whether:

1. Disparate groups are equally valued, and if not, which are not being empowered;
2. Often-unrecognized populations are recognized and provided with the support required;

3. All populations have equal access to community resources;
4. A degree of pre-existing trust or mistrust exists among different groups;
5. A population sector shares information with some or all of its constituents;
6. The degree of coordination among public and private organizations and agencies is equal;
7. Power resides with a select few or is shared among many;
8. Members have worked together on projects of similar concern; and
9. The community recognizes its pre-disaster issues, such as crime, transportation, socioeconomic disparity, and healthcare.

Regardless of the approach and extent of your assessment process, the following should be kept in mind:

1. Assessment is simply about taking a thorough look at the situation, seeing what is needed, detailing the available resources, and determining where other support systems can be attained. Well-conducted assessments can increase the effectiveness of recovery efforts. Without understanding the needs and assets of a community, there is a risk of providing less-than-effective forms of help;
2. Assessments strengthen efforts over time to ensure needs are addressed and the most vulnerable individuals helped. Too often, assessments only measure how well physical health needs are met and not those impacting mental health. Even if the right type of help is provided, it may not reach those most at risk without identifying all segments of the community. This is where time and resources are needlessly lost;
3. Assessments can increase perceived recovery and build community trust. When volunteers are seen as outsiders, their efforts to help may be rejected and regarded as insensitive and disparaging; residents may think their needs and strengths are inadequately understood. Therefore, assessments can be especially beneficial when rightly inclusive of everyone;
4. Assessments can provide input to other community services by offering knowledge about local projects, location of at-risk populations, and additional resources for support efforts;
5. Assessments can enhance individual and community pre- and post-disaster resiliency, which is a major part of disaster mental health planning; and
6. Assessments distinguish the disparity between the "haves" and "have nots," which continues to grow in the U.S., as reported by Psychologists for Social Responsibility (2019). As power, resources, and opportunity are increasingly owned by the very few, negative outcomes grow for the

many. Inequality in healthcare blocks the way to life improvement and wellbeing.

Although the way assessments are conducted may vary considerably and the approach definitely is not set in stone, some objectives are typically similar, such as (Community Tool Box, 2018):

1. Clarifying issues and the exact focus of recovery efforts. What community population can most benefit from assessment efforts? Focus is important given how mental health resources are almost always limited. To more fully narrow direction, consider other critical situational factors involved, such as the different types of disasters possible and the stages of recovery;

2. Compiling a list of remaining needs. Although a community starts with certain assets, many of them can be lost when a disaster strikes. What needs remain? Can any of these be taken care of through the previously identified assets or by external sources? Even in later term stages of recovery, it is possible that food; housing assistance; and physical, mental health, social, and/or spiritual support may be needed. Compile that list;

3. Locating remaining resources. Given the lists of community strengths and remaining needs, how can residual resources be located? This step is frequently overlooked. What other individuals have access to or possess the other needs required? Instead of merely targeting an organization for possible advocacy, it is necessary to identify and directly communicate with the individuals who can provide the needed help. Also remember, the most obvious resources might not be the best ones.

    In such cases, think innovatively. Conducting an assessment includes generating as large and complete a list of alternatives as possible, moving beyond the obvious solutions, and exploring the pros and cons of each option. Then, look back at this list and determine what resources would be most beneficial. Similarly, think about the probability that, once acquired, the specific resource(s) will actually fulfill the unmet needs; and

4. Determining how to best obtain these resources. This assessment lays the ground work for creating an action plan. Obviously, your collaboration will need a great deal of information about the targeted individuals and organizations to make decisions about the best strategies for advocacy efforts. Key community members will be helpful in providing this information. However, they should not be the only source. Persons needing recovery assistance should be asked to identify required support services.

These individuals can also be useful to accurately evaluate the needs of their specific population.

Observation alone can be very helpful to gain a better idea about populations. By walking through the community as a participant, you can observe and note the way people live and relate to each other and their physical surroundings. Information on communities can also be found in the local public library and on the internet.

In most situations, your community will not have already experienced a major catastrophe. If a disaster has already occurred, consider asking the following:

1. Which populations were the most affected? How severe was the psychological damage to these individuals? If this type of crisis hits again, which people are most vulnerable? What suggestions can survivors offer?
2. What are the current threats to mental health, and how can they be addressed?
3. What are the best sources of support for mental health recovery?
4. Who else has gathered information about past or possible future disasters, and what information has been collected?
5. What coping or recovery guides exist for enhancing stress management skills and promoting post-disaster mental health?

A. Definition of Community

Before conducting your assessment, it is important to understand the meaning of "community." The word has several different meanings, depending on the individuals involved. For example, where people live, worship, go to school, shop, or work are distinct types of communities, which can be located by external visitors through a specifically named building structure, address, and phone number. However, the term "community" can also describe a group of people who share common characteristics, heritage, or purpose. Examples are Iraq War veterans, Italian Americans, and hotel employees. On a more abstract level are communities formed by shared values, norms, interests, and experiences. People can voluntarily join these communities. People may choose to join, for instance, one social organization or faith-based group over another. In addition, people can simultaneously belong to multiple communities with different types of people at different times in their lives.

Some communities are more visible than others. The following are some examples of more prominent communities:

Geography: Geographic communities, or neighborhoods, have specific land boundaries. People who live in the particular geographic area often have a common community name and identification. For example, one of the communities devastated by Hurricane Katrina is called the Lower Ninth Ward. Geographically defined communities vary by social factors that can influence the quality of life, such as area size, population density, location, resources, abundance or absence of institutions, and safety. The following more visible communities can also be within a geographic community:

Age: Communities based on age are important to recognize because both the youngest and the oldest populations may be more at risk when disasters occur. School-aged youth and younger working adults can be more visible in a community than many older residents. The youth are often seen going to school or joining friends at a local entertainment center, and working people are seen traveling to and from work and near places of employment. Older and elderly individuals may be less visible because they live in age-specific housing areas or are housebound.

Ethnicity: Ethnically similar or racially marginalized groups, which are often victims of racism and discrimination, may share challenges such as lower income levels. Those who are ethnically diverse may have varying income and education. Typically underserved communities especially should be assessed before and following a disaster since wealthier residents have access to more resources. Disaster response needs to be sensitive to issues of trust and misunderstanding based on the community's historical and current experiences.

Language: Communities where most residents do not speak English require interpreters and liaisons who help negotiate between residents and the disaster-response efforts. This type of community is visible because the spoken language is heard. However, non-English-speaking people living in communities with mostly English-speaking members may not wish to come forward to access services. Many times, this is due to the fear or a lack of understanding of the assistance being offered. Other times, it can be related to issues such as immigration status.

Some communities are invisible or not readily obvious. Their identification should help your collaboration consider groups who are not immediately apparent following a disaster.

1. Non-documented persons. Fear of deportation will make these residents difficult to reach for disaster response. These populations are also stigmatized and sometimes the last to receive help;

2. Stigmatized residents. Individuals belonging to groups who have experienced discrimination may have more difficulty accessing services. The mentally ill are a primary example;

3. Persons with disabling conditions. These individuals, who can have unseen physical or mental disabilities, are not immediately obvious; and

4. Occupational-specific areas: Community members may possess occupational skills that are helpful in a disaster. However, these skills are often not assessed. For example, engineers, carpenters, and healthcare providers can be utilized for knowledge of the community and for their help in disaster recovery.

B. Meeting Diverse Population Needs

Similar mental health treatment can be provided to most survivors, yet every community has residents who are at higher risk for being negatively impacted. Clearly, certain community populations are more at risk or vulnerable when disasters occur and may receive suboptimal healthcare. Typically, individuals who have received inadequate or diminished support services prior to a calamity are the first ones to be overlooked once the event occurs. The terms "at risk," "vulnerable," and "special needs" are applied interchangeably to specify those individuals whose needs are not fully addressed by traditional health and social service providers.

WHO (www.who.int) defines "vulnerability" as "the degree to which a population, individual or organization is unable to anticipate, cope with, resist, and recover from the impacts of disasters." The Centers for Disease Control (CDC, www.cdc.gov) define vulnerable populations as groups whose needs are not fully addressed by traditional service providers or who feel they cannot comfortably or safely access and use the standard resources offered in emergency preparedness, relief, and recovery. These vulnerable populations include, but are not limited to children and youth, the elderly, socioeconomically disadvantaged, physically disabled, mentally ill, non-English speaking, homeless, and migrants. At-risk individuals also include those on life-support systems and dialysis, having radiation treatment, and going to methadone clinics.

Disaster response research finds a number of recent examples of resource inequity. For example, Hurricanes Katrina and Rita clearly demonstrated major gaps in emergency preparedness planning for the entire population, but particularly exposed how social, physical, and economic needs of many of the community members were not met. Although organizations have tried to rectify this situation, "few have integrated the perspective and experience of local service providers to investigate the needs of these populations and create a unified framework for addressing the challenges involved" (Nick et al., 2009). A large number of the most vulnerable residents were left stranded and waiting for evacuation support, refused shelter by unprepared organizations, and faced major challenges in attaining emergency services due to pre-existing mental and physical health conditions.

During Hurricanes Katrina and Rita, individuals with psychiatric conditions faced multiple forms of discrimination (National Council on Disability, 2006), which included denial of access to housing and other services and inappropriate and involuntary placement in jails, emergency rooms, nursing homes, and mental institutions. Group home residents were removed to new locations without prearrangement or tracking systems and could not be found by family members or original providers. People with psychiatric disabilities "encountered enormous problems with general shelters" because such facilities were "crowded, noisy, chaotic, confusing, and sometimes violent, all inadequate circumstances for a person with psychosis, anxiety, or depression." Some special needs shelters were available, but designed for people with medical and physical disabilities and not prepared to support mental health needs. The existence of a special needs shelter was used as an excuse to discriminate against individuals seeking access to the general shelters, with the result that some people with psychiatric disabilities being unable to obtain shelter altogether.

In 2018, Puerto Rico was particularly devastated because of its previous socioeconomic, infrastructure, and health issues. Half the island's residents lived below the poverty level. The Environmental Protection Agency reported how severe lack of water in some cases led to drinking from wells at hazardous waste Superfund sites. The number of deaths neared 3,000, and the number of people who tried to commit suicide more than tripled.

Socioeconomically Disadvantaged

After a disaster, many low-income people are stranded because they do not have personal transportation and are unable to use emergency mass transit or get help from other residents. In addition, real-time evacuation information is not generally provided to people with limited English proficiency. The disaster leaves the disadvantaged unable or less able to prepare for, respond to, and recover from the hazards and damages. The physical and social impact on these individuals is also disproportionate. Decreased ability to buy insurance, secure temporary accommodations, repair or build a house, purchase new clothes and household goods, access ongoing medical treatment, and take time off from work clearly hinders recovery. Such limited financial options can add to stress that, in turn, adversely affects personal relationships and increases anxiety and depression. Studies of numerous people impacted by storms in the Alabama, Florida, Louisiana, Mississippi, and Texas areas show how disasters are likely to increase poverty.

Children and Youth

Children, like the impoverished, are among the most vulnerable populations when catastrophes strike. They are particularly susceptible to higher stress levels, and their symptoms may linger much longer than those of adults. They also show greater susceptibility to how adults behave after disasters. Younger children may cry more frequently, become clingy, have nightmares, change their eating habits, and show excessive fear of the dark, being alone, animals, and sounds associated with the event. They may speak with difficulty or revert to behaviors such as bedwetting or thumb-sucking.

Older children may also become more irritable, aggressive, and competitive for parental attention. Some become obsessed by what happened and talk about it continually. They may also become more withdrawn from both family and friends and lose interest in normal activities. Teenagers and young adults may become rebellious and take part in high-risk behavior, develop physical health problems, suffer from sleep problems, or turn to drugs and alcohol.

The Frail and Elderly

A host of issues may hinder the care of elderly individuals, such as lack of mobility, visual and hearing impairment, language or literacy problems, decision-making difficulty, resistance to change, stigmatization, poor health literacy, and lack of knowledge or understanding about services. In contrast to younger adults, older persons are historically less likely to complain, ask for support, and receive services or resources after a disaster.

Older adults with limited education and financial resources may find accessing such services particularly daunting. They may be reluctant, ashamed, or embarrassed to admit and discuss mental health problems. Consequently, some develop serious emotional distress that may go unrecognized, unmanaged, or inadequately treated after a disaster. Or these older individuals may interpret their psychological symptoms as physical problems and seek medical rather than mental healthcare. Some of them may also not want to accept assistance from government agencies and be more willing to receive assistance from the Salvation Army, American Red Cross, or church groups. In general, older adults are more open to accepting help in familiar settings, including senior centers and religious institutions, and from previous social networks. Your action planning group should be aware of these potential barriers to care, which can impact its outreach efforts.

The ability of the elderly to adjust and cope after a disaster is increased by their capacity to access tangible resources, such as water, food, medical supplies, medication, and social support. Formal and informal caregivers can play an important role in assisting the elderly and frail with completing required paperwork to receive aid or assistance, serving as advocates for treatment and support services, providing or securing transportation, and promoting appropriate use of services. Following a catastrophic event, your interventions should be focused on building a recovery environment that returns people to their usual sources of social support and restores normalcy.

Communities must have specific plans for facilities for the aging and elderly (Hyer & Dosa, 2017). Nursing homes and other similar care facilities need to research and write emergency management manuals that properly prepare them for arising dangers. In recent hurricanes, many community facilities for the disabled, infirm, and elderly, particularly those who were wheelchair users or on life-support systems, had not given enough thought to what to do before, during, and after a disaster. They were unprepared for the worst and not well connected to emergency response systems and plans. Quick and expedient transportation of the infirm was not considered.

Disasters can be extremely stressful for the aged because they can greatly worsen their physical and mental wellbeing. Many of the deaths from Hurricane Maria were elderly patients who could not receive vital healthcare, such as oxygen and dialysis. The suicide rate was considerably higher in this population. A year after Hurricane Maria, the storm continued to take its toll on the elderly. Many of them were living in substandard homes and anxious about additional storms. In 2017, many elderly were stranded when Hurricane Irma hit the Florida shores. Eight residents of a nursing home/rehab facility across the street from a hospital died of heat prostration when generators were not used in lieu of lost power. In 2018, assisted-living residents in a Texas nursing home were left trapped in dangerous situations without electricity and generators or simply abandoned as waters rose.

People With Physical Disabilities

More than 23 million Americans, or 12% of the population aged 16 to 64, have special healthcare needs due to some disability. There is an 80% chance any individual will suffer a temporary or permanent disability at one point in their life. Community-based organizations are underutilized resources when assessing this population's needs. Studies find few emergency managers have given thought to helping the disabled in a disaster. After the 2013 Black Forest Fires in Colorado, where nearly 16,000 acres burned, no one was prepared to help the disabled populations. Similarly, according to the National Council of Disability (2006), only one of six organizations in the Gulf area that specifically served the disabled population impacted by Katrina said it had plans to help its clients in a catastrophe—and these were verbal rather than written plans. Ideally, such organizations would have guidelines for pre-disaster to post-disaster situations.

Immediately after a disaster, it is not logical to believe people with special needs can be adequately cared for in quickly built and arbitrarily placed shelters with untrained responders. Directors of disability support service organizations said they have confronted many barriers, making effective evacuation and post-disaster response time slower and more difficult. In some instances, the personal assistants of disabled individuals were not allowed in emergency shelters set aside for this vulnerable population and could not perform tasks such as bowel and bladder routines. As a result, the disabled were then sent to overburdened hospitals. A similar issue arose during the California wildfires, when emergency personnel were sometimes not allowed to drive their accessible para-transit vans into neighborhoods to evacuate people with disabilities. Such policies and practices resulted in unnecessary hospitalizations and utilization of medical care and beds that could have been better allocated to individuals with more intensive and appropriate medical needs. Social services for the physically disabled also need to set policies allowing for support animals, required medications, and quiet areas for individuals with mental illness.

Mentally Ill

Mentally ill individuals may function relatively well immediately following a catastrophe. As with the rest of the population, a portion of these individuals show resiliency and help themselves and others in a time of serious need. However, over time, they may become more threatened than others by the disaster's social disruption. Although mental healthcare in the U.S. has improved over the past couple of decades, a disparity continues to exist between mental and physical healthcare. In many cases, the mentally ill are not considered as important as those suffering from physical injuries. Both populations need to be treated as equal and important populations to be served in a catastrophe.

Addressing the special needs of the mentally ill can alleviate or prevent negative outcomes:

1. People with serious mental illness are less likely to be prepared for a disaster. They often do not have needed emergency supplies. This makes them even more dependent on others for evacuation or taking other necessary steps to safety;
2. The emotional impact of a disaster often leads to the onset of new and recurrent stress-related symptoms and possible relapse. The mentally ill may have difficulty handling psychological distress or disruption in their social situations. Those with a history of PTSD especially may prove more vulnerable;

3. A disaster often separates the mentally ill from their family and friends who normally care for them. Acquiring the basic necessities such as food, water, and safe housing may not be possible after an emergency, and caregivers have less time to provide these resources to others;

4. When a disaster strikes, the mentally ill are also cut off from support services and medication if clinics and pharmacies are closed or transportation problems make it difficult to get to appointments; and

5. Many people with psychiatric problems also face unemployment, financial instability, social isolation, stigmatization, and unstable social relationships. They are thus less able to protect themselves from harm and need others to anticipate their needs.

C. Community Resources

Communities should be seen as more than just "bundles of needs." At times, value comes from reframing the situation and instead focusing on the identification of "assets." What are community strengths? What resources do individuals offer? These can be practical resources, such as cooking and repair expertise, or they can be people skills, such as counseling, organizing, or speaking abilities. The resources of neighborhood groups or organizations, local businesses, mental health providers, agencies, schools, and places of worship should also be considered.

A resident may recognize his or her ability to help rebuild or transform the community, including the parent who organizes a playgroup, someone who starts a neighborhood watch group, or a young adult who visits older residents. A physical structure or place, such as a community/recreation center, school, or social club, can provide a location for people to feel a sense of belongingness and to share ideas for community improvement. They can also be places for sharing and support during or after a disaster. A community service, such as public transportation, a clinic, a co-op, a park, or a cultural organization, improves community life and invites participation, and a business provides local employment and supports the economy. Identifying these assets will expand the pool of resources available to assist with recovery.

Everyone in the community, including all members of the collaboration, have skills and talents to provide needed support and be a force for improvement. They can be used as a foundation for community improvement. Determining these assets can help in many ways when a disaster strikes or when building community resiliency before an event. Since external help is not always available, communities often have to rely on their own resources for change. Identifying and mobilizing these strengths enables residents to be empowered and gain control over their lives. Feeling pride in these efforts, residents will be more positive about outcomes and work together to solve problems as they arise. Such local investment efforts become integrated into the community, with members dedicating time and abilities to making desirable change.

It is impossible to know a community without recognizing both its needs and assets. Whoever conducts your community assessment must recognize how a seeming negative can be transformed into a positive. An overgrown empty lot filled with discarded items can be seen as either an eyesore or a future neighborhood garden or park.

D. Impact on the General Population

All people, even those who are not physically or mentally disabled, can and do become susceptible in a disaster. Individuals of all ages and backgrounds may not have any history of trauma, yet they become more vulnerable when a calamity hits because of such factors as separation from or passing of friends and family, injury, or loss of a home. During catastrophic times, earlier emotional and medical problems can worsen. People at risk differ in their interests, skills, and experiences, so no single organization can be a spokesperson for all vulnerable populations.

The mentally ill, physically disabled, young, and elderly have difficulty caring for themselves in usual circumstances. So it becomes all the more difficult for them to cope with moving from their homes to shelters, fear for their safety, and being torn away from their family members. Suddenly, the typical challenges they face on a daily basis turn into a very traumatic situation. Attempting to assess and care for these individuals in the midst of the disaster is nearly impossible.

To make matters worse, some people, even the most vulnerable, do not want to comply with directives to leave their homes. Or, because of a mental illness, they are fearful of leaving their homes or the stigma of their disease. It becomes all the more dangerous to transport them, and sometimes their pets or service animals, to shelters. Keeping track of these individuals and their support systems through ongoing assessments can be of help in such situations.

E. Conducting the Assessment

Assessments can be conducted of an entire community, geographical areas, or specific neighborhoods. Or you may find parts of your community have already been assessed, and your collaboration has to fill in the gaps. If your entire community needs to be assessed, it will be necessary to find volunteers from the assets listed here. For example, many neighborhood groups can provide valuable information on the residents. The time and people/financial resources you have available will determine the depth and extent of information collected. Establish a priority list and pursue the most important items first. Always keep in mind your end goal, so you get input to answer most of your questions about needs and assets.

Once you complete your community mental health assessment, the collaboration members can determine the best ways to meet residents' needs and the best ways to utilize assets to respond to them. You may want to have a meeting where people share ideas about the information gathered and how it fits into the required action steps.

In addition to gaining insights directly from the residents, you need to gather information from written and digital publications. Evaluate all the information you acquire based on the sources. Government information tends to be quite sound. Professional organizations and college or university sources are typically reliable. The information on some websites can be worthwhile or questionable, depending on the source. Similarly, other general forms of information may seem useful but require being checked for reliability by locating the sponsoring organization's "about us" information and reading about its mandate, history, board/officer structure, and past/ongoing projects. If there is time, it is best to talk directly with a contact for further information and confirm the timeliness and accuracy of the posted material.

F. Post-Disaster Re-assessment

How you will conduct a post-disaster assessment of your action plan is a critical objective for your mental health strategy, since continuous improvement is a necessity. Your collaboration team members should determine what data will be collected, and how, after the calamity. For example, they may decide to look at the effectiveness of a mental healthcare triage tool, response time, participation rates, the number of referrals for post-disaster psychological care, and/or long-term treatment results. Records are helpful in such assessments, but observations and interviewing those directly involved with the disaster often provide the best input. The more input you receive from people in the field, the better. Part of your action plan may be having short debriefings when volunteers leave the disaster site. If cell phones are working, volunteers can spend a few minutes recording what occurred during their shift.

How long your assessment continues depends on the type of disaster and its degree and length of impact. Regardless, the assessment should begin as soon after the event as possible, since waiting too long will diminish anecdotal research. Most likely, many new ideas can be gained from the recent experience, and the community will want to make improvements based on those lessons. Setting aside a full day or more to review the collaboration's key members' thoughts and suggestions can be very beneficial. Dividing into breakout groups by areas can assist in gathering specifics for each topic of disaster preparedness. These sessions can then be followed by presentations to the whole group for their comments and input. Frequently, people who have not participated in a particular area will notice some additional ways to make an improvement.

The results can then be incorporated into a revised plan. The more specifics documented, the more information you have for another serious event. The agenda may ask some general questions:

1. How successful was the community in responding to the disaster?
2. What went well?
3. What did not go so well?
4. What improvements can, or should, be made?

The object of the tracking and evaluation process is never to be disappointed by how much work you accomplished but to better gauge whether the initial goals were realistic. Most important is reviewing the information gained and determining how to use what is learned to better align the goals and actions for another possible event. It is important to see the progression made, paying attention to the strengths of the approaches and the barriers encountered. It will be possible to see the gaps existing between what it was hoped would happen and what actually happened. That will help vary the approach for more effective results in the future.

It may also be important to survey or interview community members about the group's efforts. The key to adequate monitoring is to ask very specific questions. People can be asked to carefully review the initial strategies used and the approaches taken. Then you can determine if these strategies and the targets of different efforts were the best choices. If not, then it may be better to try another approach. The process of any effort involves taking different steps and seeing what works, monitoring efforts, and then trying again.

After all information is collected from the various meetings and interviews, a draft of this post-disaster assessment needs to be prepared, with specific findings and recommendations for each topic. This preliminary report should be presented at a series of meetings, first to the original collaboration and then to other key community leaders, as well as to the community at large. The draft should also be extensively distributed through the local media.

Copies of the revised action plan can be available online as well as through key community locations such as the town hall and the library. All residents should be encouraged to review the report's draft and provide comments and suggestions. Members of your collaboration can have copies of the report to respond to any queries or for reference purposes. Comments can also be made through the planning team's website. Public input should be recorded and summarized and act as a source for revisions. Eventually, some of these ideas will be incorporated into an updated mental health disaster response plan.

Of course, many of the steps in your action plan will be ongoing for quite some time after the disaster, particularly for the most vulnerable groups. The state of these interventions/programs can be noted in the post-event assessment, and quarterly updates can be provided. The impact of disasters is long term, and your collaboration will continually be acquiring new input over the months and even years to come.

Mental health action plans should be updated at least every two years, even when a disaster has not occurred, due to the speed of changes nationwide. A plan requires ongoing testing and updating to ensure the highest safety measures for its residents. In addition, community planners must continue to conduct realistic training and exercises on a regular basis, using different disaster scenarios. The results need to be evaluated in an objective and fair manner, and additional revisions made. Whenever new members join the collaboration, they must be brought up to date on the status of the plan either with a walk-through of the latest rendition or, at least, with a personal reading of the material and meeting for follow-up questions and discussion.

It is always important to remember how other communities are either preparing for or are actually facing their own catastrophes. Reading the lessons learned in reports from other communities can be very helpful. The contact information for one or more of the members of a preparedness group should be available online. It can also be helpful to share your community's report with area universities and attend regional and national meetings and conferences on disaster mental health response. This will greatly help others undergoing this traumatic experience. A representative of your collaboration may also be invited to visit other parts of the U.S. where disasters have occurred to lend advice.

G. Ethical Considerations

It is essential your collaboration members follow ethical guidelines with all vulnerable populations (SCRA, 2010). This is particularly important in crisis situations when stress is at its highest. How do you provide the right balance between achieving maximum gain and fairness? Such decisions must be based on sound ethical knowledge. The answer will inevitably consist of judgment and compromise. Broad ideas need to be made based on specific contexts and then refined.

Lack of resources and atypical healthcare practices to assure the immediate care and survival of a stricken population can lead to unethical inequities. It may take greater effort to uphold individual rights than in normal situations. Ethical considerations need to be included in your disaster mental health plan. Your collaboration may even want to assign a member or a committee to define and oversee these guidelines.

Emergency responders want to act in the most expedient manner. However, they also must be mindful of the victims' personal needs and requests. Responders should disagree only when such requests will be more harmful than beneficial. Also, providers must ensure intervention decisions are consistent for everyone involved, not only for those who are most susceptible. For example, all impacted community members should be required to vacate their homes when a storm is imminent, not only certain populations.

Such decisions are not easy. When catastrophes occur, many decisions need to be made in a very short and stressful time about allocation of services and resources. Consistency, fairness, effectiveness, and transparency are standards for which to strive, but this may not always be possible. It is best to talk with the individual groups being served to get their input.

It is impossible to plan for every circumstance, but the Florida Department of Health provides additional things to consider when assessing populations. The able-bodied can also be at risk (Florida Department of Health, nd):

◆ Healthy children may have family vulnerability factors, as well as a lack of transportation or phone that puts them at risk.

◆ During crises, mental health problems may occur more frequently, and pre-existing medical conditions/cognitive impairments may get worse.

◆ Vulnerable populations differ in their capabilities, opinions, needs, and situations, and no one individual or agency can speak for all groups.

◆ Do not think that, post-disaster, older people with special needs can be adequately cared for in hastily prepared shelters, which are randomly located and with untrained personnel. Requests that seem like luxuries in the time of crisis may be essential for people with disabilities.

◆ Tracking of evacuated individuals can become a concern, especially if there is no communitywide registration system.

◆ Issues with the greatest impact during disasters include notification; evacuation; emergency transport; and access to medical care, medications, mobility devices or service animals, and information.

◆ Reasons for noncompliance with evacuation directives include no access to transportation, mobility impairment, financial inability to leave, providing care to others, not hearing the warning or receiving it in time, the inability to bring pets or service animals, and thinking their location is safe.

◆ Some people do not voice their needs for fear of being stigmatized.

◆ Preparedness instructions require some level of money and resources that are not available for some populations.

◆ The higher the technology being used for messages, the fewer vulnerable population groups will be reached.

◆ Messages must be kept at a sixth-grade level because the ability to understand instructions and/or read information lessens in a disaster.

◆ Defining at-risk populations is continual since people and their needs and vulnerabilities change over time; organize data in ways that are accessible and easy to amend.

TO DO

1. A community health assessment is a systematic examination of the health status indicators for a given population to identify key community problems and assets. The ultimate goal of a community health assessment is to develop strategies for addressing health needs and identifying issues. Communities also conduct human health assessments to estimate the risk to human health associated with exposure to specific environmental chemical contaminants. These concern human-caused long-term issues that may or may not be impacting the community at the present time. Another assessment may include private healthcare through medical practices, hospitals, and medical centers. Regardless, you want to provide a snapshot of current local policy, systems, and environmental change strategies and identify areas for improvement.

    Determine whether or not your community has already completed an assessment of your residents, how long ago it was conducted, and if it is relevant to present needs.

2. Which group(s) of individuals are the most at risk in your community? What can be done to increase their resiliency prior to a possible disaster occurring?

3. Given the makeup and resources of your collaboration, what is the most expedient way to conduct an assessment?

References

Community Tool Box. (2018). *Center for community health and development University of Kansas*. Retrieved from https://ctb.ku.edu/en

Florida Department of Health. (n.d.). Vulnerable populations assessment tool.

Hyer, K., & Dosa, D. (2017). *Testimony presented to the United States senate special committee on aging*. Retrieved from www.aging.senate.gov/imo/media/doc/SCA_Hyer_09_20_17.pdf

National Council on Disability. (2006). *The needs of people with disabilities with psychiatric disabilities during and after Hurricanes Katrina and Rita: Position paper and recommendations*. Retrieved from https://ncd.gov/publications/2006/07142006

Nick, G. A., Savoia, E., Elqura, L., Crowther, S., Cohen, B., Leary, M., . . . Koh, H. K. (2009). Emergency preparedness for vulnerable populations: People with special health-care needs. *Public Health Reports, 124*(2), 338–343.

Psychologists for Social Responsibility. (2019). *Building cultures of peace with social justice*. Retrieved from https://psysr.net/inequality/

Rosenbaum, S. (2013). *Principles to consider for the implementation of a community health needs assessment process*. The George Washington University School of Public Health and Health Services, Department of Health Policy. Retrieved from http://nnphi.org/wp-content/uploads/2015/08/PrinciplesToConsiderForTheImplementationOfACHNAProcess_GWU_20130604.pdf

Society of Community Research and Action (SCRA). (2010). *How to help your community recover from disaster: A manual for planning and action*. Retrieved from https://www.scra27.org/files/2114/0605/7122/SCRA_Disaster_Recovery_Manual.pdf

Reader's Notes

6

Natural and Human-Caused Disasters

Chapter 6 Preview
A. Natural Disasters
B. Human-Made/Caused Tragedies
C. Mass Violence (Deliberate Disasters)

Disasters, also called calamities and catastrophes, often involve extreme forces of nature like earthquakes, fires, floods, hurricanes, and tornadoes. Natural disasters struck long before modern humans inhabited the planet and will likely continue as long as Earth exists. They can hit at any time and in any place, building slowly or occurring suddenly without warning. These events may have different characteristics and impacts, but they also have a common element, which is their severity. An emergency is a calamitous event that can typically be handled by a community alone; a disaster normally requires external support as well due to increased severity. In both cases, injury and loss of life are possible outcomes.

Sometimes human actions cause disaster or contribute to loss of property and lives that may have been avoidable. These human-caused disasters have changed along with the evolution of human culture and technology. Some of these human-caused disasters are due to human error or carelessness, and others are from intentional acts of violence and cruelty or to make a political statement.

Providing proper mental healthcare to those involved in a catastrophic event is a complex undertaking. This is especially true because people may react and be impacted very differently by a horrifying situation, so they may react and be impacted very differently depending on the type of disaster.

A. Natural Disasters

Statistics confirm an ever-increasing number of natural disasters. The weather in particular areas is indeed getting more extreme. The U.N. reports how weather-related disasters are bombarding the world with greater power and producing significantly more losses: 90% of disasters are due to the weather (U.N. Office for Disaster Risk Reduction, 2015). Over the past 20 years, the U.S. has been one of the hardest hit nations for such weather-related disasters (Shaw, 2015).

In the last three decades, North America has been continually battered by hurricanes, tornadoes, floods, searing heat, and drought. The worst storms are deadly. Even when disasters cause little loss of life, there is a widespread perceived and justified threat to personal wellbeing. Natural disasters in 2018 topped earlier records, from the deadliest wildfires in California's history to the worst hurricane to hit the East Coast since 1969. In fact, the U.S. led the world in catastrophes, not the type of statistic that brings satisfaction. This followed another disastrous year: In 2017, Hurricane Maria was ranked one of the deadliest natural disasters in America. An official report estimated nearly 3,000 people died in Puerto Rico. Five months after the deadly storm hit, suicide rates spiked in this U.S. territory, after two decades of decreasing numbers. Puerto Rico's Department of Health reported a 29% increase over the previous year, with 253 people committing suicide.

Storms may only last for a short time, but heavy rainfall, such as the 20 inches that Hurricane Matthew dropped on North Carolina in 2016, can cause severe flooding and significant structural damage. Also, strong winds and flood waters can carry large objects for long distances. In addition to such destruction comes the lack of potable water, food, and adequate shelter; homes are damaged, personal possessions demolished, and jobs and leisure time lost. Repairing the physical damage can take from months to years. As in cases such as Hurricane Sandy in 2012, many structures are never rebuilt. In parts of Louisiana, the same areas have been hit time and time again. Except for loss of life, dislocation is among the most disturbing of all problems that arise from such tragedies. Even when moving is planned, it is an intense stressor. Forced relocation from weather-related disasters is in every way disturbing for both primary and secondary victims. Indirect effects may be less physically intrusive but, in the long run, can cause as much trauma.

Tornadoes

Tornadoes develop from strong thunderstorms that arise as circling, funnel-shaped clouds. These rotating clouds reach downward to Earth's surface with forceful winds measured by the Fujita-Pearson ("F") scale. Introduced in 1971 by Ted Fujita, a professor at the University of Chicago, the F scale measures the intensity of the storm by the amount of damage done.

In the U.S., about 75% of tornadoes are found at the weaker end of the scale, with winds less than 110 miles per hour, according to the National Weather Service (www.weather.gov). Tornadoes may also alter their speed from remaining stationary to high F-scale speeds. Making a deep roaring sound like a train, they typically measure 500 feet across and travel on the ground for five miles. Every state in America is at some risk from tornadoes, although they occur mostly from March until June in the "tornado alley," or central Texas through Oklahoma; central Kansas and Nebraska; eastern South Dakota; and sometimes through Iowa, Missouri, and Illinois as well as Indiana to Ohio.

Oklahoma residents have faced these deadly storms repeatedly throughout their history. In 2013, an intense and destructive tornado hit Moore, Oklahoma, and adjacent areas, with peak winds reaching 210 miles per hour. The storm killed 24 people, including seven children in Plaza Towers Elementary School,

Source: NOAA. Photo by OAR/ERL National Severe Storms Lab

and injured 377 residents. In 2011, a tornado in Joplin, Missouri, killed 161 people and injured about 1,150 individuals. A study (Adams et al., 2014) found nearly 7% of adolescents suffered from PTSD from this storm. Females who previously experienced stressful incidents and/or had an injured family member were at greatest risk for trauma. Fortunately, 2018 was a relatively calm year with a record low number of deaths.

There is no way of knowing what the weather will bring from one year to the next. Nor does the arrival of tornadoes come with much warning. They frequently strike quickly, so people do not have time to escape to safe areas and prepare for the impact. Due to this unpredictability, victims often experience emotional distress, such as overwhelming anxiety, sleep problems; and depression before, during, and after the storm. Other signs of emotional distress related to severe storms such as tornadoes include:

1. Unreasonable worry and guilt;
2. Feelings of helplessness or hopelessness;
3. Fears that the worst will happen when any storms are forecast;
4. Nightmares or recurring thoughts and memories; and
5. Increased disagreements with family and friends.

Hurricanes and Tropical Storms

Hurricanes are tropical storms that form in the southern Atlantic Ocean, Caribbean Sea, Gulf of Mexico, and eastern Pacific Ocean and annually affect millions of people along the Atlantic and Gulf of Mexico coasts. In parts of the Southwest U.S. and the Pacific Coast, hurricanes often combine with tornadoes, floods, and heavy winds.

Some studies forecast climate change is already increasing the severity of hurricanes. The intensity of these storms is measured by the Saffir-Simpson scale, named after the co-developers, civil engineer Herbert Saffir and meteorologist Robert Simpson, according to the National Oceanic and Atmosphere Administration (www.noaa.gov). Wind speed is ranked on a scale of 1 to 5 to estimate the potential property damage and flooding along the coast.

By looking at the research conducted after the most recent high-grade hurricanes, it is possible to see how much the victims were then, and still are, impacted by the tremendous damage done. Over 50 people lost their lives in Hurricane Sandy in 2012, and much of the damage may never be repaired. Researchers (Adams et al., 2014) surveyed the mental health impact on more than 1,000 residents of the Rockaways, which lost about 100 homes in the storm. They found the psychological impact persisted nearly four years later. They concluded: "Given the likelihood of more frequent and intense hurricanes due to climate change, future hurricane recovery efforts must consider the long-term effects of hurricane exposure on mental health, especially on PTSD, when providing appropriate assistance and treatment."

Floods

Floods, a quite common U.S. hazard, occur when excessive rainfall from storms, failed dams or levees, and flash floods typically cause an overflow on normally dry land. Coastal areas are more vulnerable to floods, especially with hurricanes, but they take place nationwide and vary in extent and duration. The greatest emotional devastation comes from populations who experience and re-experience flooding and other weather-related tragedies over short periods of time. When Louisiana was hit by major floods in 2016, many people were faced with terrifying memories of Hurricane Katrina and the water damage in 2005. For many, as they abandoned their homes, it was like living the trauma of Katrina all over again.

Many of these people were already traumatized from their first tragic experience and still greatly troubled. Even those not as severely traumatized by Katrina were experiencing feelings of dread. On the other hand, resiliency was also seen in many individuals as they regained their pride by becoming stronger and moving on from earlier storm disasters.

Climatic patterns are continually changing in the U.S. For example, studies (Mallakpour & Villarini, 2015) show large floods are becoming increasingly

Source: FEMA: Photo by Patsy Lynch/FEMA

more frequent across the Northeast, Pacific Northwest, and northern Great Plains but decreasing in some other areas of the country, such as the Southwest and the Rockies.

Wildfires

Many scientists also believe climate change is leading to a major increase in the number of U.S. forest fires. One recent study (Abatzoglou & Williams, 2016) revealed changes over the last three decades doubled the areas affected by forest fires in the West. Since 1984, climbing temperatures and aridity have caused fires to spread across an additional 16,000 square miles, an area larger than the combined states of Massachusetts and Connecticut. Further warming will continue to increase wildfires significantly in coming years, as was seen in 2018 with the deadly California fires.

Wildfires usually start by lightning or human-caused accidents. Unnoticed when first starting, they can spread quickly and destroy woodland settings as well as nearby residential areas. The 2018 California fires just continued many prior years of the same. In 2013, over 47,500 wildfires were reported in the U.S., destroying over 1,000 homes and burning more than 4 million acres of land (National Fire Protection Association, 2015). In 2017, California was hit by a series of devastating wildfires. A total of 4,625 fires burned 309,687 acres (California Department of Forestry and Fire Protection, 2017).

The first catastrophe brings trauma, which is often compounded when it occurs again. When the 2018 California forest fires rushed in, numerous residents were still trying to get their lives in order from the previous year's disaster. Counselors were continuing to help people with reoccurring nightmares, grief, agitation, and high levels of stress (NPR, 2018). Children are especially impacted by these fires, having difficulty sleeping, clinging to their parents, and feeling fearful when hearing the sound of the wind or sirens. Parents often disregard such emotions after disasters because they are so greatly involved with rebuilding physical structures.

Earthquakes

Earthquakes are caused by the shifting of the Earth's plates or shell, leading to a sudden shaking of the ground lasting from a few seconds to several minutes. In 1935, Charles Richter (1935) created a scale to mathematically compare the size of earthquakes. At a higher Richter magnitude, damage can be considerable after only a few seconds. Even when signs occur that an earthquake is going to take place, there is no way to know exactly when or how severe/mild it will be. Earthquakes happen without warning and at any time of year. Certain states have a greater risk of these events, such as California, Hawaii, Nevada, and

Source: FEMA. Photo by Bob McMillan/FEMA

Washington. These disasters often lead to other deadly catastrophes, such as tsunamis and fires, as well as damaged infrastructure, such as highways.

On August 24, 2014, a magnitude 6.0 earthquake struck California. With its epicenter in Napa County, it was the largest to affect the San Francisco Bay area in 25 years and led to two deaths; widespread power outages; five residential fires; and damage to roadways, waterlines, and 1,600 buildings. Researchers (Attfield et al., 2015) conducted a household-level community assessment for Public Health Emergency Response in two impacted counties. One fifth of respondents—27% in Napa and 9% in western Vallejo—reported one or more traumatic psychological responses in their households; Napa County Public Health made decisions on immediate-term mental healthcare resource allocation for public training sessions and education campaigns to support persons at risk following the earthquake, as well as community resilience and future disaster preparedness.

Drought

Although drought was widespread in the Great Plains in the 1930s, an era commonly referred to as the Dust Bowl, few studies have been conducted on the long-term psychological impact of such events. Given the fact that the frequency and intensity of droughts are steadily increasing in the Southeast U.S. along with rising temperatures, mental health interventions for such disasters may become the norm in the future.

A drought is a normal, reoccurring nationwide weather event that can vary in intensity and duration geographically and within a specific state. Drought takes place with reduced precipitation over a significant period of time, typically a season or more, or a delay in the rainy season. Low water availability creates shortages in water supplies that impact various activities and the environment. Unlike other weather phenomena that occur quickly and in one specified location, drought is a slow-moving hazardous event over larger areas. Thus, the mental health effects are more subtle and last longer than with other natural disasters. The effect becomes even greater as people place more demands on water supplies. Research (Padhy, Sarkar, Panigrahi & Paul, 2015) found changes in temperature and effects such as drought are likely to increase rates of aggression and violent suicides by farmers.

Volcanoes

Volcanoes are points in the Earth's crust that have erupted, spilling lava, ash, rocks, and gas during periods of seismic activity. Although many volcanoes are located under the ocean, those on land can pose considerable danger to life and property depending on how close they are to inhabited areas and the extent of the eruption. Volcanoes are generally classified as being active, dormant, or extinct based on their level of activity. They may appear dormant on land but be very active beneath the surface. Historical records provide input on activity, since those that have recently erupted will most likely do so again in future years or centuries.

Volcanic gases that pose the greatest potential hazards are sulfur dioxide, carbon dioxide, and hydrogen fluoride. Sulfur dioxide can cause acid rain and air pollution downwind from a volcano. Ash, which is gritty and abrasive, can travel hundreds to thousands of miles downwind from a volcano. Although not highly toxic, it can lead to health problems in children, the elderly, and those with respiratory ailments.

Kīlauea in Hawaii tops the list as the most dangerous volcano in the U.S., with Washington's Mount St. Helens and Mount Rainier following in second and third place (Wei-Haas, 2018). In 2018, Hawaiian farmers lost up to $30 million in damage, and numerous people needed to be evacuated. Fortunately, there were no fatalities. Despite this positive news, loss of personal homes and businesses has led to trauma similar to those at other locations (Hughes, 2019). The state provided mental health outreach at shelters, clinics, and community meetings, where hundreds of residents showed signs of trauma from the volcanic eruptions. The most common psychological issues are a sense of confusion, emotional numbing, anger, frustration, difficulty sleeping, and anxiety.

B. Human-Made/Caused Tragedies

If it is not bad enough that nature bombards the U.S. with deadly storms, humans add to this devastation in their own destructive ways. Industrial, chemical, biological, and radiological accidents result directly or indirectly from one or more deliberate or negligent human actions. Natural disasters may cause terror, severe anxiety, and stress, but Siegrist and Sutterli (2014) note that people are even more disturbed by catastrophes perpetrated by humans.

Such human disturbances are anything but recent. Anthropologists (Moris et al., 2013) have found what they believe to be the oldest polluted river in human history. About 7,000 years ago, humans were contaminating Southern Jordan through pyrometallurgy, or extracting metals, in this case copper from stone. More recent hazards have occurred with technology misuse, infrastructure damage, transportation accidents, hazardous materials spills, fires, and explosions. The most recent devastating example is the water crisis in Flint, Michigan, which was entirely preventable. As many as 9,000 children are victims of lead poisoning with no one knowing what physical and developmental problems are to come in their future.

Oil train accidents are skyrocketing, and growing numbers of people are being injured or dying from commuter train accidents, such as the one in Hoboken, New Jersey, which injured 100 passengers; another in Los Angeles injured 16; and a derailment in New Hyde Park, New York, harmed 33 riders (PW Parker, 2017). All these calamities also included major physical damage to buildings and infrastructures, adding up to billions of dollars over time. Psychological trauma goes hand in hand with these accidents. With underlying anxiety and depression come anger, feelings of vulnerability, perceived lack of control, and a sense of helplessness.

An oil spill in the Gulf of Mexico starting over a decade ago may be the worst of all such U.S. human-caused disasters. Somewhere between 300 and 700 barrels of oil were ejected off the Louisiana coast after a mudslide sank a Taylor Energy platform in 2004 during Hurricane Ivan. Since some of the wells are still not capped, the federal government warns such spillage could continue throughout the 21st century (Tousignant, 2018). The BP oil spill in 2010 also competes for top place in worst disasters of this type. The explosion and sinking of the Transocean Deepwater Horizon oil rig—once again in the Gulf of Mexico—killed 11 people and spewed more than three million barrels of oil in 87 days.

The BP well was located more than 5,000 feet beneath the water's surface, in the deep ocean, which accounts for approximately 75% of Earth's total ocean volume. Immediately following the explosion, BP workers, the oil company and Transocean contractors, and many government agencies attempted to control the spread of oil to coastal ecosystems such as beaches. Floating booms were used to contain oil from breaking down in the water. Researchers are still trying to understand the spill and its impact on marine life, the Gulf coast, and human communities. After the BP calamity, several studies reported on the emotional decline of impacted residents, including significantly increased depression, particularly closer to the epicenter; severe distress; and increase in domestic conflicts. Researchers have compared mental health outcomes in two fishing communities—Baldwin County, Alabama, which was directly exposed to spilled oil, and Franklin County, Florida, which was indirectly impacted although it never saw oil on its shore. During the spill, between one-third and one-half of both populations were clinically depressed. Two years later, about 20% of the population was still depressed. It took three years for the spill levels to drop back to where they were before the accident (Weir, 2014).

Hydraulic fracking is another more recent area of human interference. California used to have the largest number of earthquakes, but now Oklahoma holds this record due to the horizontal drilling and hydraulic fracking process. A mixture of water, sand, and chemicals is pumped through the ground at high pressures, which cracks open rocks that release oil and natural gas. This process produces earthquakes so small they can only be detected through sensitive instruments. Earthquakes may also occur when the wastewater is injected into the Earth's crust. As fluids move away from the initial site, they sometimes cause deeper faults to slip and more serious earthquakes to occur.

A review of mental illness and fracking studies (Hirsch et al., 2018) found that, although people living in fracking areas may experience minimal initial benefits from the sale of their land for this process, they may soon also feel higher levels of worry, anxiety, and depression about lifestyle, health, safety, and financial security. Entire communities may jointly experience collective trauma from the "boom/bust cycle." The most vulnerable populations, including the poor, rural, and indigenous, are often impacted the most and may suffer for generations.

Climate Change as a Stressor

In the past, questions arose about whether or not climate change was impacting catastrophes. Now, most climate models predict rising temperatures may lead to greater risk of drought and increased storm intensity. Over the last 50 years, much of the nation has seen increases in prolonged periods of excessively high temperatures, heavy downpours, and severe floods and droughts in some regions. Studies are just beginning to be conducted on the relationship between climate change and mental health, as seawaters rise; storms become stronger;

droughts spread; and increasing numbers of Americans lose their homes, jobs, family members, friends, and communities. The negative mental health effects of climate change range from simple anxiety due to minor emotional issues to PTSD because of displacement and to the death of friends and family members.

Surveys report approximately 69% of Americans are at least somewhat concerned about changing climate (Lavelle, 2019). This threat is associated with a greater sense of insecurity about the future. A large number of people experience a range of negative mental health responses to what is considered a "hybrid risk" of climate change, or an ongoing threat or event that will demonstrate both natural and human causes and processes. These emotional responses include greater risk perceptions, general anxiety, pessimism, helplessness, lower self-esteem, stress, sadness, feelings of loss, and guilt.

Media reports about serious climate change may elicit strong emotional responses, based on how the information is presented. If the media coverage is scientifically inaccurate or discouraging, the stress increases; yet more effective, constructive communication furthers adaptive and preventive individual and collective action.

Research also shows a slowly growing environmental disaster negatively impacts the physical and psychological health of individuals and their families and communities. For example, in Libby, Montana, a number of residents have become victims of amphibole asbestos (Cline, Chung, Chung, & Hernandez, 2014). In 2011, a state judge approved a $43 million settlement for over 1,000 victims, agreeing that Montana officials knew that dust from a mine was killing people but failed to intervene. In this case, residents who felt conflicted about their community's response also reported increased family conflict. These concerns caused people to withdraw from their social life and reduce direct and indirect communication with others about their disease. Victims felt they needed to keep quiet about their illness in order not to be stigmatized.

One male victim, for instance, did not even talk with his best friends about his disease. He noted, "And there's lots of people that are afraid to admit they have it to anyone. . . . One of my best friends, I saw her at Dr. Black's office, and I said, 'Well, what are you doing here?' And she said, 'Well what are you doing here?' And I said, 'I have asbestos poisoning. What are you doing here?' She said, 'So am I.' She whispered, like it was a secret."

A previous study (Erikson, 1994) showed similar results with gas leaks, mercury poisoning, and nuclear waste that contaminates communities, or what was called a "new species of trouble." Erikson suggested divisiveness creates additional disaster-related trauma. Edelstein (1988) noted how community conflict impacts families and social relationships which, in turn, enhance people's perceptions of the tragedy's severity. The trauma from the resulting conflict can be so great that victims may experience "a loss of confidence in the scaffolding of family and community." It must be remembered, however, that individuals who do not fall into these prescribed categories may still develop mental health problems, particularly when they become vulnerable in more severe disasters.

C. Mass Violence (Deliberate Disasters)

Mass violence is also increasing nationwide. In fact, some are calling this an epidemic. Mass shootings are defined differently, depending on the source, but they are broadly recognized as consisting of any situation in which at least four people are injured or killed, potentially including the shooter. The U.S.

Source: Wikipedia. Photo by Rm Visuals

experienced an average of one mass shooting a month in 2018. The shootings at the Marjory Stoneman Douglas High School in Parkland, Florida, and the Tree of Life Synagogue in Pittsburgh were highly reported in the media, but many other, smaller deadly shootings were just as notable. These included a Rite-Aid in Maryland, Mercy Hospital in Chicago, a Western Pennsylvania car wash, a Detroit gas station, a Nashville Waffle House, and Santa Fe High School in Texas.

While the U.S. has 5% of the world's population, it has recorded 31% of all public mass shootings. Despite such a high incidence of gun violence, few communities have any plan to support the mental health needs of those primarily or secondarily impacted by the tragedy. Each new incident tends to rekindle a national debate on mental illness, gun control, safety, violence prevention and response, and the media's role. Questions immediately arise about what the mental health impact of the shooting will be on the survivors, witnesses, families, first responders, and entire community. The psychological consequences of directly experiencing or witnessing a mass shooting are often serious.

Although some research was conducted at the Columbine High School shooting in Colorado in 1999, few studies provide "lessons learned" about how to enhance mental health after such tragedies. Newtown, Connecticut, has the most statistics on the mental health impact, with residents requesting counseling services for the first time even six years later.

Terrorism

The U.S. experiences fewer terrorist attacks than many other countries. In the 15 years post 9/11, acts of political terror have killed fewer than 100 Americans nationwide, but again these numbers have little to do with the impact on mental health from such events. Terrorist attacks are illegal, planned, sociopolitical actions taken through force, violence, or intimidation by a person or group of individuals. In such cases, terrorists are purposely using panic and lack of situational control as psychological weapons.

Terrorism is a form of psychological warfare. Most terrorist groups lack the resources, expertise, and manpower to assume political supremacy. Instead, they promote their agenda through violence that shapes perceptions of political and social issues. "Political" is the primary word here. These terrorists have a political agenda and are typically foreign based. As seen with the Russian collusion in the 2016 Presidential election, this terrorism can take a variety of forms.

The Russians used social media to gain virtual access to American voters and alter or reinforce their political decisions. The internet has also been used to encourage American citizens to carry out attacks and/or travel to other countries for training.

In addition, America has been the victim of domestic terrorism or, as defined by the American Patriot Act (U.S. Department of Justice, 2001), attempts to "intimidate or coerce a civilian population; to influence the policy of a government by intimidation or coercion; or to affect the conduct of a government by mass destruction, assassination, or kidnapping." This terrorism is primarily locally based. Homegrown terrorist acts include the Denver shooting of transit officer Scott Van Lanken by Joshua Cummings, a Muslim convert and former Army sergeant, and the violent rampage at Pulse nightclub in Orlando, Florida, by Omar Mateen. The latter pledged allegiance to the Islamic State during the attack that left 49 people dead before he was killed.

Both terrorist and natural events can occur without warning, but the latter are more predictable; many times, weather experts provide several days' notice of these events. Hurricane warnings typically give people time to prepare and increase their sense of control over the situation. Sometimes, an important factor in psychological impact is whether those responsible for the terrorist act are killed or held accountable through a criminal trial.

Terrorism counteracts feelings of security and safety for both individuals and communities, because it makes people believe they do not have control over what is happening in the world. This lack of control usually enhances stress and trauma and causes longer-lasting mental health effects than natural disasters or accidents. A sense of personal violation leads to anger, frustration, helplessness, fear, and a desire for revenge, which furthers greater resentment, guilt, and distress.

When a terrorist attack occurs, people quickly focus on reuniting and caring for their family members, not personal emotional needs. At such time, communities need to keep abreast of the public's psychological needs and encourage therapy to lower incidents of severe trauma. After the Oklahoma City bombing, most symptoms of PTSD were believed to have developed relatively quickly.

Because the Boston Marathon is typically a very enjoyable event, the traumatic impact of the bombing was more severe. The terrorist attack quickly turned a joyful family experience into a time of horror and pain. One study (Comer et al., 2014) found that the proportion of youth with attack/manhunt-related PTSD was about six times higher among those attending than not attending the event. In addition, PTSD symptoms and psychosocial problems were linked to youth who watched more than three hours of TV coverage on the day of the bombing; this once again demonstrated the impact of such indirect exposure.

Cyberattacks

These are attacks via cyberspace purposely for the disrupting, disabling, destroying, or maliciously controlling a computing environment. In addition to hackers and spammers in the U.S., Russia and China present the most sophisticated cyber threats. The U.S. implicated Russia in efforts to hack political entities such as the Democratic National Committee.

TO DO

1. If not already done, conduct a community hazard vulnerability analysis to identify the types of natural, human-caused, and deliberate incidents to which your community is exposed. Emergency planning needs to be based on accurate knowledge of the threat and likely human responses. Part of knowing the threat necessitates understanding the basic characteristics of these hazards, such as degree of predictability; speed of onset; scope and duration of impact; and potential for producing casualties, injuries, and property damage.

    Rate possible exposure from 1 (LOW CHANCE OF EXPOSURE) TO 5 (HIGH CHANCE OF EXPOSURE). For example, communities in the Southwest have a greater chance of tornadoes.

2. List any community disasters over the past decade. What actions were taken after the event? How well did the emergency response team respond to each disaster and meet each specific need? How well did the team members work together? What was the extent of the physical damage? What, if anything, was done for the psychological needs of the victims? Lessons learned?

3. If your community has already faced major emergencies, what impact has this had on the residents? Do you believe such experiences made them more or less resilient to future events?

4. Think about the demographics of your community and who will be the most vulnerable and in need of most care based on type and location of disaster. If planning needs to be done on a step-by-step basis, it may be best to start with those residents who need the most support.

References

Abatzoglou, J. T., & Williams, A. P. (2016). Impact of anthropogenic climate change on wildfire across western US forests. *PNAS, 113*(42), 11770–11775.

Adams, Z. W., Sumner, J. A., Danielson, C. K., McCauley, J. L., Resnick, H. S., Grös, K., & Ruggiero, K. J. (2014). Prevalence and predictors of PTSD and depression among adolescent victims of the spring 2011 tornado outbreak. *Journal of Child Psychology and Psychiatry, 55*(9), 1047–1055.

Attfield, K. R., Dobson, C. B., Henn, J. B., Acosta, M., Smorodinsky, S., Wilken, J. A., . . . Roisman, R. (2015). Injuries and traumatic psychological exposures associated with the South Napa Earthquake—California, 2014. *Morbidity and Mortality Report*, *64*(35), 975–978.

California Department of Forestry and Fire Protection. (2017). *Fire incident by year*. Retrieved from http://cdfdata.fire.ca.gov/incidents/incidents_statsevents

Cline, R. J., Chung, O. H., Chung, J. E., & Hernandez, T. (2014). The role of social toxicity in responses to a slowly-evolving environmental disaster: The case of amphibole asbestos exposure in Libby, Montana, USA. *American Journal of Community Psychology*, *54*(1–2), 12–27.

Comer, J., Datowitz, A., Chou, T., Edson, A. L., Elkins, R., Kerns, C., . . . Greif Green, J. (2014). Adjustment among area youth after the Boston Marathon bombing and subsequent manhunt. *Pediatrics*, *134*(1), 7–14.

Edelstein, M. R. (1988). *Contaminated communities: The social and psychological impact of residential toxic exposure*. Boulder, CO: Westview Press.

Erikson, K. (1994). *A new species of trouble: Explorations in disaster, trauma, and community*. New York, NY: W. W. Norton.

Fujita, T. T. (1971). *Proposed characterization of tornadoes and hurricanes by area and intensity*. Satellite and Meso meteorology Research Paper 91. Chicago, IL: Department of Geophysical Sciences, University of Chicago.

Hirsch, J. K., Smalley, K. B., Selby-Nelson, E. M., Hamel-Lambert, J. M., Rosmann, M. R., Barnes, T. A., . . . LaFromboise, T. (2018). Psychological impact of fracking: A review of the literature on the mental health consequences of hydraulic fracking. *International Journal of Mental Health and Addiction*, *16*(1), 1–5.

Hughes, T. (2019, May 8). A year after lava began flowing in what would become Hawaii's most destructive volcano eruption in decades, thousands are still struggling to recover. *USA Today*. Retrieved from www.usatoday.com/in-depth/news/nation/2019/05/03/hawaii-volcano-eruption-recovery-stalled-tourism-down-1-year-later/3486120002/

Lavelle, M. (2019, January 23). Americans increasingly say climate change is happening now. *Inside Climate News*. Retrieved from https://insideclimatenews.org/news/22012019/climate-change-survey-impact-now-americans-extreme-weather-george-mason-yale

Mallakpour, I., & Villarini, G. (2015). The changing nature of flooding across the central United States. *Nature Climate Change*, 250–254.

Morris, J. G., Grattan, L. M., Mayer, B., & Blackburn, J. K. (2013). Psychological responses and resilience of people and communities impacted by the Deepwater Horizon Oil Spill. *Transactions of the American Clinical and Climatological Association*, *124*, 191–201.

National Fire Protection Association. (2015). *Fire loss in the U.S. by year*. Retrieved from www.nfpa.org/News-and-Research/Data-research-and-tools/US-Fire-Problem/Fire-loss-in-the-United-States

National Public Radio. (2018, August 5). *California wildfires reignite old trauma for survivors of last year's blazes*. Retrieved from www.npr.org/sections/health-shots/2018/08/05/635475707/wildfire-trauma-revisited

Padhy, S. K., Sarkar, S., Panigrahi, M., & Paul, S. (2015). Mental health effects of climate. *Indian Journal of Occupational Environmental Medicine, 19*(1), 3–7.

Parker, P. W. (2017). *Train crashes raise questions about safety*. Retrieved from www.yourlawyer.com/accidents/train/train-crashes-raise-safety-questions/

Richter, C. F. (1935). An instrumental earthquake magnitude scale. *Bulletin of the Seismological Society of America, 25*(1–2), 1–32.

Shaw, J. M. (2015, November 24). The U.S. has more natural disasters than any other country in the world. *Market Watch*. Retrieved from www.marketwatch.com/story/the-us-has-more-natural-disasters-than-any-other-country-in-the-world-2015-11-24

Siegrist, M., & Sutterlin, B. (2014). Human and nature-caused hazards: The affect heuristic causes biased decisions. *Risk Analysis, 34*(8), 1482–1494.

Tousignant, L. (2018, October 23). 14-year-long Gulf of Mexico oil spill to become worst in US history. *New York Post*. Retrieved from https://nypost.com/2018/10/23/14-year-long-gulf-of-mexico-oil-spill-to-become-worst-in-us-history/

United National Office for Disaster Risk Reduction. (2015). *Human cost of weather-related disasters*. Retrieved from https://reliefweb.int/sites/reliefweb.int/files/resources/COP21_WeatherDisastersReport_2015_FINAL.pdf

U.S. Department of Justice. (2001). *USA patriot act*. Retrieved from www.justice.gov/archive/ll/highlights.htm

Wei-Haas, M. (2018, October 26). These are the most dangerous U.S. volcanoes, scientists say. *National Geographic*. Retrieved from www.nationalgeographic.com/environment/2019/03/partner-content-charting-their-own-course/

Weir, K. (2014). *After the spill researchers study the lingering effects of the BP oil spill*. American Psychological Association. Retrieved from www.apa.org/monitor/2014/07-08/spill

Reader's Notes

7

Essential Mental Health Services

Chapter 7 Preview
A. Immediate Interventions After a Disaster
B. The Importance of Trauma-Informed Care
C. Effective Brain-Based Trauma-Specific Interventions
D. Other Trauma-Informed Therapies
E. Effective Wellness Activities
F. Helping First Responders
G. Types of Mental Health Providers

A disaster affects people differently. The impact depends on a variety of factors, including:

1. Physical and emotional proximity to the center of the event;
2. What is seen and experienced;
3. Prior personal experience with trauma;
4. Current physical and mental health condition;
5. Degree of resiliency with such coping skills as exercise, yoga, and meditation;
6. Level of vulnerability due to risk factors; and
7. Concerns about the future (e.g., health, job, and family).

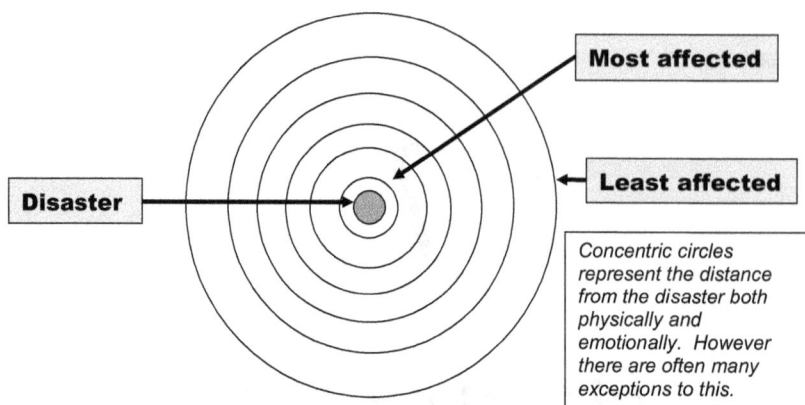

Concentric circles represent the distance from the disaster both physically and emotionally. However there are often many exceptions to this.

FIGURE 7.1 The relationship between proximity and emotional impact

People who at first appear not to be connected to a disaster can also be affected if they had a relationship with those who lost their lives. In Newtown, for example, relatives, friends, neighbors, bus drivers, and even babysitters for the children who died were all severely impacted. Human-caused events, such as shootings, have been found to be more personally traumatic than natural disasters (Butler, Panzer, & Goldfrank, eds., 2003).

Terrorism is especially disturbing; it is intended to provoke collective fear and uncertainty, which can spread quickly and is not limited to individuals with firsthand experience. Others in the community may be impacted, such as family members of victims and survivors and even those exposed through broadcast images (Silver, Holman, & Andersen, 2013). Natural disasters bring their own form of trauma since they are often widespread, affect a large portion of the population, and often include the loss of a family member or friend as well as a home. Prolonged flooding and droughts are associated with elevated levels of anxiety, depression, and PTSD (Clayton, Manning, & Hodge, 2014).

Ideally, an evaluation by a trauma-informed therapist should be offered to anyone who is struggling after a disaster. That clinician can determine if an individual is suffering from anxiety, depression, or Acute Stress Disorder (ASD) and provide appropriate care. If this person does not have trauma but rather suffers from general anxiety, the therapist can offer appropriate care. However, treatment will most likely take longer if the individual has a history of trauma, anxiety, or depression. Whatever the case, the sooner someone seeks professional help, the better. If a person is diagnosed with trauma, it will not go away in time. The expression, "Time heals all wounds" does not apply when it comes to trauma because, as explained in Chapter 2, the brain actually changes.

Trauma takes its toll on the community as well because many traumatized residents become dysfunctional. They lose the ability to work, provide for their families, and have a healthy marriage and personal relationships. Those who ignore their symptoms frequently try to self-medicate with alcohol or drugs. Although suicide rates vary depending on the location and population studied, suicidal behavior increases following both human-caused and natural disasters. In Puerto Rico, there were an average of 19 suicides per month in the eight months prior to hurricane Maria in 2017 and 25 suicides per month in the three months immediately after Maria (Alfonso, 2018). A current long-term study (Institute for Safe Families, 2013) revealed how children exposed to adverse experiences such as trauma exhibit more health problems throughout their lives and have shorter life spans.

Mental health providers are continually acquiring new information on and insights into the best ways to care for trauma. In recent years, a great deal has been learned about effective treatments for trauma and maintaining wellness. The newer "brain-based" techniques, as described in this chapter, have been used successfully for treatment in addition to traditional cognitive approaches. Your collaboration members are not expected to be experts on all the types of treatments but should have a general knowledge of each so they can be a source of general information to the community.

A. Immediate Interventions After a Disaster

Immediately following a disaster, many individuals will experience anxiety and depression. For this reason, it is important to provide emotional assistance as soon as possible. Although people helping after a disaster are often called "crisis counselors" (CCP), they do not provide counseling in the traditional sense. They are volunteers from all walks of life who go through a training program to learn how to address the basic physical and emotional needs of individuals post-disaster. Their job is to support, inform, and educate survivors. These crisis counselors may also recommend trauma-informed care from a licensed professional, but they are not trained to provide treatment. Only licensed trauma-informed therapists with instruction in trauma-specific interventions can treat others (FEMA, 2016).

Crisis Counseling and Psychological First Aid

Disaster mental health volunteers may go through the PFA program or the Crisis Counseling and Training Program (CCP). The National Child Traumatic Stress Network (NCTSN) offers a six-hour interactive online course in PFA. CCP is a federally funded supplemental program administrated by the U.S. Department of Homeland Security and approved by FEMA. CCP training is also available online. Local chapters of the National Red Cross have a great deal of experience in mental health support and can be extremely helpful in training volunteers. Communities may also offer their own PFA training sessions for volunteer recruitment.

In situations where people are evacuated to temporary housing, such as after Hurricane Florence in 2018, crisis counselors or PFA volunteers need to be assigned to all shelters for the entire time they are open. As time goes on, family needs and personal concerns may become more pressing, and support should be available. Crisis counselors can also canvas neighborhoods after a disaster to assess whether homebound survivors need food, water, medication, or medical help.

Both PFA and CCP training address the basics all humans need to feel more secure after a disaster. They emphasize making people feel safer by giving them food, water, and clothing; stabilizing them; and, if possible, connecting them with lost loved ones or providing information on those who have been injured or passed away. Even those people who make it safely through a disaster may become anxious, exhausted, and very worried about the future, particularly if their house and/or place of employment was damaged or lost (FEMA, 2016). Survivors are concerned about the length of time before they can go back to their previous lives. Mental healthcare professionals agree that early intervention can prevent more serious long-term problems and enhance resiliency. In many cases, PFA or CCP can minimize any psychological care required in the future (NCTSN, 2019).

Free Psychological Services Center(s)

The Mental Health Volunteer Coordinator on your collaboration should compile and continually update a list of licensed trauma-informed clinicians. Prior to a disaster, this list is posted online and shared with the media. Crisis counselors can also distribute it at shelters. The same collaboration team member is also in charge of setting up a free psychological services center staffed by licensed trauma-informed therapists who volunteer to provide therapy. Unlike the crisis counselors, these therapists can recognize trauma and provide appropriate treatment. Many people may need treatment but not know where or by whom it is provided. They may not have access to mental healthcare because they do not have insurance or money to pay for services. Offering free psychological services encourages people who need assistance to get help. Individuals who remain in shelters for an extended period of time may be grieving or showing signs of ASD. It is a good idea to assign some licensed therapists to go to the shelters to offer help.

The authors feel very strongly that the free psychological services center is essential to the healing of the community after any type of disaster. Communities sometimes call them "crisis centers" (not to be confused with "crisis counselors"), which follow a "triage" format. People arriving at the center share their personal information and concerns with the facilitator, who is a licensed therapist. The facilitator prioritizes the needs of these people interviewed and allows those most affected to obtain help first. The facilitator shares the information with fellow therapists, and the one who feels the most qualified counsels the individual or family. A list of licensed trauma-informed therapists is distributed to the families, who can then set up future appointments with the therapist they have just met or choose another one from the list. After the Pulse nightclub shooting in Orlando, Florida, the community offered a free counseling resource guide, which included providers who offered free counseling.

The Communications/Media Coordinator should publicize the crisis centers' locations. The disaster call center should also have the information. It is suggested that these psychological services centers be kept open as long as possible, encouraging people to get the help they need. In Sandy Hook, Connecticut, the center was open for three months. When the number of people coming begins to dwindle to a few, it is time to close the center.

The graph demonstrates the average progression of emotional reactions a person experiences after a disaster. Each individual's journey is unique but follows a similar path. Triggering events, such as learning about another similar disaster, and anniversary reactions are typically low points in emotional healing.

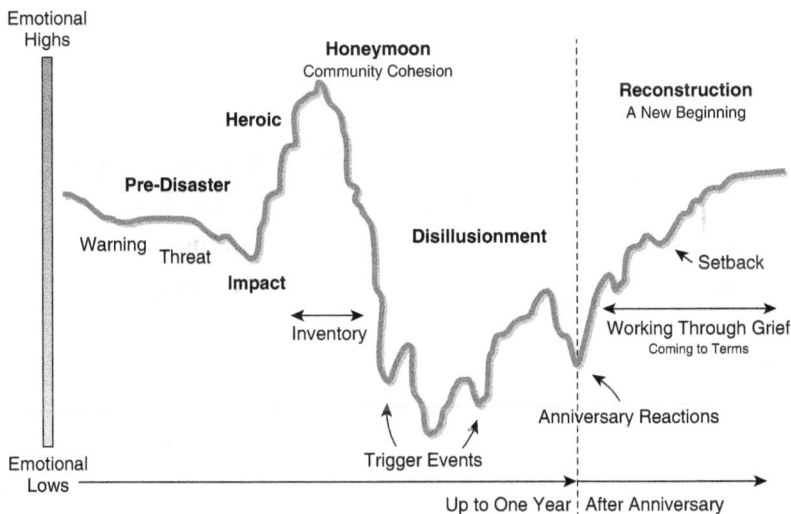

FIGURE 7.2 Emotional Impact Graph After a Disaster (FEMA, 2016)

Source: Department of Veterans Affairs, National Center for Post-Traumatic Stress Disorder, Palo Alto, CA. Adapted from Young B.H., Ford J.D., Ruzek J.I., Friedman M., & Gusman F.D.

PsySTART Program

Psychological Simple Triage and Rapid Treatment or PsySTART (2019) was developed by Merritt Schreiber, PhD. It is used mainly by hospitals, clinics, and emergency medical services. The program is more geared to people who have some medical background. Many emergency medical technicians (EMTs) receive this training because they are the first ones to arrive after a disaster. The program has four components:

1. Solutions to link mental health to "disaster systems of care" in real time;
2. Mental health triage, decision support at point of care;
3. Cloud-based/smartphone application; and
4. Population based.

PsySTART Measures

1. Severe/extreme stressors (not symptoms);
2. Severe/extreme exposures;
3. Traumatic loss (including missing family members);
4. Ongoing or persistent stressors;
5. Injury/illness;
6. Peri-traumatic severe panic; and
7. Prior history of PTSD.

B. The Importance of Trauma-Informed Care

It is now widely recognized that anyone suffering from trauma should only be treated by a trauma-informed therapist who is trained in trauma-specific interventions. A clinician who is not trauma-informed risks the possibility of re-traumatizing an individual. Re-traumatizing occurs when people feel the intense emotions from the original trauma all over again. They become "flooded" with emotions and have difficulty functioning. Talking about a traumatic experience with an untrained therapist may be harmful and could prolong the healing process.

A trauma therapist needs to have thorough training before working with a patient and ideally in more than one trauma-specific intervention. A particular intervention may work well for one person but not work for another. Learning to apply trauma-specific interventions is not something a therapist can learn quickly. Some clinicians erroneously believe that taking an online course is adequate preparation for providing trauma treatment.

Trauma-informed treatment addresses an individual's memories in a careful, gradual, and gentle way. It is different than what is commonly called "talk therapy," in which individuals talk about what is happening in their lives and how they feel about it. This manual offers information on a wide variety of trauma-specific treatments to provide your collaboration with a thorough overview of effective approaches.

Traumatic Grief, Complex Trauma, and Complicated Grief

There are also types of trauma that are helpful for collaboration members to know about, such as traumatic grief, complex trauma, and complicated grief. With traumatic grief, a person suffers because of a death or traumatic distress (Jacobs, 2006). Complex trauma occurs when an individual is repeatedly traumatized over time. The most common examples of complex trauma are soldiers who have been continually deployed to war zones, victims of repeated abuse, and first responders who deal with human suffering on a regular basis. Special attention needs to be given to police, firefighters and EMTs after a tragic event. Typical symptoms of complex trauma are (Firestone, 2012):

1. Difficulty regulating emotions;
2. Persistent sadness;
3. Suicidal thoughts or self-harm;
4. Feeling isolated;
5. Guilt; and
6. Alcoholism or substance abuse.

Complicated grief can affect an individual physically, mentally, and socially. Although there are some similarities and patterns in the grief process, in reality, everyone grieves differently. However, when people have experienced a loss and they are unable to move on in a reasonable amount of time, complicated grief should be considered.

Complicated grief can occur when the following conditions are present:

1. An unexpected or violent death (murder, suicide, car accident);
2. Death of a child;
3. A close or dependent relationship to a person who died;
4. Past traumatic experiences;
5. History of PTSD, depression, or chronic anxiety; and
6. Serious life stressors, such as financial problems or a physical handicap.

In complicated grief, painful emotions are so long lasting and severe that the individual has trouble recovering from the loss and resuming a normal life. People who have experienced loss from a disaster and are still in constant emotional pain should be referred to a therapist (Mayo Clinic Online, 2017).

C. Effective Brain-Based Trauma-Specific Interventions

In recent years, much has been learned about trauma, the symptoms, and the treatments.

It is important to understand there is no "one-size-fits-all" therapy for trauma. However, the latest studies indicate how the newer "brain-based" therapies are effective because they address the part of the brain affected by trauma. Researchers cite several references elaborating on that point (Sharp, 2013). Later in this chapter, results from surveys done by the Newtown Sandy Hook Community Foundation provide additional input.

Remember, people requiring therapy must make sure the therapist selected is licensed to practice in the state, is trauma-informed, and knows how to use trauma-specific interventions. People should check with their insurance company before making an appointment, to see if they are covered. Some therapists may not be on an insurance company's panel but are willing to fill out the insurance forms and submit them to the insurance company. People also need to know it is okay to try a new therapist or approach if, after a few sessions, they are not comfortable.

Below are some examples of brain-based trauma-specific therapies. They have been used by therapists after disasters in Sandy Hook, Connecticut; Orlando and Parkland, Florida; Oklahoma City, Oklahoma; Las Vegas, Nevada; and New York, New York, as well as several international sites.

Eye Movement Desensitization and Reprocessing (EMDR)

Background

EMDR was discovered in the mid-1980s by Francine Shapiro, PhD. It is an integrative psychotherapy approach with eight treatment phases and is APA approved for trauma. EMDR has a set of standardized protocols incorporating elements from several treatment approaches. Through its eight phases and deliberate focus on past, present, future memories, and content, EMDR can foster mindfulness, increased presence in the here and now, emotional tolerance, self-compassion, and personal growth. The therapist uses bilateral, or binaural, stimulation (left and right side of the body) with a hand movement, sound, vibration, or tapping. EMDR gained popularity when it was successfully used to treat survivors of 9/11. EMDR centers are found nationwide (EMDRIA, 2018).

Theory

The foundation of EMDR therapy is the Adaptive Information Processing (AIP) model, which classifies processes and integrates information in an ongoing manner. Traumatic memory is stored differently from normal memory; it lacks language and rational understanding. Therefore, it is stored as sensory information (what is felt emotionally and physically at the time). These sensory memories form traumatic information networks, which are unable to participate with normal adaptive memory networks.

How It Works

Bilateral stimulation can be experienced through eye movements, tappers that emit a vibration held in the patient's hands, or listening to bilateral sounds with headphones. While patients are experiencing the bilateral stimulation, the therapist helps them gently revisit distressing memories from the traumatic event. The sensory information stored with the memories are then re-experienced in a new and less distressing way. Bilateral stimulation is gentle and rhythmic, and most patients find it relaxing.

Emotional Freedom Techniques (EFT)
Also Known as Tapping

Background

Gary Craig created EFT in the 1990s, and it became very popular after Nick Ortner published the *New York Times* best seller *The Tapping Solution* in 2013. EFT is also called tapping because the patient gently taps on several acupressure points. Specific tapping protocols have since been developed for treating trauma. APA approved for trauma and stress, EFT has been delivered to well over ten million people in 24 countries to treat PTSD resulting from natural disasters, genocide, and extreme violence (Morina et. al, 2017; Robson et. al, 2016; Connolly & Sakai, 2011).

Theory

Magnetic Resonance Imaging (MRI) scans have shown how the stimulation of certain acupressure points on the body calms the amygdala and stops the fight/flight/freeze response (Zimmerman, 2013). The hippocampus and other bodily fear sensors are similarly and often very quickly affected and discharged. As a result, distressing memories are retained but no longer carry the emotional intensity to trigger a trauma response in the body. EFT can be an effective way to dispel negative feelings and release limiting beliefs, thus making room for more positive beliefs and emotions to emerge (Stapleton, 2019).

How It Works

After interviewing the patient, a therapist selects one aspect of the traumatic situation and develops a "set-up statement." The therapist says the statement out loud while the patient repeats it and taps on nine or more acupressure points. The therapist repeats the "round" with the client until the negative feelings decrease to a comfortable level. Research has shown that EFT can reduce the production of cortisol, the stress hormone, by 24% in just one hour of treatment (Church, Yount, & Brooks, 2012).

Brainspotting (BSP)

Background

This newer brain-based approach was discovered in 2003 by David Grand, PhD. While using EMDR to treat survivors of 9/11, Grand discovered how holding a particular eye position helped patients more readily access traumatic memories. Brainspotting has been used with excellent results in trauma therapy and the treatment of PTSD. Surveys and research conducted thus far have shown Brainspotting to be highly effective, and it is currently being used worldwide to treat trauma (Grand, 2017).

Theory

Brainspotting helps people access, process, and overcome trauma, negative emotions, and physical and psychological pain. Evidence demonstrates that trauma is stored in the brain and alters the way in which the brain works by interfering with emotion, memory, and physical health. By working on the limbic system (amygdala, hippocampus, and hypothalamus), Brainspotting accesses both the physical and emotional aspects of negative emotions.

How It Works

A "brainspot" is an eye position that tends to activate a traumatic memory or painful emotion. The eye position differs from person to person, and only a trained therapist can locate this spot. During Brainspotting, a therapist helps patients correctly position their eyes and target the source of the negative emotions. The therapist may also employ BioLateral Sound (BLS), developed by Grand. With headphones, the biolateral sound can be music or nature sounds gently shifting from the left ear to the right ear. The therapist is able to access emotions on a deeper level and reduce the physical effects of trauma (Grand, 2013).

Masgutova Neurosensorimotor Reflex Integration (MNRI)

A Nonverbal Body-Centered Trauma Treatment

Background

MNRI, also known as the Masgutova method, was first developed and used in Russia by psychologist Svetlana Masgutova, PhD, for treating trauma, MNRI is a nonverbal brain-based technique that releases tension in parts of the brain affected by trauma. Although not yet APA approved, it can be a very helpful adjunct to psychotherapy. Growing numbers of individuals are being trained in the procedure, as increasing numbers of people experience the positive results of this treatment worldwide. There is currently an MNRI national headquarters in Orlando, Florida.

Theory

MNRI addresses primary reflex patterns. When people experience trauma, their primary reflexes are activated for protection. PTSD coincides with these primary reflex patterns remaining in an active state, and individuals may experience various symptoms (e.g., anxiety, irritability, difficulty sleeping, difficulty focusing, sensitivity to sounds, and decreased immune system). MNRI targets the emotional center of the brain in a gentle and noninvasive way without talking to achieve proper realignment of the sensory-motor reflexes.

How It Works

A reflex is a conscious or non-conscious response to input. When reflexes fail through trauma, the brain's neural networks function improperly. The MNRI professional identifies specific reflex problem areas in the patient and develops a treatment of movement, stretching, and gentle touch to address trauma-impacted memory. Patients are often provided with a simple home program and instructions on how to apply basic MNRI techniques between visits.

D. Other Trauma-Informed Therapies

Trauma-Focused Cognitive Behavioral Therapy (TF-CBT)

Background

TF-CBT was developed by Anthony Mannarino, PhD; Judith Cohen, MD; and Esther Deblinger, PhD in the 1980s to treat children who were sexually abused. In the last 15 years, the APA approved therapy has been used for other groups of traumatized youth, as well as for both children and adults exposed to violence, murder, suicide, fire, accidents, and major disasters (TF-CBT Therapist, 2019).

Theory

Cognitive Behavioral Therapy (CBT) stems from the belief that perception of events, rather than the events themselves, determines how a person will feel and act. It rests on the theory that behavior and emotions are directly influenced by adjustments in thought patterns. It is a short-term, problem-focused form of treatment that helps a person see the relationship between beliefs, thoughts, and feelings and the resulting behaviors and actions.

How It Works

Through TF-CBT, patients are helped to unlearn negative reactions and relearn new, positive emotional and behavioral responses to challenging situations. Through goal setting, people set goals, break larger problems down into small manageable parts, and adjust the way they think, feel, and react in challenging situations.

Equine Therapy or Animal-Assisted Therapy

Background

Although it was not specifically created for treating trauma, equine therapy has received very positive reviews from trauma specialists. It is practiced with a licensed therapist and an animal trainer. The psychological and physiological benefits of equine and animal-assisted therapy have been well documented (Johnson et al., 2018). The improvements in health can include decreased stress; reduction of anger, heart rate, and blood pressure; and improved social interactions, sense of trust, and empowerment. Young children in particular can see significant improvements in interpersonal relationships with equine therapy. Children unable to experience physical and emotional comfort with others may find they are able to freely form that bond with a horse or other animal.

Theory

Equine and animal-assisted therapy involve the use of horses and other animals to help people gain self-awareness and emotional healing. The benefits of the natural bond between animal and human being are fostered in an effort to facilitate emotional recovery. Animals can elicit a number of nurturing emotions, and therapists find that many people, especially children, respond positively to the idea of caring for another living being.

How It Works

Equine therapy involves much more than simply spending time with the animal and does not typically involve riding the horse. There are specific therapeutic goals, strategies, and outcomes to measure. Therapeutic experiences can include walking, brushing, petting, and caring for the animal. The therapist, as part of a growing relationship with the patient, incorporates care of and exercises with the animal.

Trauma-Informed Art Therapy

Background

Art therapy uses the individual's creativity to help develop physical and emotional health. Self-expression can frequently awaken someone's inborn problem-solving capacities. The therapy combines traditional techniques found in psychotherapy with the creativity of producing visual art. Trauma-informed art therapy takes into consideration how the mind and body respond to traumatic events, recognizing that symptoms are coping strategies rather than pathology. It aims to help individuals thrive through skill building, support networks, and resilience building.

Theory

People of all ages can benefit from trauma-informed art therapy, particularly those experiencing such issues as anxiety, depression, addiction, and trauma. This therapy approach is helpful for individuals who may prefer focusing on another task while discussing complex issues or who are challenged with expressing these issues verbally.

How It Works

Art therapists are trained professionals with a master's degree in art therapy. In order to practice, they must understand psychotherapy and counseling. Artistic theories combined with clinical techniques are used to enhance the healing effect the creative process has on the patient. Therapists are aware of the body's reactions to stressful events and/or memories and can thus incorporate sensory-based artistic activities. They are mindful of reinforcing a sense of safety by making and maintaining a positive attachment and an individualized care plan.

Trauma-Informed Music Therapy

Background

Music therapy integrates the elements of music with therapy to help provide healing. A trained music therapist uses the nonverbal language of music to initiate contact with the patient, fostering a relationship that allows the growth of self-awareness, personal development, and self-expression.

Theory

Research in music therapy supports its effectiveness in many areas such as overall physical rehabilitation and facilitating movement. Music therapy often enhances or increases motivation to become engaged in treatment. Involving a more holistic and creative level, it often elicits responses from individuals who may not otherwise respond to traditional therapy.

How It Works

After assessing the patient's needs, a qualified music therapist can provide treatment including creating, singing, moving to, and/or listening to music. Through musical involvement in the therapeutic context, patients' abilities are strengthened and transferred to other areas of their lives. Music therapy also provides avenues for communication that can be helpful to those who find it difficult to express themselves in words.

Play Therapy

Background

Play therapy works to transform current life issues by accessing past, present, and unconscious experiences through play. During play therapy, the therapist and child (and sometimes adults) form a relationship in which they are encouraged to explore life situations utilizing play materials in a manner and pace of their choosing. Play is the primary tool used; language is secondary.

Theory

A caring environment is created to allow the child to play with as few limitations as possible, with the exception of physical or emotional safety. Sessions may be with an individual or groups of children. A variety of play techniques are used according to the child's wishes and the skills of the therapist.

How It Works

Through play, rather than conversation, children are given strategies to cope with difficulties they may be powerless to change. It can also provide the therapist with valuable insights into what the child is experiencing, as many children can or will better express their needs and feelings through imagination and play.

Prolonged Exposure Therapy (PE)

Background

PE was developed by Edna Foa, PhD, director of the Center for the Treatment and Study of Anxiety at the University of Pennsylvania. It is another form of Cognitive Behavioral Therapy (CBT).

Theory

The theory is based on the cognitive techniques of gradual desensitization to the traumatic events in a safe, supportive environment. The expectation is that the patient will eventually cease to be triggered by the negative thoughts and memories of the traumatic experience.

How It Works

PE slowly exposes patients to trauma-related memories and triggers (sounds, smells, events, etc.) in order to desensitize them. Traumatized individuals typically avoid situations that trigger their trauma, but in PE, the therapist guides the patient to gradually confront those memories (US Dept. of Veterans Affairs, 2019).

E. Effective Wellness Activities

Wellness activities are helpful as a supplemental intervention during and after therapy in order to maintain emotional balance and resiliency. However, it is understood wellness activities are not a replacement for trauma-specific interventions administered by a licensed, trauma-informed therapist who applies trauma-specific approaches.

Yoga

There is considerable scientific research showing the positive effects of yoga. The following seven characteristics relate to trauma (Link, 2017):

1. Can decrease stress;
2. Relieves anxiety;
3. Improves quality of life;
4. May fight depression;
5. Could reduce chronic pain;
6. May promote sleep quality; and
7. May relieve migraines.

Meditation

There are three popular and effective forms of meditation. Transcendental Meditation and mindfulness require a good deal of practice before the person can feel the full benefits of meditation.

1. Transcendental Meditation (TM): While sitting in a comfortable relaxing position, the individual repeats a mantra (a sound or word) over and over to block out other thoughts and allow the mind to rest.
2. Mindfulness meditation: The person focuses on an awareness of the present experiences. This includes breathing, body sensations, sounds, smells, etc.
3. Guided imagery or visualization meditation: This is an excellent way for a beginner to practice meditation. The individual listens to a recording in which the narrator helps the listener relax his/her body. The narrator

may also take the person on a relaxing journey. Many of these recordings also have soft music playing in the background. The recordings can easily be found on the internet. (Some appropriate websites can be found in the Appendix.)

Research on meditation shows 12 positive changes in the brain and the body (Thorpe, 2017). All these benefits are extremely helpful for an individual dealing with ASD or PTSD:

1. Reduces stress;
2. Controls anxiety;
3. Promotes emotional health;
4. Enhances self-awareness;
5. Lengthens attention span;
6. May reduce age-related memory loss;
7. Can generate kindness;
8. May help fight addictions;
9. Improves sleep;
10. Helps control pain;
11. Can decrease blood pressure; and
12. Can be done anywhere.

EFT/Tapping

In addition to a therapist's office, tapping can also be used as an effective self-help technique for stress and anxiety. Tapping at home is not a replacement for trauma-specific treatment, but an adjunct to the treatment provided by a trauma-informed therapist. The tapping protocol for treating trauma is more involved, requires specific training and mentoring, and should only be done with a licensed professional.

Bio*Lateral* Sound Healing (BLS)

Developed by David Grand, PhD, creator of Brainspotting, Bio*Lateral* sound can help a person relax and/or relieve anxiety. The recordings are soft music or nature sounds that gently sweep from left to right ear in a gentle irregular pattern. It is very helpful for stress, anxiety, sleep issues, and depression but is not a substitute for trauma-specific interventions by a licensed therapist. Without headphones, it can help an individual relax and fall asleep.

MNRI (Musgatova Neuro-Reflex-Motor Integration)

Patients who are receiving MNRI treatment can be provided with a simple home program and instruction on how to apply the techniques between visits. There is also protocol for nontraumatic treatment that is very calming and provides stress relief.

Therapeutic Aromatherapy

When inhaling an essential oil, an individual can become calm in just 20 seconds. Many therapists use aromatherapy in conjunction with other trauma-specific treatments in their practice. Scents containing linalool (basil, lavender, and bergamot) seem to be most effective. It is important that only essential oils from a reputable company are used.

Therapy Dogs

Therapy dogs are very effective in helping children and adults feel calm and safe. Many mental health clinicians use comfort dogs in their practice. It is a good idea for the collaboration to gather names of therapy dog associations and local individuals having therapy dogs so they can be contacted right after a disaster. After the Sandy Hook tragedy, therapy dog owners volunteered their time to come to the crisis center. School administrators also asked the owners to bring comfort dogs to the Newtown schools. Likewise, comfort dogs from other U.S. locations headed to California after the 2018 wildfires.

Cardiovascular Exercise

Regular exercise (e.g., jogging, power walking, Zumba, and weightlifting) is very helpful for keeping both the body and mind fit. Gym memberships provide an excellent variety of cardiovascular activities people can do individually or with others. Research (Carek, Labstain & Carek, 2011) has shown exercise to decrease symptoms of depression and anxiety.

CASE STUDY: NSHCF Surveys on Trauma Treatments

New brain-based trauma-specific interventions are increasingly being used to treat trauma, although there is very little data on trauma-specific interventions after a tragedy. Online surveys of Newtown residents conducted by the Newtown Sandy Hook Community Foundation (NSHCF) in 2016 and 2017 shed additional light on this topic.

The results indicated Newtown residents favored the brain-based therapies over the cognitive approaches. Although this study technically did not fit the guidelines for scientific research, it is certainly worth considering. It is recommended that collaboration members keep abreast of the latest research on the topic. It is also helpful to get feedback from survivors about the effectiveness of the programs supported by collaboration members, always remembering that when and how these survivors relate their experiences must be taken into consideration. (See article in Chapter 9.)

The NSHCF survey asked participants to rate therapeutic interventions for adults as highly effective, effective, somewhat effective, or not at all effective. (Other techniques were listed on the survey, but the ratings, or number of people who responded. were insignificant.) The highest rated were the brain-based therapies (Brainspotting, MNRI, EFT, and EMDR) art therapy, play therapy, and equine therapy.

TABLE 7.1 2016 NSHCF Adult Survey

TECHNIQUE	Number of People who Responded	HIGHLY EFFECTIVE
Brainspotting	22	59.09%
MNRI	22	40.9%
Equine Therapy	18	38.89%
Music	17	38.09 %
Art	30	37.93%
EFT: Tapping	48	37.5%
EMDR	54	31.48%
TF-CBT	34	26.5%
Talk Therapy	223	25.11%

The results of the 2017 survey were similar to those in 2016, but traditional talk therapy scored higher than TF-CBT. This seems unusual but may be because it was five years after the tragedy, and a large number of people still needed therapy but were no longer suffering from trauma.

TABLE 7.2 2017 NSHCF Adult Survey

TECHNIQUE	Number of People who Responded	HIGHLY EFFECTIVE
Equine Therapy	24	54.17%
MNRI	25	40%
Brainspotting	24	41.67%
Music	21	38.09%
Art	29	37.93%
EMDR	58	32.76%
Talk Therapy	217	30.88%
EFT: Tapping	50	26%
TF-CBT	41	12.2%

Key Points

Very little research has been conducted on the results of therapy on those impacted by disasters. Longitudinal studies for disaster victims are few, not only regarding long-term mental health, but also other areas such as prior medical conditions, living environment, exodus of residents from impacted location, and changes in lifestyle such as alcohol consumption and divorce.

Newtown is a small (approximately 27,000) New England town. In 2016 it had a median household income of about $127,000; median property value of $407,500; and poverty rate of 3.34%. In other communities where a technique such as equine therapy is not available or is cost prohibitive, surveys would be of value to determine what works with other populations.

There were 20 first-grade students and six educators who lost their lives at Sandy Hook Elementary School. All the people at the school were affected that day, including their family members and the first responders. According to the Office of Victim Services, anyone who was in the school was considered a victim of a crime. There were also 12 first-grade children who were eyewitnesses to the shooting but either ran out of the classroom or hid when the gunman stopped to reload. Those children survived, but they and their families were seriously traumatized. Although some of the primary victims moved out of Newtown following the event, the majority of this population has remained and can be followed through studies. Organizations such as Newtown Center for Support and Wellness, which was formed after the tragedy, are currently maintaining these statistics.

One of the most challenging aspects of disaster mental health is the wide variety of factors and inconsistencies among events. The Boston Marathon bombing, which occurred right after Newtown's shooting, was much more difficult to study because the primary victims were a diverse mix of characteristics such as age, gender, and ethnic and cultural backgrounds from all parts of the country and even from other countries. About 260 people were physically injured, many seriously as amputees. Participants came to the event from all over the world, and most left Boston immediately after receiving medical care. It is much more difficult to track what happened to these runners and the type of support services they received, if any, once they returned to their communities. Then the Oklahoma tornado occurred, and once again the country faced children dying in their elementary school—this time from a natural disaster.

F. Helping First Responders

According to Adler-Tapia (2011), so much is focused on the psychological needs of those impacted directly by a disaster that first responders, who also are significantly exposed to acute stress, are forgotten. Volunteer residents, public employees, mental and healthcare workers, police officers, firefighters, search and rescue workers, paramedics, clergy, and child and family support professionals can all suffer trauma from their experiences. Their work can truly be an emotional and physical burden. In the U.S., hundreds of thousands of people provide support in these high-risk situations. Some regularly face emotional trauma in their daily work; others only assist at the most traumatic times. Even in their own work, these individuals are more at risk for suffering from PTSD and developing physical illnesses such as heart disease and diabetes.

Members of your collaboration need to understand the unique traits common to these first responders. Studies show the greatest trauma is caused by responding to and viewing several highly distressing events over time. This can often develop into complex trauma. The degree of impact varies depending on the individual involved, but any significant disaster can have a major impact. First responders frequently use specific defense mechanisms to deal with their daily employment stressors. They often depersonalize or detach themselves from what is taking place around them; however, suppressing these memories will not make them go away and may contribute to an emotional breakdown.

First responders rely on their own personal strengths or support systems for dealing with stress and often do not feel comfortable seeking help from therapists. They also do not want to be seen by their peers and supervisors as being weak. They need to recognize the normalcy of their feelings. After Hurricane Katrina, several first responders told mental health providers it was important that their circumstances be viewed and understood firsthand. Clinicians thus met first responders in the field rather than in a therapeutic setting. Trust between therapists and responders developed by maintaining appropriate boundaries yet increasing informalities, such as eating together and talking to each other on the job. (Adler-Tapia, 2011)

Chopko and Papazoglou (2017) found guilt may be one of the most difficult emotions for first responders. They relate the story of a female responder who nearly killed herself trying to save the lives of two other people in an emergency. She then developed PTSD, believing she had not done enough to help these people. When asked to rate her guilt on a scale of 1 to 100, with 100 being the worst, the woman responded, "100."

G. Types of Mental Health Providers

What follows is a list of the many different titles and credentials of mental health professionals who can help those impacted by a disaster. Each of these individuals may volunteer to serve at the free psychological services center as well as provide the long-term mental health services needed for trauma recovery. Their credentials are based on a determined level of education, training, experience, and code of ethics. Mental health providers are licensed by a board or state licensing body. These professionals include:

Remember, it is imperative that therapists are not only licensed but are also trauma-informed and have training in one or more trauma-specific interventions if they are treating someone for ASD or PTSD.

---

1. **Psychiatrists** are medical doctors (MDs) trained in the diagnosis and treatment of psychological and emotional illness and allowed to prescribe medications. They may also specialize in certain fields, such as child/adolescent or geriatric psychiatry.

2. **Psychologists** are counselors with a doctoral degree (PsyD) and at least two years of supervised work experience. They diagnose, administer, and interpret psychological tests and provide individual, family, and group therapy.

3. **Psychiatric Nurse Practitioners** (PsyNP) or advanced practice nurses (APRN) are registered nurses who have completed postgraduate training in the diagnosis, management, and treatment of mental illness. They may also prescribe medication.

4. **Licensed Clinical Social Workers** (LCSW) have earned a master's degree in social work. They can diagnose, and provide individual, family, and group therapy.

5. **Licensed Professional Counselors** (LPC) or (LC) also called Clinical Mental Health Counselors, possess a master's degree with supervised work experience. They can diagnose and provide individual, family, and group therapy to children and adults.

6. **Licensed Marriage and Family Therapists** (LMFT) complete a master's degree in their specialty, diagnose, and provide individual, family, and group counseling.

7. **Pastoral Counselors** (MAPC) are ordained clergy with advanced training and certification in Level II Clinical Pastoral Education (CPE) and a master's degree in theology required by most American denominations for ordination. They counsel and offer spiritual and sacramental ministry. Make sure to ask your clergypersons if they have a degree in counseling and are trauma-informed because not all members of the clergy are.

8. **Community Psychologists**, who typically pursue advanced degrees after receiving their bachelor's degree, research and respond to problem situations in a community to uncover ways to make improvements. Some, but not all, provide therapy for individuals.

TO DO

1. Select a person in the collaboration to contact mental health professional organizations in your state, such as counselors, social workers, psychologists, marriage and family therapists, psychiatrists, and psychiatric
   nurses. Ask the organizations for lists of trauma-informed therapists in
   the area who have training in trauma-specific interventions and their
   contact information. Keep these lists on hand and continually update
   them.

2. It is also helpful to reach out to the following organizations for listings of
   people in the area who are trained in these techniques. (See the Appen-
   dix for contact information.)
   ◆ EMDR International Association
   ◆ EFT/Tapping: Create Global Healing
   ◆ Brainspotting: David Grand's website
   ◆ MNRI National Center: Orlando, Florida

3. What type of wellness activities does your community offer its residents
   to help with their mental health? Do you have enough of these programs, or should others be started? Are any open to community members free of charge?

References

Adler-Tapia, R. L. (2011). Early mental health intervention for first responders/protective
  service. *Journal of EMDR Practice and Research, 3*(4), 232–247.

Alfonso, C. A. (2018). PTSD and suicide after natural disasters. *Psychiatric Times*. Retrieved
  from www.psychiatrictimes.com/ptsd/ptsd-and-suicide-after-natural-disasters

Butler, A. S., Panzer, A. M., & Goldfrank, L. (2003). *Preparing for the psychological
  consequences of terrorism*. Retrieved from www.ncbi.nlm.nih.gov/books/
  NBK221643/

Carek, P. J., Labstain, S. E. & Carek, S. M. (2011). Exercise for the treatment of depression
  and anxiety. *International Journal of Psychiatry in Medicine, 41*(1), 16–28.

Chopko, B., & Papazoglou, C. (2017). *The role of moral suffering (moral distress and moral
  injury) in police compassion fatigue and PTSD: An unexplored topic*. Retrieved from
  www.ncbi.nlm.nih.gov/pmc/articles/PMC5694767/

Church, D., Yount, G., & Brooks, A. (2012). The effect of emotional freedom techniques on
  stress biochemistry: A randomized controlled trial. *Journal of Nervous and Mental
  Disease, 200*, 891–896.

Clayton, S., Manning, C., & Hodge, C. (2014). *Beyond storms and droughts*. American Psychological Association. Retrieved from http://ecoamerica.org/wpcontent/uploads/2014/06/eA_Beyond_Storms_and_Droughts_Psych_Impacts_of_Climate_Change.pdf

Connolly, S. M., & Sakai, C. E. (2011). Brief trauma symptom intervention with Rwandan Genocide survivors using thought field therapy. *International Journal of Emergency Mental Health, 13*(3), 161–172.

EMDRIA. (2018). *What is the actual EMDR session like?* Retrieved from www.emdria.org/page/120

FEMA. (2016, July). *Crisis counseling assistance and training program guidance: CCP application toolkit*. Retrieved from www.samhsa.gov/sites/default/files/images/fema-ccp-guidance.pdf

Firestone, L. (2012, July 31). Recognizing complex trauma. *Psychology Today*. Retrieved from www.psychologytoday.com/us/blog/compassion-matters/201207/recognizing-complex-trauma

Grand, D. (2013). *Brainspotting: The revolutionary new therapy for rapid and effective change*. Louisville, CO: Sounds True.

Grand, D. (2017). *What is Brainspotting?* Retrieved from https://brainspotting.com/

Institute for Safe Families. (2013, September). *Philadelphia urban ACE survey*. Retrieved from www.instituteforsafefamilies.org/sites/default/files/isfFiles/Philadelphia%20Urban%20ACE%20Report%202013.pdf

Jacobs, S. (2006). *Traumatic grief: Diagnosis, treatment, and prevention* (Series in Trauma and Loss). New York, NY: Routledge.

Johnson, R. A., Albright, D. L., Marzolf, J. R., Bibbo, J. L., Yaglom, H. D., Crowder, S. M., . . . Harms, N. (2018). Effects of therapeutic horseback riding on post-traumatic stress disorder in military veterans. *Military Medical Research, 5*(3), 1–13.

Link, R. (2017, August 30). Thirteen benefits of yoga that are supported by science. *Healthline*. Retrieved from www.healthline.com/nutrition/13-benefits-of-yoga

Mayo Clinic Online. (2017, October 5). *Complicated grief, overview*. Retrieved from www.mayoclinic.org/diseases-conditions/complicated-grief/symptoms-causes/syc-20360374

Morina, N. Nickerson, A., Malek, M. & Bryandt R. (2017). Meta-analysis of interventions for posttraumatic stress disorder and depression in adult survivors of mass violence in low-and middle-income countries. *Depression and Anxiety, 34*(8), 679–691.

National Child Traumatic Stress Network. (2019). *About PFA*. Retrieved from www.nctsn.org/treatments-and-practices/psychological-first-aid-and-skills-for-psychological-recovery/about-pfa

Ortner, N. (2013). *The tapping solution: A revolutionary system for stress free living*. Carlsbad, CA: Hay House Inc.

PsySTART. (2019). Retrieved from https://tn.psystart.net/

Robson, R. H., Robson, P. M., Ludwig, R., Mitabu, C. & Phillips, C. (2016). Effectiveness of thought field therapy provided by newly instructed community workers to a traumatized population in Uganda: A randomized trial. *Current Research in Psychology, 7*(1), 111.

Sharp, C. (2013, September 9). *Stumped on trauma treatment? Start with the brain, says Bruce Perry*. Retrieved from https://www.thenationalcouncil.org/BH-1365/2013/09/stumped-on-trauma-treatment-start-with-the-brain-says-bruce-perry/

Silver, R. C., Holman, E. A., & Andersen, J. P. (2013). Mental and physical health effects of acute exposure to media images of the September 11, 2001 attacks and the Iraq War. *Psychological Science, 24*(9), 1623–1634.

Stapleton, P. (2019). *The science behind tapping: A proven stress management for the mind and body*. Carlsbad, CA: Hay House Inc.

TF-CBT Therapist. (2019). *About trauma-focused cognitive behavior therapy: Certification program*. Retrieved from https://tfcbt.org/about-tfcbt/

Thorpe, M. (2017, July 5). *12 Science based benefits of meditation*. Retrieved from www.healthline.com/nutrition/12-benefits-of-meditation

US Dept. of Veterans Affairs. (2019, January 23). *Prolonged exposure for PTSD*. Retrieved from www.ptsd.va.gov/understand_tx/prolonged_exposure.asp

Zimmerman, R. (2013, July 23). Trauma update: On the tipping point for tapping therapy. *Harvard News*. Retrieved from https://hms.harvard.edu/news/trauma-update-tipping-point-tapping-therapy

Reader's Notes

8

Resilient Individuals and Communities

Chapter 8 Preview
A. Building Pre-Disaster Resilience
B. Re-establishing Post-Disaster Resiliency
C. Building Community Capacity
D. Focus on First Responders

Throughout this manual, you have seen the debilitating impact that disasters can have on the everyday life, physical wellbeing, and mental and emotional state of many individuals for the long term. Yet a large number of people suffer when the calamitous event occurs but, after a relatively short time, are able to "get through it" relatively unscathed. This ability is called resilience, or the "process of adapting well in the face of adversity, trauma, tragedy, threats, or significant sources of stress," according to the APA (www.apa.org). Studies show that resilience is ordinary, not extraordinary, in humans. They have the innate capacity to rebuild their lives, despite the effort it takes. This does not mean these people do not have high levels of stress or face life with difficulty. They continue to feel the pain that others who have suffered major adversity or trauma in their lives do. The APA has noted that resilience is not a trait that people either have or do not have. Rather it involves behaviors, thoughts, and actions that can be learned and developed by anyone.

Just as insights are being learned by neuroscientists about the changes the brain undergoes with PTSD, so, too, are these scientists learning about what occurs in resilience. While studies of neurobiology are relatively few, animal research provides beneficial information about the mechanisms occurring in the brain when it overcomes the stress and responds with normalizing changes. This information shows how resilient brains react to stress but are making corresponding adaptations to cope. Resilience brings the focus back to the amygdala, or an early part of the brain that recognizes fear, anger, trauma, and aggression and is the center for the fight-or-flight response, and the frontal lobe where the logic, decision-making, and problem-solving occur. Resilience represents an interchange among these two parts of the brain. When faced with danger, the frontal lobe activates the amygdala to prepare for the threat to come. Resilience consists of a complex engagement of different physical and psychological stressors that are processing different circuitries in the brain. Where one person undergoes extreme stress, sometimes leading to PTSD, another person is able to overcome the stress and handle the situation.

While such neuroscience studies continue, researchers are also determining ways people can enhance their resiliency. Many of these basic points are reinforced in this manual and recommended to be part of your disaster mental health action plan. Based on the key studies on this topic, Sandifer and Walker's (2018) recommendations to reduce stress and build resiliency include the following:

1. All government levels must clearly recognize the impact of disaster-related stress and increase the number of post-disaster mental health treatment programs;
2. Preparedness plans must include a means of measuring the connection between disasters and increased stress as well as evaluating recovery through treatment;
3. Communities nationwide need to build on PFA, which reduces immediate disaster anxiety, by creating new ways that first responders and organizations can detect and reduce negative mental health consequences. This must be a coordinated effort that includes public education on the risks of heightened anxiety and distrust;
4. Natural infrastructures, such as dunes, wetlands, and islands, should be successfully utilized to reduce disaster injury and protect health and wellbeing. Narayan et al. (2017) studied how coastal wetlands helped circumvent about $625 million in possible flood damage from Hurricane Sandy;
5. Due to the far-reaching displacement of people after a natural disaster, response teams need to expand their geographic area of care. Hurricane

Source: Wikimedia Commons. U.S Fish and Wildlife Service

Katrina hit both Louisiana and Mississippi, an area larger than the U.K., leading to about 485,000 evacuees. This basically included the whole population of New Orleans (Schumacher et al., 2010). Some 13 million people suffered from Hurricane Harvey and 32,000 of them were displaced. Greater difficulties arise with islands such as Puerto Rico, where evacuation is more problematic. Yet following Hurricane Maria, Melendez and Hinojosa (2017) estimated that the territory could lose over 470,000 people or about 14% of its population by 2019;

6. Communities must develop long-term commitments to help the most vulnerable populations who are displaced following a disaster, including a variety of healthcare, housing, and income-generating options, until it is possible to return to homes and work; and

7. The processes in place for providing assessments, litigation, and housing for those impacted must be equitable. The means for distributing assistance and funds following a human- or natural-caused event must include ways to identify and avoid fraud.

A. Building Pre-Disaster Resilience

Resiliency is an important factor in building your residents' capacity to confront and react better to a catastrophic event. A number of ways can be utilized to increase resiliency after a disaster strikes, which are noted in the post-disaster section of this chapter. From a more proactive stance, your collaboration can also develop practical tools that encourage your community to better prepare for such disasters and, it is hoped, lower the emotional impact.

Decisions on how to increase resilience involve collaboration and short- and long-term planning as well as investment of time and resources. As with any other proactive venture, however, communities may not see the value and may decide to wait until if/when a disaster occurs. The payoff can be sizeable if you take steps to integrate resiliency into your action plan. Bottom-up planning, as you are doing with your disaster mental health plan, is essential since local conditions vary greatly from one part of the U.S. to another, and each community is unique in its geography, demography, culture, infrastructure, and inherent risks.

According to the U.S. Department of Health and Human Services (www.hhs. gov), resiliency consists of the knowledge and resources to know how to care for oneself and others in both routine and urgent situations. Resilient people have strong social networks to support recovery and are ready to take deliberate, collective action that responds to the negative effects of these catastrophes.

The core components of community resilience are:

1. Social connectedness for resource communication, unity, response, and recovery;
2. Effective risk communication for all populations, including vulnerable individuals;
3. Integration and participation of government and nongovernmental parties in planning, response, and recovery;
4. Physical and psychological health of the residents; and
5. Socioeconomic wellbeing.

Individuals build resilience as they learn productive ways to manage stress and life's challenges. This involves finding personal strengths and being supported by family, colleagues, and friends. Some suggestions for residents include:

1. Learning more about mental health and how to handle difficult situations, using stress- management activities, and exercising daily;
2. Encouraging entities such as employers, schools, and faith-based organizations to hold drills, discussions, and tabletop exercises for potential community-relevant disasters;
3. Building neighborhood/geographic networks and collaborating on similar goals;
4. Considering new ways to build neighbor-to-neighbor connections, including block parties to encourage people to meet one another;

5. Furthering neighborhood and community identity and pride to enhance psychological connections to place and people;
6. Talking with family and friends about preparations for a potential disaster;
7. Sharing stories with other community members who have experienced disasters to learn more about response and recovery;
8. Taking inventory of people's strengths, even the most vulnerable, that can be utilized in extreme conditions;
9. Following healthy eating and sleeping habits;
10. Determining what leads to positive feelings, such as spending time with family, reading, or enjoying the outdoors;
11. Making a list of individuals to provide support in stressful times, even if it is not in person;
12. Finding a healthy balance between work, family, and personal activities; and
13. Spending more time speaking face to face with others rather than on the phone and less time online and watching television.

Source: Photo by Bill Branson

When people are faced with a disastrous event, it is very difficult to think clearly and make sound decisions. No one expects all people can be completely prepared for a highly traumatic situation, but with an understanding of a typical reaction to high-level stress, there is a better chance to be more in control and reduce the risk of having serious injury or loss of life. If people have the coping skills to be more composed in a traumatic situation, they can express how they feel without being judged and take some responsibility for themselves rather than blindly following others—especially if these others are not acting rationally. This is sometimes called stress inoculation, in which individuals, often mentally ill patients, are prepared in advance for stressful situations. It includes anticipating that, although it is normal to feel worried and anxious, overreaction can lead to greater problems; identifying the specific psychological feelings associated with anxiety and whether frightening thoughts are accompanying this fear; and gaining control over negative thoughts by taking smaller breaths, remaining as calm as possible, and focusing on the steps needed to be taken.

The degree of individual resilience, or the ability to recover from adversity, depends on a number of personal characteristics—strengths and/or vulnerabilities. Resilient people:

1. Gain assistance from a social support network and close relationships with family and friends. They are helped through difficult times and enjoy their relationships during everyday life;
2. Take control of their personal feelings and desires and are less likely to be overwhelmed, anxious, or frustrated;
3. Still feel sadness and grief but find ways to restore health and wellbeing;
4. Problem solve and make decisions, which adds to their feelings of self-worth, independence, and competence;
5. Feel in control even when faced with a chaotic environment where no immediate answers exist;
6. Are confident they can face the present and the future while not being glued to the past;
7. Understand they do not have all the answers and are not afraid to seek others for their input. Yet they see themselves as having the power to make decisions and not rely solely on the input of others to take action;
8. Cope with stress in healthy ways such as meditation, physical activity, and yoga, and
9. Desire to help others and gain personal satisfaction knowing they are making other people's lives better.

As part of your collaboration plan, you can recommend pre-disaster community activities and programs to improve preparedness; mental health and wellness understanding and enhancement; risk-response education for pre-, during and post-disaster; community unity and communication; and decision-making for planning, response, and recovery.

B. Re-establishing Post-Disaster Resiliency

Especially with major disasters in which there is great infrastructure damage, displacement of residents, and/or high levels of personal grief and trauma, the amount of pre-disaster resiliency is critical to how quickly the community rebounds. Regardless, returning to earlier ways typically takes time, and the town or city is forever changed in some ways. In order to rebuild your community as quickly as possible, you should encourage different neighborhoods to meet and share with one another. Survivors are bolstered when spending time with family and friends. The support system provides them added strength to move forward and to share their concerns with those they trust. As with support groups, they know they are not the only ones trying to cope with the chaos in their lives, and others understand the difficulties they face.

Once your post-disaster assessment is completed, you will want to share it with the wider community. Disasters lead to many problems and difficulties and a great deal of uncertainty. Although a community conversation about recovery can be overwhelming, it is also vital to restoration. It is critical to heal the psychological wounds remaining in the wake of a disturbing event. Public engagement builds hope, trust, and confidence in relationships and opportunities to improve long-standing community challenges. It also provides a time to offer personal gratitude to those who gave their time and efforts to help others.

To capture these benefits, public engagement must have no agenda other than enhancing communication and sharing. This will be a time when residents have the opportunity to express their feelings about what occurred, the help they received, the resources they wish to share with others, and ways to improve response and recovery if/when another disaster arises. Effective community outreach after a catastrophe requires recognizing community needs and vulnerabilities, establishing appropriate forms of communication during routine operations, creating trust through information updates at familiar facilities, and discussing future steps to be taken. Attendees should feel they have some way to participate meaningfully in decisions being made about their lives. This enhances their relationships with each other, makes the community more equitable, and focuses on aspects of injustice and deprivation that have been invisible.

Your collaboration also has a responsibility to ensure that mental health services are being provided and that the people who need these services are aware of them and feel comfortable getting help without fear of being stigmatized. A range of support should be provided from wellness centers that assess needs and offer suggestions for treatment to trauma-informed therapists and mindfulness activities. Those who cannot afford these services or do not have insurance must be helped either through reimbursement funding, income-based costs, or free-of-charge public health support. The school system, facilities for at-risk populations, houses of worship, and local government need to develop programs that promote resiliency and psychological wellbeing. The public library, community agencies, and schools should regularly plan on holding disaster preparedness education programs throughout the year.

C. Building Community Capacity

Resilience is not only for individuals. One community may be more or less resilient than another community. One of the primary goals of your mental health plan is to ensure you are building a more resilient population to better face future challenges.

Nor is resilience something innate to a community, but rather something that can be developed and encouraged. The strength of the community can have a great influence on the relative frequency of positive or negative outcomes. Success or failure in coping after disasters depends in large part on the extent of the disaster and other unchangeable factors, but it also depends on the characteristics and actions of affected individuals and their communities.

What resources can best help facilitate recovery at the community level? What features encourage more community resilience? The concept of resilience is critical in thinking about disaster recovery. The idea of resilience should never be used to judge a particular person or community as a success or failure. It simply refers to the ability to adapt to change and the process of bouncing back after a challenge. People do not immediately return to the way things were before the disaster, but rather look for opportunities and potentials or growth. Post-disaster community action and a return to social participation with others, for example, reflect this adaptability and potential.

Resilience also takes time and exists in waves of stronger and weaker periods of time. Just as resources associated with resilience can be developed, skills associated with resilience can be learned and practiced. Thinking about the factors that create community resilience can help your collaboration decide on positive actions they can use to help others. This should be true regardless of whether the group is working toward preparedness or response.

At the beginning of the 21st century, an international team, led by Stevan Hobfoll et al. (2007) and supported by the National Institute of Mental Health Traumatic Stress Research Program and SAMHSA, recognized how many of the recommended psychosocial interventions for immediate- to mid-term post-disaster phases were either ineffective or even harmful. This team rightly offered general principles for successful intervention at different phases rather than specific interventions because of the number and diversity of therapy approaches, as well as the many different types of disasters and the variety of people's psychological needs and impacts from the event. The team recommended that caregivers promote a sense of safety, calming, self- and community efficacy, social connectedness, and hope. These "essential principles" have influenced the thoughts of policymakers, care providers, and scholars worldwide and are now embedded in several guidelines.

A Sense of Safety

Safety includes promoting both actual wellbeing and, when true, the perception of a secure environment. This is often accomplished together with firefighters and police officers, government officials, and organizations such as religious organizations, community centers, and private associations. If people are not placed in relative safety and reminded of this security, it will be hard for further psychological support and recovery-related actions to take place.

The principle of the sense of safety is related to the objective or perceived reality by those impacted. Many of the immediate responses to disaster, such as high stress levels, depression, separation anxiety, and lack of sleep, frequently lessen over time with a feeling of safety. Even when the threat persists, a relative sense of safety helps lower the risk of PTSD in the first months after the disaster. This sense of safety is critical to diminishing the fight-or-flight reaction so embedded in a person's mind.

Several interventions on the individual, group, or communitywide level may be used to promote this increased feeling of safety, such as reuniting family members as soon as possible and offering information about missing loved ones. The safety of family is just as important as personal safety, if not more so. Such immediacy offers a sense of relief and renewed hope that the danger has passed. Similarly, particularly with children, perceived safety is derived from maintaining contact with parents and other caregivers. Evacuation and removal of children from caring adults were once considered helpful to keep young ones safe, but it is now recognized as increasing separation anxiety.

Preparing for traumatic events also necessitates having plans in place for reliable and thorough information as soon as possible. Such accurate communication can reduce stress and the number of disturbing rumors that quickly begin to arise in such fearful situations. For example, after the 2004 Indian Ocean earthquake and tsunami, researchers studied a group of Norwegian children who were watching news shows that repeatedly ran the same footage of the tsunami hitting the beach. The children actually believed that each of these broadcasts was another tsunami, and the country was being hit time and time again by this massive wave (Heir, Hussain, &Weisaeth, 2008). Interventions must limit the degree of inaccurate information that can increase anxiety or depression and reduce the fear for friends and family members.

Calming

It is not abnormal to feel anxiety. Some degree of apprehension and fear is normal, but for their own wellbeing, people need to be calm enough to begin functioning normally, which includes sleeping, caring for themselves and loved ones, and returning as much as possible to normal routines within days and weeks, based on the nature and extent of the disaster. Calmness can and should be encouraged through responsible public messaging, coping recommendations, and authorities putting the threat into proper perspective. Victims can learn anxiety management techniques that are directly connected to specific post-disaster reactions, such as loss of appetite, sleep problems, forgetfulness, and abnormal fears. A variety of calming techniques also exist, ranging from direct and targeted to indirect and for general usage. Direct treatment, such as deep breathing, deep muscle relaxation, and yoga can be helpful. (See Chapter 7 for more information.)

When people realize they are not alone in their fearful reactions to a tragedy, they feel calmer. After a disaster, many may feel uncomfortable talking about their emotional state because of the associated stigma. Some individuals do well in small groups or one-on-one situations, while others feel more at ease with larger group discussions and education about post-disaster reactions. This information can also be made available online for those who are not ready to leave the safety of their homes. People find that their reaction is not only acceptable but also shared by others. Such education through religious organizations, schools, nonprofit organizations, and businesses, which confirms and normalizes emotional reactions, should be included when planning public health interventions.

Sense of Self- and Collective Efficacy

The more people can take charge of their own care and recovery, the more they will feel a sense of confidence in themselves, their families, and their communities. Too much of a dependence on authorities and relief agencies can be counterproductive, making residents feel less, rather than more, capable. To foster collective efficacy, survivors should be included in planning and recovery decision-making, which needs to be repeatedly emphasized.

Long studied by psychology professionals, self-efficacy is the belief by individuals that their actions will likely lead to generally positive outcomes. This will primarily occur through self-regulation of thoughts, emotions, and behavior. After traumatic events, people are at risk of feeling less competent about their ability to handle personal events. Although such feelings begin with the trauma of the original event, they may quickly expand to more general situations.

Successful interventions can be helpful in reducing such negative self-efficacy and make it easier to overcome difficulties. Often, it may not be the actual self-efficacy, but rather the perception of how one can handle trauma-related situations, that can be helpful. The ability to enhance self-efficacy does not occur in a vacuum. This is another reason collaboration is critical at the time of trauma-related events.

Partners need to work together to solve communitywide problems going far beyond the abilities of an individual or one organization to face such complex issues. Collective efficacy, which refers to the capacity of a group of people to work together for shared goals, occurs when a population in a mass casualty situation recognizes they can succeed only by sharing with others. Collective efficacy may be most effective on the family level, where psychological, material, or social losses are felt deeply by loved ones. Families are frequently the main source of social capital within any community and the main provider of mental healthcare after disasters, particularly in rural areas. Competent communities promote perceptions of self-efficacy among their members; they foster perceptions that others are available to provide support to families who then provide sustenance to their members.

In the case of self-efficacy, empowerment without resources is counterproductive and demoralizing. Individuals who lose the most personal, social, and economic resources are the most devastated by mass trauma, but those able to sustain their resources have the best ability to recover. People wrongly assume they, and not the circumstances, are the failure, and intervention will over- or underestimate people's capabilities. People need to believe not only that they can effectively evacuate, gain access to temporary housing, and find a job on their return, but also that they will have the resources to meet their goals. It is not surprising that attempts to send trauma victims home with self-help pamphlets are likely to backfire. Outcomes are greatly influenced by population vulnerability factors and already depleted resource reservoirs.

Also, because disasters and situations of mass violence may undermine already fragile economies, it must be understood how efforts to return things to normal may be doomed to failure; public mental healthcare programs need to interact with development initiatives to help local populations enhance survival capacities and increase resiliency and quality of life.

Promotion of Connectedness

Social support is one of the most important ingredients in recovery. Some promotion of connectedness is helped by technology and common sense. Getting individuals in touch with loved ones is critical. The more people work together, the more they feel connected to others. People may need some quiet or alone time, but continued isolation can also be a warning sign of mental health concerns. Social support and sustained attachment to loved ones and social groups combat stress and trauma. Such personal interaction increases opportunities for knowledge that is essential to disaster response and myriad social support activities, such as problem-solving, emotional understanding, and acceptance leading to community efficacy.

Connecting with others is of critical importance, particularly for children and adolescents. It is of considerable importance that support providers identify those individuals who most lack social support and are at greatest risk of being socially isolated. Keeping these individuals connected, giving them opportunities to access support as needed, and providing formal help when informal avenues fail is essential. Also, it is necessary to consider the specific disaster's impact; floods and other weather-related events, in which there are greater risks of destruction and evacuation, have a higher priority for support networks that may be fragmented.

Instilling Hope

It is not helpful to promote unrealistic optimism about the future, but where there is room for hope, it should be encouraged. Messages of hope are best when they are realistic. Things may never be as they were, especially with loss of life. Yet, to the extent that positive planning and recovery efforts are put into place on individual, family, and community levels, more hope will be instilled. Survival stories can be helpful. Volunteers who come from formerly affected communities and who have recovered can share recovery stories, ideas, and plans. Not surprisingly, retaining hope after a mass trauma can be very therapeutic. Those who remain optimistic are likely to have more positive outcomes because they hold a reasonable degree of hope for the future. They can combat feelings of resignation and despair and offer a coping mechanism. Hope can be facilitated through a wide range of interventions for individuals to larger groups.

To instill hope on a large group or community level, it can be beneficial for participants to share their common problems and ways of coping. Collaborative networks, such as schools, community groups, religious institutions, and social service organizations, help people share their stories, personally assess their situations, establish goals, regain and build strength, and move from self-blame to constructive thinking and actions.

D. Focus on First Responders

First responders also need to know the impact a catastrophe may have on them, even with extensive training. Sometimes, it just is not possible to emotionally handle what is being faced. Communities can establish their own first-responder mental health programs. Fire Rescue 1 of the Houston Fire Department (Pfeffer, Buser, & Tran, 2018) provides information specifically related to first responders and post-disaster stress. It tells its firefighters how each disaster has unique factors influencing the nature, intensity, and duration of this stress and anxiety. These are some of the issues first responders can jointly talk about after the disaster is over:

1. **Control:** Many first responders experience anger and frustration about resources and feelings of heightened anxiety and helplessness from the random, uncontrollable nature of the event. It is important for first responders to recognize that no one can control a natural disaster, and they are not alone in their feelings of distress.

2. **Exposure:** First responders typically live in the same community they are helping and face their own personal challenges, such as the loss of a loved one or their own home. They feel a combination of grief and trauma, which may develop into post-trauma or physical symptoms and substance abuse. First responders need to build networks with local schools and religious organizations where they may turn for help. They are part of a community, not isolated from it.

3. **Vulnerability:** Hurricane Irma brought intense wind and rainfall for 37 consecutive hours and resulted in 132 deaths. Hurricane Maria devastated the entire island of Puerto Rico, leaving residents without power, water, or access to medical care. When entire communities are affected, survivors may become disoriented; it is critical to offer social support that maintains a sense of community and occurs in familiar settings. Such situations are even more difficult for first responders because of the extent of support they need to give. Someone needs to be available at the disaster site to provide help to these individuals—a peer, a chaplain, or a sanctioned volunteer. A respite center for volunteers can be a very helpful addition to a disaster mental health plan.

4. **Remain Active:** Once the disaster passes and the threat ends, the recovery and rebuilding process can begin. For first responders, this conclusion is not clear. Hurricanes and floods often remain "active incidents," and first responders continue to look for survivors and the deceased for several weeks. First responders must understand that their needs are as important as those of the people they are saving. Meeting the basic needs of sleeping, eating, and taking downtime for wellness activities such as yoga and breathing exercises is critical.

5. **Recurrence:** The end of the catastrophe is also not concrete for first responders because anniversaries of critical incidents can trigger PTSD

symptoms. Communities need to ensure support for first responders continues far after the event occurs.

Your collaboration's action plan should include a recommendation for first responder pre- and post-disaster support and training. Psychological first aid, originally developed for civilians, is now being used with first responders as well, immediately after an event. Then these first responders should be assessed by trauma-informed health providers, recognizing that stress is not due to a personal weakness but is an ordinary response. Communities should not wait until a responder seeks out help—many do not—but rather, these individuals should be contacted and their trauma symptoms reviewed. They should be contacted regularly to see if their emotional needs are being met. In the past, responders attended debriefing sessions, which have proven ineffective or even harmful. These volunteers should instead be given options of where they can go for help; their managers need to be trained to recognize symptoms.

It is critical that first responders get rest after a 12-hour shift. Too often, they ignore the need for rest. Many will not stop their work until they are directed to do so. First responder training needs to explain how the physical and psychological factors work together toward personal debilitation. Members of the clergy, counselors, and volunteer laymen need to be included in this directive as well. Most people rush to help when the disaster first occurs and then are exhausted in a few days when help continues to be needed. If possible, some volunteers should wait for the second wave of requests for help when the emotional and physical toll takes place with those arriving earlier. This can all be part of the disaster mental health plan.

Too often, first responders needlessly suffer alone in the days and weeks following the disaster, with denial, embarrassment, or a belief they can cure themselves. There should be no reason first responders or others in the community cannot request help if needed.

HEART 9/11

The Sandy Hook 12/14 shooting negatively impacted several of the town's police officers, and the Newtown Police Department asked HEART 9/11 to assist its officers in their wellness and recovery. The HEART 9/11 organization, which helps communities cope with disasters and related trauma, assembled six teams of two members each to work with the Newtown officers for several days a week during 2015. The program successfully helped officers recognize issues personally affecting their emotional state, job performance, and relationships with family and community members. Nine of the officers then participated in train-the-trainer courses and are now training first responders in other towns and cities.

First responders are not the only group of individuals who frequently fall through the cracks when disasters occur. Compassion fatigue may be experienced by counselors, clergy members, teachers, family, and friends, who are personally involved with helping others deal with fear, pain, and grief. Over time, many of these providers of support may become as traumatized as the people they are trying to help. They may feel exhausted and overwhelmed and believe anything they do will not be helpful. If these feelings are not addressed, they can worsen over time.

CASE STUDY: Building a Healthy Community

Shortly after the Sandy Hook Elementary School shooting in December 2012, the town of Newtown was determining how to implement the World Health Organization's (WHO) Healthy Community Initiative. "Wellness is the overarching principle that makes all citizens enjoy a good quality of life," explained Pat Llodra, first selectman from 2009 to 2017, who supported introducing this new concept to Newtown. "We want to ensure all Newtowners receive the factors that influence community health and development."

According to WHO, there are three overarching determinants of health: Income equality, which significantly impacts the life expectancy of the residents; social connectedness, in which "belonging" is related to longer life and better health; and a sense of personal or collective efficacy. These determinants are then broken into ten characteristics:

1. The social gradient—difference between the "haves" and "have nots";
2. Stress;
3. Early life experience;
4. Social exclusion (the opposite of social connectedness);
5. Work;
6. Unemployment;
7. Social support;
8. Addiction;
9. Food; and
10. Transport.

With strong social determinants, a community has the capacity to take action and control its own fate. It becomes resiliently strong enough to promote social change that positively impacts all residents for the long term.

As is often the case, life did not happen as planned. The idea for the Healthy Community Initiative quickly altered course after the shooting. The town received a three-year grant from the U.S. Justice Department in 2013, and a team provided trauma treatment for approximately 900 residents. "This was about building a safety net of ongoing support for those in the mental health system and to capture new people who have needs," Llodra said at the time. When the federal grant came to an end, Newtown formed the Center for Health and Wellness (CSW), hired professionals certified in social services, and developed partnerships with two local nonprofits to ensure there would be no gaps in services. Additional funding came from the Victims of Crime Act (VOCA).

The mission of CSW was "to lead the development and realization of a shared vision of a healthy community. Through advocacy, referrals, program development, and outreach, we will ensure Newtown's individuals and families have access to a comprehensive system of behavioral health and wellness support." It was clearly recognized that mental health services were going to be a long-term need, particularly since some residents were seeking help for the first time even four years later.

According to then-CSW Director Jennifer Crane, the center provided assessment and referrals for at least another 1,700 people living or working in Newtown from 2016 to 2019. The Newtown public school counselors and guidance staff refer families to CSW when a student's challenges are outside the scope of the school. In addition, both the Newtown Police and Social Services Departments utilize CSW for referrals and as a partner when responding to community behavioral health issues.

"The CSW is a unique organization, in that it is funded by the town, not a grant," noted Crane. "Most municipalities do not have services such as CSW that functions as a town department. This was intentional, because the future of the organization depends on fund availability." Because CSW's primary service is as a referral center, it has also created a valuable database of local providers that can be searched by demographic information such as the types of insurance accepted and treatments utilized. It has also formed strong partnerships with many municipal and nonprofit organizations.

In 2018, CSW was able to implement Llodra's first vision of establishing a healthy community effort, stating: "The Town of Newtown strives to provide a healthy community that encourages schools, businesses, and organizations to support wellness through the delivery of services promoting: Healthy Life Choices, Connections with Others, Awareness and Education, and Positive Emotional Well-Being." A healthy community is one where all individuals and families have access to opportunities for social, physical, and emotional health. CSW formed a task force to look at a variety of health community categories, and residents were surveyed, and public meetings held for additional input.

"Newtown has many attributes of a healthy community," noted Llodra, "such as good schools, parks, and resident participation in a host of organizations, sporting activities, and volunteering. Yet we always need to think about the future and how our population's needs are always changing." As Newtown has learned well since 2012, preparedness is essential for ever-challenged modern-day communities.

CASE STUDY: Free Trauma Center for Disaster Victims

After the Sandy Hook Elementary School tragedy on December 14, 2012, Stephanie Cinque, a Newtown, Connecticut, social worker, created the Resiliency Center of Newtown (RCN). As executive director, she solicited donations, found a location, and established a vital service that treated children and adults with a wide variety of therapies. RCN looked to Tuesday's Children (an organization started after 9/11) for support and backing to get up and running. Though the healing models are not exactly the same, they had similar missions to help people for the long term. Since then, Cinque and music therapist Jennifer Sokira have traveled to many other communities affected by disaster to provide consulting services and assist them in building this unique resiliency center model.

RCN has continued to offer excellent state-of-the-art trauma services without charging any fees. In this way, the center has been able to help many disaster-impacted individuals who would not have sought treatment because of financial issues or were too overwhelmed to look for a local trauma-informed therapist. RCN has thus played a crucial role in Newtown's healing process.

From the start, it was RCN's mission to offer trauma-informed therapeutic services focused on long-term individual and community healing for children and adults impacted by the Sandy Hook Elementary School shooting. It was Cinque's goal to offer programs and treatments not readily available in the local area. She talked to members of the community and mental health professionals and learned of Brainspotting, developed by David Grand, PhD, which was successfully used to treat 9/11 survivors, and Masgutova Neurosensorimotor Reflex Integration (MNRI).

When RCN first opened its doors, it was staffed with certified volunteers and used Stanford University's Creative Insight program, which focuses on developing tools and skills helping build resilience by assisting participants in identifying their own abilities and strengths after difficult life circumstances. Newtown Resiliency Center now offers the following services:

◆ Bereavement counseling;
◆ Art therapy;
◆ Music therapy;
◆ Play therapy;
◆ Brainspotting (David Grand);
◆ Masgutova Neurosensorimotor Reflex Integration (MNRI); and
◆ Enrichment programs such as Camp Creativity and a girls' empowerment group.

In 2016, Cinque and her team did a critical analysis of what was needed to maintain RNC's sustainability. Their strategic plan outlined strategies for each goal and identified who would be responsible when it was completed.

1. Financial Sustainability
   ◆ To secure public and private funding necessary to support operating needs and provide a health reserve for the future.
2. Marketing and Outreach
   ◆ To increase awareness of RCN's programs and services to clients and donors.
3. Governance
   ◆ To create a sustainable governance structure.
4. Community Collaboration
   ◆ To strengthen relationships with other community providers to improve community healing.

The team saw the value of being a part of and remaining connected to the community collaborative established by the Newtown Sandy Hook Community Foundation. Their plan is to close the center in 2025, but many community members would like to see it remain open and continue to provide services for trauma as well as other mental health issues.

RCN Mission Statement

"Resiliency Center of Newtown is a non-profit, 501(c)(3) organization. RCN was founded by a community member and offers long-term healing to anyone impacted by the tragic events of December 14, 2012, providing the resources so every individual reaches their full potential. The center is a welcoming place where people feel comfortable connecting with others while finding appropriate services to assist in the healing process."

TO DO

1. What data collection and research can your community investigate to understand the skills and education for resiliency that already exist with individuals and population groups?
2. What activities can be conducted in your community at a low cost to increase resiliency efforts before or after a disaster?
3. When you envision a resilient community, what do you see? How would it be different from what currently exists? How will you get from here to there?
4. How would you rate your community in terms of acceptance of mental health issues? Are people willing and open to discussing their problems and seeking help, or do they feel stigmatized?

References

Heir, T., Hussain, A., & Weisaeth, L. (2008). Managing the after-effects of disaster trauma—The essentials of early intervention. *Touch Briefings*. Retrieved from www.researchgate.net/profile/Trond_Heir/publication/256605332_Managing_ the_after-effects_of_disaster_trauma_-_the_essentials_of_early_intervention/ links/00b49523774095f9b1000000/Managing-the-after-effects-of-disaster-trauma- the-essentials-of-early-intervention.pdf

Hobfoll, S. E., Watson, P., Bell, C. C., Bryant, R. A., Brymer, M. J., Friedman, M. J., . . . Berthold, P. R. (2007). Five essential elements of immediate and mid-term mass trauma intervention: Empirical evidence. *Psychiatry, 70*(4), 283–314.

Melendez, E., & Hinojosa, J. (2017). *Estimates of post-Hurricane Maria exodus from Puerto Rico* (pp. 1–7). New York, NY: Center for Puerto Rican Studies, Hunter College, CUNY Centro RB2017-01.

Narayan, S., Beck, M. W., Wilson, P., Thomas, C. J., Guerrero, A., Shepard, C. C., Reguero, B. G., . . . Trespalacios, D. (2017). The value of coastal wetlands for flood damage reduction in the Northeastern USA. *Scientific Reports*, 7, Article 9463.

Pfeffer, K., Buser, S., & Tran, J. (2018, January 8). Disaster mental health: Meeting the unique needs of first responders. *Fire Rescue 1*. Retrieved from www.firerescue1.

com/health/articles/372450018-Disaster-mental-health-Meeting-the-unique-needs-of-first-responders/

Sandifer, P. A., & Walker, A. H. (2018). Enhancing disaster resilience by reducing stress-associated health impacts. *Frontiers in Public Health*, *6*, 373.

Schumacher, J. A., Coffey, S. F., Norris, F. H., Tracy, M., Clements, K., & Galea, S. (2010). Intimate partner violence and hurricane Katrina: Predictors and associated mental health outcomes. *Violence Victims*, *25*, 588–603.

Reader's Notes

9

Lessons Learned

Chapter 9 Preview
A. Nationwide Longitudinal Study of Psychological Responses to September 11, 2001
B. Assessment, Crisis Intervention, and Trauma Treatment: The Integrative ACT Intervention Model
C. The Role of Social Science in Preparedness Response
D. Pediatric Disaster Preparedness in the Wake of Katrina
E. Community Resilience: Lessons From New Orleans and Hurricane Katrina
F. The Mental Health Effects of Hurricane Sandy
G. Coordinates of Resilience: On the Nimbleness of Community and Faith-Based Organizations in Disaster Response and Recovery
H. Psychosocial Recovery After the Oklahoma City Tornadoes
I. Ethical Considerations for Conducting Disaster Research With Vulnerable Populations
J. After-Action Report for the Response to the Boston Marathon Bombing
K. Post-Trauma Recovery of Children in Newtown, Connecticut Using MNRI
L. Natural Disasters and Mental Health: Lessons Learned in Puerto Rico
M. Not-So-Happy Anniversaries (Columbine)

Fewer articles have been written about the state of mental health after a disaster than most other areas of study, although the number has increased in the past few years. Even fewer reports address long-term effects. Only a handful of studies have researched the impact on survivors more than five years after the calamitous event. As noted in one of the following articles (Ferreira et al., 2015, see below in I), this often is because of ethical considerations.

The increasing frequency and severity of disasters and their subsequent impact on the U.S. population provide excellent reasons to study these experiences and how to make improvements in care. Too often, humans do not learn from history. Decisions are often made without meaningful input, and mistakes are repeated from one incident to the next. Although mental health is complex and every disaster situation is unique, similarities in response and recovery can be ascertained and used to enhance future wellbeing. Preventative plans can limit inadequate policies, communication breakdown, population generalizations, and poor first-responder training. Learning from the experiences of others and applying that information are among the main reasons for this manual.

The importance of avoiding duplication of errors and repeating successes cannot be stressed enough. Organizations need action plans that clearly identify, document, and communicate lessons gained to learn from past experiences and improve future responses. Part of your preparation is reviewing what has already been learned by researchers and other communities facing tragedies.

Following are several overviews of recent studies and articles providing input on the topic of mental health interventions and disasters. The conclusions and recommendations can help determine your collaboration's own goals and expectations.

A. Nationwide Longitudinal Study of Psychological Responses to September 11, 2001

Silver, R. C., Holman, E. A., McIntosh, D. N., Poulin, M., & Gil-Rivas, V. (2002). Nationwide longitudinal study of psychological responses to September 11, 2001. *Journal of American Medical Association*, 288(10), 1235–1244.

After researching the acute responses to the 9/11 terrorist attacks, Silver found the psychological effects of a major national trauma are not limited to those who experience it directly, and the degree of response is not predicted simply by objective measures of exposure to or loss from the trauma. Instead, use of specific coping strategies shortly after an event is associated with symptoms over time. In particular, disengaging from coping efforts can signal the likelihood of psychological difficulties up to six months after a trauma.

Six months after 9/11, the entire U.S. population, including individuals not directly affected by the attacks, was still dealing with the impact of such a significant event. Although PTSD symptoms decreased over those six months, they continued to remain high. Also, people were still anxious that future terrorist attacks would affect them or someone close to them. The degree of PTSD symptoms and the general stress of the population as a whole were impacted by such factors as demographics, a person's mental/physical health prior to the event, and exposure to and loss from the disaster itself.

Even when adjusting for these factors, this study showed how the degree of use of coping skills after the attacks, such as conversations with others for support, relaxation techniques, and physical activity, most strongly predicted the severity of trauma. Sometimes, coping mechanisms are the only approach that appears to protect against ongoing stress. On the other hand, negative actions, such as giving up, denial, and self-distraction, seem to increase the likelihood of continued stress.

> **TAKEAWAYS: Studies show that many different factors cause the increase and decrease of trauma. By best understanding your residents' vulnerability, particularly with different forms of human-caused and natural catastrophic events, your mental health planning collaboration can determine what factors will lead to the most trauma after a disaster and put greater resources toward these areas. Such information can specifically be included in your plan, so the community will know what steps to take to address traumatic responses.**

B. Assessment, Crisis Intervention, and Trauma Treatment: The Integrative ACT Intervention Model

Roberts, A. R. (2002). Assessment, crisis intervention, and trauma treatment: The integrative ACT intervention model. *Brief Treatment & Crisis Intervention*, 2(1), 1–21.

Albert R. Roberts was known for his work in the fields of criminal justice, social work, and mental health. He also developed the Assessment Crisis Intervention Trauma Treatment (ACT) model in response to the September 11, 2001, terrorist attack.

In this article, Roberts showed how some of the therapists involved with 9/11 wanted to "rush to action" as soon as they heard about the terrorist attacks. A therapist without training in trauma or crisis intervention, for example, could possibly convince a survivor to quickly make major life changes, such as moving from New York to New Jersey. Such decisions can bring a whole new set of challenges. Instead, Roberts said it is better when counselors "pause and assess" so they do not engage in well-intentioned but misguided and possibly harmful responses.

According to Roberts, with the increased threat of terrorist attacks, mental health educators and practitioners must develop the following:

1. Training and certification programs for responders and trauma specialists;
2. Tested procedures for disaster response, crisis intervention, and trauma treatment; and
3. Coordinated inter-agency disaster mental health teams that are on call and can quickly travel to community disasters in their respective regions.

TAKEAWAYS: Roberts's comments emphasize one of the main themes of this manual—ensuring that only trauma-informed mental health professionals are responsible for the assessment and suggested treatment of those impacted by the catastrophe. Your community must also utilize local, state, and federal services to be better prepared for meeting the mental health needs of your residents. Although Roberts's article only addresses terrorist attacks, his advice can easily be extended to any trauma-causing event.

C. The Role of Social Science in Preparedness Response

House Hearing 109 Congress. (2005, November 10). *Role of social science in preparedness response.* Retrieved from www.govinfo.gov/content/pkg/CHRG-109hhrg24463/html/CHRG-109hhrg24463.htm

Several psychologists testified in front of the Research Subcommittee of the U.S. House of Representatives Committee on Sciences to explain how the social sciences can inform planning for, response to, and recovery from natural hazards and disasters. The following is based on an excerpt by Dan O'Hair, chairman of the Department of Communications at the University of Oklahoma, on risk vulnerability and disasters.

Risk Perception

Risk and crisis communication have formally been studied over the past several decades, but more recently a renewed emphasis is being placed on understanding how officials communicate risks and warnings to the public. For example, during President George W. Bush's administration, studies were conducted on risk messages about the avian bird flu pandemic.

Many studies have been carried out on what impacts the level of risk perception and how seriously people believe they are threatened. Such factors include an individual's perception of dread and sense of control; whether the threat is human-caused, natural, or novel and new; how the situation affects children, and whether or not "this could happen to me." Sociopolitical factors such as gender, power, status, ethnicity, culture, education, and, perhaps most importantly, trust, are known to influence people's perception and acceptance of risk.

The proximity of the threat to a person is also pertinent. For example, if individuals from a non-metropolitan area are introduced to risk messages about the potential for an avian flu pandemic, they may think their exposure rate is minimal and not feel obligated to take suggested precautions. Similarly, risk perception is also based on the extent to which recipients find a risk important when hearing about it. Do their perceptions lead them to believe the risk is going to have any impact on their own lives? Individuals were asked to rank the importance of various news items during a television broadcast. Researchers found that the items ranked highest for risk perception included an 18-wheeler turning over on a local highway. Conversely, the viewers ranked an item focusing on the tragic deaths of U.S. servicemen much lower. The TV audience experienced perceptual nearness to the trucking accident but not to the soldiers' deaths. Likewise, studies on temporal factors demonstrated the more time that went by after an event, the less significant people found it to be in their lives. Too often, risk and crisis communicators overestimate what the public is going to perceive as important simply because they think the issue is important.

Role of Media

People depend on multiple sources for risk information, including TV, radio, newspapers, and friends. More recent studies indicate that some people first learn of disasters from others through electronic sources, such as the internet and instant messaging. Others first turn to broadcast media and then to print, the internet, and interpersonal sources. These latter sources confirm and assure people get more in-depth information. Other research has shown that women are more apt than men to seek information on family management needs from the media; they appear to assume more responsibility for adapting to a crisis.

However, there are other groups of isolated and impoverished, minority, and rural populations who first rely on interpersonal and community sources of information. News media may also be biased toward higher income, more educated, and less vulnerable populations and direct most of their information toward these viewers.

Although people turn to the media for answers, broadcast organizations and journalists do not seem to be any better prepared for disasters and emergencies than other members of the at-risk community. One study found only 33% of radio stations, 54% of TV stations, and 60% of newspapers reported any kind of disaster plans. Media organizations with disaster plans did not provide sufficient thought to critical issues; in many cases, plans consisted of brief procedures and a list of phone numbers, but not necessarily the most relevant local emergency agencies. Another study found that media representatives were among the least prepared of those involved in local response and exhibited the greatest amount of fear and stress under simulated emergency conditions.

Uncertainty and Media Access

Most individuals assume they live in an uncertain if not risky environment. Multiple studies demonstrate people cope by blocking information from their awareness and strive for a "new normalcy." When risk probability is low, individuals have little motivation to seek or process information from the media. Risk messages are unlikely to resonate with them. When risk probability is higher, individuals become curious, process risk messages more directly, and may seek additional information. As the threat of risk becomes increasingly meaningful, people have a more immediate desire for information and increase media exposure. Lastly, when a threat seems imminent, the process of information seeking becomes acute, and media access becomes vigorous if not frantic.

Media Sensationalizing and Framing

The media often operate on a sensationalism basis, in which their interest is in casting the context of risk through political and human-interest lenses, frequently omitting risk factors. For instance, during Hurricane Katrina, opinionated journalism became accepted among some of the harsher media critics. Journalists found it difficult to separate human emotions from their reporting.

Message framing, or how a message is described, is an essential characteristic of risk communication. For example, the public does not want to be patronized, as in "Don't worry. We're from the government; we're here to help." Most people know how to frame messages. They do not frame messages in the same way to their spouses as to their children or with constituencies or colleagues. The media and political managers have become very skilled at message framing.

Studies indicate three ways the media typically frame messages: 1) general issues are relayed in a thematic frame; 2) episodes emphasize specific people, perpetrators, and victims and use episodic framing; and 3) stories are slanted in a certain way—often negatively—and rely on strategic framing. Using the same basic message but with varying framing will evoke different cognitive and emotional responses. In Hurricane Katrina, for example, the media used a strategy framework by portraying an America divided along racial lines. Two-thirds of African Americans, but fewer than one in five whites, said the government warning and response would have been faster had most victims been white.

Constructive Media

Journalistic and broadcast activities can create a "paradox of media coverage." On one hand, media often frame their messages in ways that omit critical information, overemphasize certain circumstantial features, sensationalize the situation, stimulate distrust among those whose role is to mitigate the threat, and politicize the context of the disaster event. However, media can also serve a number of valuable if not essential functions for consumers, government officials, and organizations. After Katrina, the media provided much-needed information, emotional support, and companionship to victims.

Following the storm, many reporters became interviewees rather than interviewers. Media also provided emotional support and companionship to victims who felt isolated and alone and imparted helpful information to them. Effective warnings in the media reduced casualties, spread assistance to disaster-stricken areas, and provided reassurance to people concerned about the wellbeing of their loved ones.

Effective Messages

Successful messages do the following: 1) Promote survival: Tell people what to do, where to go, and what to expect; 2) Provide meaning: Tell people why they need these things; and 3) Offer assurance: Tell residents something is being done by someone or some organization.

A government report on risk communication suggested how the most important principles for communicating risk and threat information involve the following: 1) Messages should be consistent, accurate, clear, and offered repeatedly through multiple methods; 2) Information should be timely; and 3) Information should be specific about the nature of the threat, when and where it is likely to occur, and directions on preventive measures or protective responses. Jargon, euphemisms, and acronyms do not always resonate with people. Do most people understand the difference between "tornado warning" and "tornado watch?" What about the terrorist warnings of different colors? "Shelter in place" wrongly means "go to a shelter" to some people.

Risk/Crisis-Source Match

The risk/crisis-source match is also an important element in disaster communication. Is the right person communicating for the right crisis and the right risk? Research indicates that the public has very definitive ideas about who ought to be delivering risk and crisis messages. When the event is national, federal spokespersons are preferred. When the event is more local, someone from the community is desirable. Also, whenever the risk or crisis is medical, residents want to hear from medical personnel. The public does not accept messages at face value. People continuously make judgments about all facets of the message, its source, and the context in which it is delivered.

Trust

The preeminent issue in risk communication is trust. Research identifies different variables that influence trust: perceived openness, competence, objectivity, fairness, consistency, independence, and care. Trust is reduced by disagreements among experts, lack of coordination among risk management organizations, insensitivity to the audience's communication needs, lack of information access or disclosure, and nonparticipation of the public in risk management plans. It is necessary to build a preparation mindset among the public through planned, evolving, and cooperative activities such as school programs, public education, participation in the planning processes, training citizen's groups, and small personalized learning environments.

Literacy and Intercultural Issues

America is increasingly becoming a diverse culture or network of cultures. An increasingly diverse citizenry will not respond to the same risk/crisis message in similar ways. Language diversity is an obvious issue for communication accuracy, but literacy and cultural issues are just as important. How can risk messages be designed for low-literacy receivers? What intercultural variables are most prominent in communicating risk? For example, studies suggest that certain cultures in the U.S. are more concerned about climate change than others.

Inter-Organizational Communication

Much research indicates the way public organizations fail to communicate effectively with one another. Future research must focus on their collaboration. What is the best way to handle inter-organizational conflict and territoriality, especially when funds are continually being reduced? The key is determining how to best utilize this complex system with multiple players and their politics, mindsets, perspectives, goals, fears, entrenched behavior, stakeholders, and obligations. Better metrics are required to understand communication among agencies, communities, and residents.

Organizations need to develop and test strategic communication models that will improve inter-organizational/agency cooperation. These models include assessing community and organizational risk and crisis communication programs and strategies, as well as developing standardized measurement tools to see where improvements are most needed.

> **TAKEAWAYS:** Risk and crisis communication programs must be designed, tailored, and executed at the community level. Rather than having residents rely on state or national media, you need local spokespeople to relay informative and accurate messages. Also, media use is often considered a moving target, with new services and tools continually rolled out through alerts, blogs, and instant messaging. Your mental health intervention plan needs to look at both the positive and negative aspects of external media and messaging. The goal is for your messages to be heard, understood, and followed by all community members. It is also necessary to provide the media with objective information that can be communicated nationally.

D. Pediatric Disaster Preparedness in the Wake of Katrina

National Association of Child Care Resource and Referral Agencies. (NAC-CRRA, 2006). *Is child care ready? A disaster planning guide for child care resource and referral agencies.* Retrieved from https://emilms.fema.gov/IS0366a/lesson6/L6_print.htm

Recent disasters such as Hurricane Katrina have demonstrated to emergency planners, healthcare officials, social service agencies, and volunteers that children have unique needs in response and recovery efforts. Lessons learned and knowledge gained from such situations should be utilized to better prepare for and respond to these special needs.

When tragedies occur, intervention plans immediately go into action. They mobilize response teams and notify key agencies, including schools and childcare providers, by maintaining a list of community professionals who need to be notified of potential or pending disasters.

Following a sudden-onset event such as an earthquake, educational facilities must quickly evacuate and relocate children and youth to a new location. Emergency managers should team with local school officials and childcare providers to develop plans for how such an evacuation will take place and the way parents will be notified about their children's new location. For families and community members, one of the most stressful aspects of a disaster is not being aware of the status of a child in a lockdown situation or, worse, in a fatal emergency.

Regardless of the type of disaster, family unity is the most important aspect of providing for the children's physical safety and emotional stability. Children can and do become separated from their families and other caregivers. It is thus important to identify protocols for reuniting families as quickly as possible. During and after Hurricane Katrina and more recent hurricanes, numerous children were found wandering and searching for their family members. Some of these children described swimming past bloated human and animal corpses and cutting their legs on unseen objects in the water.

During evacuation efforts, some parents have placed their children on the first available buses, believing they would follow on the next bus and be driven to the same location. This became a problem. Some of the younger children who arrived without a parent could not give their names or were too traumatized to talk. Also, investigators did not have pictures of some of the children because these were back in their flooded homes. This impeded the important reconnection of parents and their children. Recognizing this problem, Hurricane Katrina volunteers took digital photos of each child in the Houston Astrodome and focused on reuniting families. The photos and accompanying information were placed in the database of the National Center for Missing and Exploited Children. In addition, volunteers kept a list of parents who were looking for their children.

The evacuation plan for children should address the following questions:

♦ Who can direct an evacuation?
♦ How will the parents be notified?
♦ What will the children be told?
♦ What signal will be given to notify everyone in the facility?
♦ How will all staff, children, volunteers, and others in the facility be accounted for?
♦ What medications, supplies, and records will be taken during evacuation?
♦ To where will children, staff, and others be evacuated?
♦ How will children and staff be transported?
♦ What coordinating actions with community public safety and/or emergency management officials are necessary?
♦ How will utilities be shut off?
♦ Who is responsible for each action?

Every childcare facility should have evacuation kits containing the following:

♦ First-aid kits;
♦ Critical medications for staff and children;
♦ Emergency contact information for each child:
♦ Parents' work phones;

- ◆ Parents' cell phones;
- ◆ Parents' home phones;
- ◆ Parents' home and work email addresses;
- ◆ Two emergency contacts in the area (preferably individuals who live or work with parents);
- ◆ Two emergency contacts out of the area;
- ◆ Phone numbers and email of parents' supervisors;
- ◆ Critical medical information; and
- ◆ Permission to transport and seek medical treatment.

Dolan, M. & Krug, S. (2006). "Pediatric disaster preparedness in the wake of Katrina: lessons to be learned." In *Clinical Pediatric Emergency Medicine.* **Atlanta, GA: Elsevier.**

In their article, Dolan and Krug, both in pediatric medicine, wrote of the problems arising when families are evacuated to shelters when disasters hit. Vulnerable children most often do not receive the care needed. The authors noted how children in shelters need to have their mental and emotional as well as their physical needs supported. Although organizations such as the American Red Cross help set up and manage emergency shelters, it frequently takes days before they arrive at the scene. In the meantime, local voluntary agencies must help community members. These volunteers need to be specially trained to provide a safe and supportive environment amidst the external upheaval. Those who volunteer to work with children require training on the unique psychological needs of and social activities for this age group. These caregivers may be the first to communicate with the children and have a significant impact on their resilience in and recovery from such a traumatic experience.

For example, thousands of children were included in the 25,000 Hurricane Katrina survivors who were evacuated to the New Orleans Superdome and the Convention Center. These ad hoc locations often report unsafe environments with violence, excessive heat, poor sanitation, inadequate beverages and food, and medically and mentally ill persons. Because of this, it is difficult for volunteers to provide the evacuees with the basic essentials needed, especially for mental health services. In Hurricane Katrina, mental health services, including play and art therapy for the children, started days after the disaster—and many did not receive necessary care. In one case, neighborhood women contributed crayons and paper so evacuated children could begin to express their experiences and feelings. Some volunteers were trained in what to expect after a disaster and reassured parents about their child's adjustment, provided resources about trauma, and made referrals to community resources.

Dolan and Krug cited the example of a valuable group of disaster volunteers formed a considerable time ago. In 1979, Maryland was declared a disaster area because of tornadoes and severe storms. R. Jan Thompson, who was the disaster response director at the time, noticed children waiting in line with their parents for disaster assistance. Everyone was very tired, and fights broke out. Thompson recognized the need for establishing a child-centered response team, gathered with a group of educators and psychologists, and formed Children's Disaster Services (CDS). Since then, CDS has grown into a strong network of volunteers and partners nationwide, helping care for children in disasters such as floods, earthquakes, hurricanes, fires, ice storms, tornadoes, mudslides, terrorist attacks, and aviation incidents. All volunteers are trained and undergo a rigorous screening process to respond to traumatized children and offer them a calm, safe, and reassuring presence amongst this chaos. CDS, now under the umbrella of the Church of Brethren, deployed a specially trained team of volunteers to Las Vegas, Nevada, following the mass shooting, for example.

> **TAKEAWAYS: Although the support provided to children is somewhat comparable regardless of the type of disaster, differences may occur. In addition, different age groups and genders of children and youth will react differently and sometimes for the long term. Even after the floodwaters recede, power is restored, buildings are repaired, and daily routines restart, many children struggle and find it difficult to concentrate, do schoolwork, and sleep. Some are scared to leave home for school, fearful something will happen to them or their families. After major fires, such as the ones in California during 2018, some younger children may wet their beds or develop a fear of the dark. Teens, who have symptoms closer to those of adults, may become anxious, irritable, or depressed and have trouble falling asleep or concentrating. They may also experience some flashbacks and intrusive thoughts about the fire. Some older children may want to stay out of school or self-medicate with drugs and alcohol.**
>
> **Children are one of the most vulnerable populations in a disaster. Their trauma may last for many years if not treated soon after the event. If their parents also suffer from PTSD and the home situation is stressful, it will take even longer for resolution of mental health issues. Your planning group needs to work closely with the schools, childcare organizations, and child service providers to establish an expedient and effective way to address such issues.**

E. Community Resilience: Lessons From New Orleans and Hurricane Katrina

Colten, C. E., Kates, R. W., & Laska, S. B. (2008). Community resilience lessons learned from New Orleans and Hurricane Katrina. *Community and Regional Resilience Initiative*. Retrieved from https://biotech.law.lsu.edu/climate/docs/a2008.03.pdf

When these authors wrote this article on the condition of New Orleans five years after Hurricane Katrina, they agreed the city was no better prepared for another major storm because "none of the sociological factors have changed—denial is still the operative planning assumption." The authors explained how New Orleans has had a long history of hazardous threats and resilience, with its location on the Mississippi River Delta. With much of this city falling below sea level, the city experienced 27 major floods in its first 290 years. This was in addition to 19th-century invasions, yellow fever epidemics, 20th-century water pollution, and floundering population growth and economy. New levees and improved internal drainage were added after Hurricane Betsy in 1965, which encouraged development in low-lying areas and increased the city's most exposed population by 170,000 households. Organizations then developed protection systems to promote flood and hurricane forecasting and evacuation plans.

When Hurricane Katrina hit the city in 2005, it devastated the levees and flooded 80% of New Orleans. It led to about 1,300 deaths, damage to 70% of the city's residences, evacuation of 100,000 residents, and an estimated loss of $40 to $50 billion. By 2009, about 70% of the pre-storm population returned, rebuilding permits for 30% of residences were issued, and the hospitality economy was restored. In 2010, although organized reconstruction was continuing, large areas of New Orleans still remained empty, leading medical and educational economic sectors were unrecovered, and some neighborhoods were considered "lost forever."

In the past, New Orleans's resilience to repeated floods and hurricanes mostly relied on short-term flood protection levees, rather than a well-considered strategy of enhancing overall community resilience. Resilience allows communities to reduce long-term vulnerability, recover from disasters, and move toward greater sustainability.

The authors stressed that New Orleans was not adequately prepared for the future impact of climate change and its associated hazards and listed several specific lessons on resilience: How can the city prepare for these potential threats?

The Greatest Overall Disaster in U.S. History

Both scientists and the media were regularly warning that a major storm would eventually hit New Orleans. It was not the hurricane itself that surprised everyone, but the actual impact—failure of complete evacuation, collapse of the levees, inadequate rescue operations, outmigration, and, most of all, the plight of those remaining in the city: The burden fell heaviest on the African American, poor, aged, and infirm populations. Such results were expected in developing countries, but not the most powerful and wealthiest nation in the world.

Creating Community Resilience Takes Time

The emergency response period of six weeks following Hurricane Katrina was the longest of any similar disaster in American history. Existing emergency response plans were amazingly deficient, and their intended improvement was incomplete at the time of Katrina. It took 21 months to develop a community-acceptable reconstruction plan, and the city would continue to repair Katrina's damage for at least a decade to come.

Such time periods are typical: Creating the elements of community resilience—anticipation, vulnerability reduction, response, and recovery—takes numerous years. It took 40 years to create an effective tracking and warning system and almost as long to inform the community about the catastrophic threat. The same amount of time was needed to reduce levee and drainage vulnerability with a failing system that was only partly completed before the hurricane.

Surprises Should Be Expected

All hazardous events bring surprises and every disaster even more so. With Hurricane Katrina, the main unanticipated occurrence was levee failure along the major canals. Levee spillage had been expected, but not as much as the 20 feet of water that flooded 80% of New Orleans. These surprises came from unanticipated events, correctly anticipated events but failed responses, or wrongly anticipated events. Resilient communities expect surprises, try to learn from those experienced in other disasters, attempt to anticipate unexpected problems, and plan for duplication in emergency response and recovery.

Best Knowledge Does Not Get Used Widely

The New Orleans experience did not utilize the technology and knowledge previously invested in climate change research. The new engineering designs from Hurricane Betsy in 1965 were based on the estimated frequency and magnitude of a standard hurricane and considered the effects of storm surge, land subsidence, and rising sea levels of that time. These estimates were still used nearly two decades later, when sea levels, storm waves, and surges had risen by seven inches, and levee subsidence had lowered the land surface by ten feet. Already, enhanced global warming was having its own effect. In addition, the widely used FEMA risk assessment maps of the 100-year floodplain had never included sea-level rise or land subsidence effects.

Response Resources Were Invisible or Poorly Used

It is said that partnerships can help communities become more resilient after a disaster. Unanticipated or unaddressed needs occur in every catastrophe, and "shadow responders" frequently emerge from households, friends and family, neighborhoods, nongovernmental and voluntary organizations, businesses, and industry. Yet after Hurricane Katrina, government officials sometimes refused or inadequately utilized such support systems. This denial of support occurred even though these same individuals and organizations helped in most of the initial evacuation capacity, sheltering, feeding, healthcare, and rebuilding, as well as in search and rescue, cleanup, and post-storm funding. Resilient communities need to effectively use, collaborate with, and coordinate the combined public and private efforts of city, state, and federal emergency response support.

Disasters Accelerate Existing Pre-Disaster Trends

When considering the effects of climate change, it is necessary to look at the context of where it is occurring in terms of the economy, nature, and society. Previous disasters can accelerate future problems. Prior to Hurricane Katrina, New Orleans had already declined in population by 31% since its 1960 peak. Then it lost two-thirds of its population after this major storm and had regained only 70% of its pre-storm population by 2010. In addition, before the hurricane, the city's economy was already declining and not recovering.

Despite 290 Years of Effort, Vulnerability Has Grown

In New Orleans, it is not only natural geophysical vulnerabilities causing major problems, but also social issues coming from new development in low-lying areas. In addition, after the storm, the city faced the loss of population, "white flight," enhanced social vulnerability, and subsequent failure to respond to the distinctive needs of the elderly, impoverished, and households without transportation.

Efforts Increased Vulnerability to Rare Catastrophic Events

One of the questions about adapting to climate change is whether successful short-term adjustments may lead to greater long-term vulnerability. This appeared to be true from the 40- year period between Hurricanes Betsy and Katrina, when enhanced levees, drainage pumps, and canals successfully protected New Orleans against three hurricanes in 1985, 1997, and 1998. However, these same changes allowed the massive development of previously unprotected areas; the flooding of these areas when the works failed actually caused the Katrina catastrophe.

> TAKEAWAYS: The question arises as to what was learned from New Orleans in terms of geophysical disaster preparedness, climate change and resilience, and whether the U.S. is actually utilizing any of this new knowledge. Although some changes have been made based on the experiences of Hurricane Katrina, nearly two decades later, some of the same problems remain. One of the worst hurricane seasons occurred in 2017, which brought much destruction as well as significant disparities among survivors. The most vulnerable, once again, took the brunt force of the storm in Texas, Florida, and Puerto Rico.
>
> Although resilience relies on preparedness, those who barely have enough money to live from one month to the next do not have the ability to stock up for a disaster. Also, once again, supplies for those most in need were significantly delayed. Even weeks after the storm, some Puerto Ricans did not have clean drinking water, food, or electricity. Many residents of a nursing home in Hollywood, Florida, died from heat prostration. Climate change is expected to increase the frequency and severity of storms in the coming years, and adequate policies do not exist to support those at greatest risk. The most vulnerable must be placed at the top of the priority list for resilience to succeed.

F. The Mental Health Effects of Hurricane Sandy

Neria, Y., & Shultz, J. M. (2012). Mental health effects of Hurricane Sandy. *Journal of the American Medical Association, 308*(24), 2571–2572.

During Superstorm Sandy, an estimated 60 million people across 24 American states experienced storms with varying intensities, each with a different mix of wind, rain, floods, coastal surges, and blizzards. The storm led to 113 deaths, 200,000 damaged homes, and a cost of about $50 billion. Sandy's impact ranked second only to Hurricane Katrina as the nation's costliest natural disaster. A number of studies have been conducted to look at this natural disaster's mental health effects and the varying risks for specific populations and communities.

When such large unpredictable and extensive storms are forecast, mental health planning groups need more than ever to identify and support high-risk populations who may develop early psychiatric symptoms and are at a higher risk for long-term emotional problems. The mental health impact of any given disaster is related to the degree of exposure to the event. Experiencing personal injury or the death of a loved one especially indicates how much a person is affected. Studies have also shown how disaster-related displacement, relocation, and loss of property and personal finances are risk factors for trauma and depression. The actual psychological effects vary depending on the population's risk factors.

Immediately following an emergency, before clinically significant psychiatric symptoms emerge, steps of prevention include:

1. Promoting a sense of safety;
2. Calming anxiety and decreasing physiological arousal;
3. Increasing self- and collective efficacy;
4. Encouraging social support and bonding with others; and
5. Instilling hope to promote a sense of a positive future.

Utilizing such an approach among high-risk groups, such as children, the elderly, disabled individuals, and first responders, may improve impaired functioning and reduce risks for long-term psychiatric illness. When trauma-related symptoms such as PTSD last well beyond the initial month after the event, a more direct, trauma-focused intervention is required to address fear-related symptoms, such as intrusive thoughts, avoidance, sleep problems, and nightmares.

> **TAKEAWAYS: Exposure to major storms such as Hurricane Sandy often causes PTSD symptoms that persist over time. Given the likelihood of more frequent and intense weather due to climate change, your collaboration's plan may want to address the steps that must be taken as storm severity increases, and the risk of long-term trauma grows.**

G. Coordinates of Resilience: On the Nimbleness of Community and Faith-Based Organizations in Disaster Response and Recovery

Ealy, L. T. (2013). *Coordinates of resilience: On the nimbleness of community and faith based organizations in disaster response and recovery.* **Retrieved from http://localknowledge.mercatus.org/articles/coordinates-of-resilience**

Resiliency, or the ability to recover and deal effectively with new challenges, is a critical aspect of disaster care. In his report, Ealy stressed how federal and state bureaucratic systems hindered resilience and recovery in Hurricane Katrina. However, these barriers to recovery were overcome through the actions taken by numerous individuals and community grassroots and faith-based organizations that stepped in and nimbly helped coordinate resources. Many community discussions following Hurricane Katrina revolved around the idea of these "nimble" organizations that adapted, improvised, and created new approaches when situations bogged down.

Ealy stressed it often takes the greatest possible involvement of grassroots efforts to cultivate resilient communities that can successfully withstand disasters. Local associations are knowledgeable about and wish to restore the community to what it was prior to the catastrophe. Disaster intervention plans must therefore ensure these local groups are not displaced by federal or state governmental agencies.

Barriers to care can often arise because of differences between faith-based groups. Approximately 10,000 Muslim families from five Baton Rouge mosques were among those displaced after Katrina; many of these individuals faced unique challenges because of their religious beliefs. For example, Muslims normally segregate by gender in social surroundings. However, the American Red Cross did not provide separate shelters for males and females. At night, many of the Muslim men stayed awake while the women and children slept, and then the women did the same for the men. Also, the shelters' food, consisting of such items as sausage and ham, was unsuitable for Muslim dietary needs. One family said they ate very little for three days since they did not want to break their dietary laws. The situation was very different at shelters provided by the mosques, where men and women had separate sleeping facilities and were served foods following dietary regulations. The mosques also acted as information centers, particularly for those individuals not fluent in English.

Such incidents were common during Katrina. Local organizations, like the mosques, frequently proved more flexible than bureaucratic systems, such as FEMA and the Red Cross, in delivering emergency resources and providing the human touch. Katrina showed that too much confidence on nationalized disaster response may be detrimental. Although FEMA and other government agencies tried to handle the chaos, many compassionate local volunteers creatively assisted with the survivors' needs.

Local efforts relied on the personal knowledge and social networks that were unmatched by large government agencies. Residents led search-and-rescue operations and saved numerous lives with their boats; this was similar to the watercraft that evacuated hundreds of thousands of people after the World Trade Center attacks. While the military helped hold back the damaged levees and coordinated large airlifts away from the floods, civilians and voluntary organizations collaborated to provide relief for the myriad displaced Gulf Coast residents. Such actions were in line with the four critical resilience factors of economic development, social capital, information, and community competence. Grassroots efforts tapped into existing social networks and created new ones, shared information through formal and informal channels, and developed new economic and social approaches for fostering community strength.

When a government study of Katrina was conducted in 2006, it was presumed the findings would show:

1. The efforts of voluntary organizations largely supplemented the government and American Red Cross response;
2. The impact of these local efforts was minimal compared to those by the government and American Red Cross; and
3. The reach of local efforts was limited to mental health and spiritual services.

However, all these assumptions proved false. Instead, the report found the "FBOs' and NGOs' successes . . . are a stark contrast to the many chronicled deficiencies and failures of government during the catastrophic 2005 hurricane season. By studying these organizations' successes, we can learn lessons that may make the nation better prepared for, and thus more responsive to, such disasters."

Lessons learned through Katrina included:

1. The vision of local organizations goes beyond merely sheltering people. In Katrina, volunteers hoped to make life even better for residents than it was before the disaster. For example, the Plaquemines Parish built new playgrounds and created T-shirts saying "Build a Louisiana Better than Before." The Rebuild Iberia group hoped to renovate New Iberia's West End neighborhood, which was becoming increasingly blighted.
2. Local groups organized their activities around intimate knowledge of the human, social, and cultural assets of the served communities. Bureaucracies operate around standardized processes and procedures, but grassroots organizations tend to operate around people. The director of family and community development at the Southern Mutual Help Association in New Iberia said:

    We didn't want to go in with a pad and pencil and ask questions. The government does that. So we first went in and listened to their story. . . . When you listen to the story first, there is a bond there immediately, and with that bond then the most unbelievable questions could be asked . . . and from there you talk about mutual understanding and mutual helping each other get something built and ready to move back into.

3. The local organizations' resourcefulness allowed them to discover and coordinate varied support systems while identifying, prioritizing, and meeting continually changing needs. Although victimized by disaster, many community associations can become more resourceful in emergencies.

4. The local organizations can continue to help residents over time, unlike the state chapters of the American Red Cross, which were replaced by national groups and relatively disempowered soon after the devastation. The resourcefulness and community spirit of both local organizations and residents promoted a nimbleness and thus greater resilience. Within hours of the hurricane, the Greater Baton Rouge Food Bank readied 18 trucks loaded with water, Gatorade, and snacks throughout southern Louisiana; they also uploaded goods for volunteer rescue boats on the Mississippi River. This effort occurred days before FEMA and the Red Cross arrived at the scene. Katrina's devastation was focused on working with existing partner parishes familiar with the residents, the geography, and those individuals with the greatest need. The food bank even helped acquire generators for refrigerators and freezers, which continue to be available for future emergencies.

   The food bank suggested it would have been better for the state and federal governments to team with local organizations than to set up a redundant distribution process that did not effectively utilize the National Guard or help those most in need. Using the local infrastructure was found to be the best way to proceed. Baton Rouge area staff quickly assessed community needs and met every night to review the shelters' services. The following day, each foundation then sent out checks to the individuals, religious organizations, and community agencies doing an effective job. Within a month, the foundations gave nearly $2 million in grants to support relief programs.

   On the other hand, many large national private foundations were slow or unwilling to support efforts after the storm because they did not have relationships with local organizations or know where best to provide funding. This was a lesson that organizations such as the Oklahoma City Community Foundation, the Community Foundation for the National Capital Region, and the New York Community Trust learned after previous local disasters.

5. Individual volunteers can be just as effective in response efforts as organizations. One woman in New Orleans established the Beacon of Hope to further one-on-one assistance to people needing support with home

rebuilding. In addition to being a vital information source, she helped establish physical order and a neighborly spirit.

Ealy concluded it is necessary to find new ways to work with community groups that can ably support local residents even in the most difficult times through an understanding of their issues of concern, resourcefulness, and collaborative spirit. The efforts of neighbors, volunteers, and organizations offer the best resilient outcomes. No one designated pathway exists for enhancing resilience, and each population has its own risk characteristics. Those most associated with a community will understand the residents best and know the most productive way to proceed. "Coordinating resilience happens best when local knowledge, vision, resourcefulness, and an emotional stake in the community converge," Ealy concluded

TAKEAWAYS: Too often, communities believe larger national organizations and the federal government will be able to provide the best support following a catastrophe. Your mental health plan needs to recognize the strengths of the local residents, neighborhoods, and organizations in knowing what is best for their community's residents. Long after the larger national organizations have left the area to confront the next disaster, the local town or city must rely on its own abilities to build resilience and prepare for future issues that may arise.

H. Psychosocial Recovery After the Oklahoma City Tornadoes

Diaz, P. (2013). Psychosocial recovery after the Oklahoma City Tornadoes. *Psychology*. Retrieved from www.webmedcentral.com/wmcpdf/Article_WMC004269.pdf

In this article about Oklahoma tornadoes, Diaz introduced the importance of place in the recovery process. Place attachment is the emotional bond between person and place and a main concept in environmental psychology. Place includes cultural identity, family connections, and the safest location in a person's life.

When people are notified a hurricane is approaching their community, they may be able to leave their homes and travel to a safer location. However, there is typically little advance warning with tornadoes, and residents need to quickly find safety someplace in the immediate area. They do not know the condition of their home or even if it remains standing until after the storm passes. When houses are significantly or completely damaged or destroyed, people feel emotionally, spiritually, and physically depleted. This same feeling occurs in other natural disasters, such as a forest fire or earthquake. Displaced individuals feel lost and no longer an integral part of their normal surroundings. The degree of this feeling may differ from one type of disaster to another.

Place is often the key to meaning. It helps people develop new beginnings and promotes and strengthens the sense of belonging; it is where resilience begins after a traumatic experience. Loss of place equates to being uprooted and separated from neighbors and friends; it is about being invisible and excluded. Sense of place is thus critical to disaster recovery. After the search and rescue efforts are over, people often return to the wreckage of their homes to look for "dear objects," which may connect family generations. Survivors are often pictured weeding through the storm's debris. Cleaning up and finding what is left of place is the beginning of recovery.

Diaz suggested six steps to help relieve suffering and foster wellbeing in such situations:

1. Alleviate fear by connecting with family, neighbors, community, and friends;
2. Initiate mental health and spiritual care activities promoting calmness;
3. Engage those impacted by assessing the area and prioritizing the replacement of natural and built structures, such as schools, daycare facilities, hospitals, senior centers, churches, and community stores;
4. Help survivors identify their immediate needs and receive assistance with finding temporary shelter, cleaning up neighborhoods, and defining steps of recovery. This provides guidance to external partners and other concerned people;
5. Promote neighbor-to-neighbor support and activities for children, the elderly, and those with functional needs, and
6. Take time to rest. Celebrate when improvements are made and hold information-gathering events. At first, have residents appreciate the little steps they are making in the recovery process. Later, hold community-wide collaborative activities such as celebrations and fairs.

TAKEAWAYS: After a major natural event, it is easy to think of homes as purely brick and mortar. People contact their insurance companies or agencies such as FEMA for financial support. Rarely do residents think of their places from an emotional perspective, or they may need to go through a grieving process for the loss of a roof over their head and the security it provided. Counselors can help in this process and further resiliency.

I. Ethical Considerations for Conducting Disaster Research With Vulnerable Populations

Ferreira, R. J., Buttell, F., & Ferreira, S. B. (2015). Ethical considerations for conducting disaster research with vulnerable populations. *Journal of Social Work Values and Ethics, 12*(1), 29–40.

To learn more about the impact of disasters on survivors and their communities, researchers believe it is necessary to conduct empirical studies. Yet this is a double-edged sword. Although many lessons can be gained by researching those involved with catastrophic events, these studies may be intrusive, take advantage of those already impacted and more vulnerable than others, and verge on unethical interests. In this article, the authors suggested ways of approaching this research dilemma.

These authors discussed two complementary theories underscoring research with vulnerable populations after a disaster: Utilitarianism and social justice. Utilitarianism stresses how any effort should strive to attain the greatest amount of benefit for the greatest number of people. The moral worth of any action is only determined by its resulting outcome. When considering the importance of utilitarianism and disaster reports, researchers must not only pursue their own goals but also consider the impact of their actions on those being studied. In order to be utilitarian, the emphasis must lie on the final results attained through research. These results need to benefit the greatest number of people possible.

Social justice is the second ethical principle that must be considered in disaster research. The needs of marginalized individuals can be determined and addressed when researchers identify ways of thoughtfully treating those studied and not furthering their oppression. Incorporating social justice practices can help address societal inequalities and ensure people's rights are not ignored. Social justice relies on the principle of equality, in which each person has an equal right to the same amount of liberty. Equality is a necessity when conducting disaster research to limit bias and ensure balanced allocation of resources.

The authors made recommendations based on the following factors:

Timing

There is no set amount of time—weeks to years—that researchers "should" wait before beginning post-disaster research. Instead, it is necessary to look at each situation separately. Some researchers believe if studies are conducted too soon after a catastrophe, participants may still be too consumed by their own personal situations. The degree of trauma for each person is different; some people continue to suffer grief, emotional stress, and anger months or years later.

Some researchers have argued it is best to start studies right after the disaster occurs; if too much time goes by, part of the population, such as those who have moved away from the disaster area, will not be included. Starting research immediately can ensure the identification of PTSD, where starting too late may miss some cases. Also, participants can more readily respond to critical questions if not much time has gone by. On the other hand, some evidence has suggested that studies can still be successful well after the disaster. What is lost in evidence is gained in the specific information provided about long-term effects.

Researchers also disagree on the best time to end a study. Most importantly, they need to consider their ability to complete their study. A study's time line may differ from one disaster to the next due to the incident's severity, the willingness of the local community to participate, and accessibility to the impacted site. Researchers have found it is necessary to determine time points representing the critical period of 2 to 6 months, intermediate period of 12 to 18 months, and long-term period of 2 to 3 years.

Federal Regulations

The government has developed a framework for the protection of participants in disaster research. The Institutional Review Board, also known as the Ethical Review Board or Research Ethics Board, reviews research methods proposed to ensure they are ethical.

Screening Participants

Possible screening methods can include paper-based assessments and observations of participants. This process helps researchers determine which potential participants may have cognitive impairments or be at greater risk for a serious mental health outcome. Disaster researchers must be trained to identify emotional problems in those they assess.

Participant Vulnerability

Social scientists need to identify the traits of disaster-exposed participants to determine their level of vulnerability. The definition of risk must be wide enough to include all factors.

Risks and Benefits

The Institutional Review Board can help determine the participants' associated risks and benefits and know whether or not the benefits derived from a study outweigh the possible risks. These benefits include greater awareness of material resources, the state of medical and mental health services, empowerment, learning and insights, altruism, kinship with others, feelings of satisfaction from participation, and favorable attention from other researchers. Risks may consist of physical harm, legal action, participant inconvenience, economic hardship, psychological discomfort, loss of dignity, confidentiality and exposure concerns, unwanted media attention and social media exposure, and emotional distress.

Gender, Cultural Norms, and Traditions

Researchers may be faced with challenges based on gender and culture that hinder the legitimacy of the final results. They must be sensitive toward such differences and adhere to levels of respect for all involved.

Code of Ethics

All researchers must adhere to the fundamentals of their governing organization's ethical standards.

Gaining Permission

Voluntary informed consent is the foundation of ethical research. All studies must be viewed as optional, and all participant refusals should be respected. Separate consent forms are required when children are research participants. All consent forms should be at the participants' reading level and in their language. All their questions should be answered.

Confidentiality and Anonymity

Privacy and confidentiality are critical in all forms of research, but even more so in disaster studies, particularly with vulnerable individuals.

Assistance to Participants

Researchers must be sensitive about the stress and anger some participants may express during post-disaster research. Those conducting a study should be familiar with the survivors' needs after a disaster, such as the necessity of a safe shelter, as well as being able to provide information on available resources. Participants can feel a sense of belonging if their questions and concerns are answered at this difficult time.

> TAKEAWAYS: It is essential for your collaboration to conduct a post-disaster assessment to determine the strengths and weaknesses of your mental health plan. However, you need to first consider the interests of those who may be included in the study. By making it clear to possible subjects that their best interests are at stake, they will be more willing

to participate and provide a vehicle to help others in need. Similarly, when your planning group requests information from another community that has experienced the trauma of a disaster, it must recognize that some information may not be shared until it is ethically best.

J. After-Action Report for the Response to the Boston Marathon Bombing

City of Boston. (2015). *After-Action report for the response to the Boston Marathon bombings.* Retrieved from www.policefoundation.org/wp-content/uploads/2015/05/after-action-report-for-the-response-to-the-2013-boston-marathon-bombings_0.pdf

This report by the city of Boston and its community organizations found improvements needed in the area of "better mental health services for non-public safety personnel, healthcare, and human services providers."

Because Boston did not have a disaster mental health coordination plan, there was initial confusion among public health and counseling agencies about the availability of mental health resources, which were required where, and who was serving as the lead coordinating agency. It was challenging to coordinate the many dozens of mental health providers and to identify the most relevant specialties for addressing current needs. The lack of a centralized source providing a detailed listing of credentialed mental health providers in the Boston area made the situation worse.

There were many resources provided for the psychological wellbeing of public safety personnel, the public, employees of impacted businesses, and family members of those impacted by the bombings. However, the level of support for non-public safety employees, healthcare providers, and human services providers was not as adequate. Some first responders did not have their mental health needs properly addressed, for example, although many of them had first-line interactions with survivors and their families and committed long hours over many days to provide support services and to restore Boylston Street back to normal. While a few city offices and some healthcare and human services employers set up debriefing sessions, some departments did little more than refer staff to an employee assistance program.

Based on its findings, the city of Boston made the following recommendations for disaster mental health services:

1. Develop a disaster mental health coordination plan to delineate roles and responsibilities for coordinating the activation of a disaster mental health support system. The plan should also address the availability of services for extended periods of time and recognize the roles of local, state, federal, and private-sector entities.

2. Develop a centralized source to identify disaster mental health specialists that includes contact information, credentials, and specialized training. The responsibilities for managing mental health resources must be made clear. At the bombing, some providers placed personnel on standby pending a request to deploy them, and others activated personnel on their own. This led to duplication of services for some locations, and it was difficult to know if, when, and where mental health providers were needed.

3. Ensure access to mental health services for all employees involved in disaster response and recovery activities. Healthcare and human services employers, the commonwealth, and the city of Boston should explore opportunities to provide post-disaster services for employees. Employee assistance programs should not serve as the sole resource for employees who have had direct contact with survivors, families, and impacted individuals or have worked directly in the area of impact. Managers should receive psychological first aid training to have the skills necessary to identify signs of trauma in their employees.

TAKEAWAYS: Boston's experiences clearly demonstrate the importance of having a mental health plan prior to a potential disaster. No one could have predicted such a catastrophe would occur. When a plan is not in place, the first responders as well as other volunteers suffer greatly if adequate mental health support is not available. This suffering can go on for years if not quickly and adequately addressed.

K. Post-Trauma Recovery of Children in Newtown, Connecticut Using MNRI

Masgutova, S. (2015). Post-trauma recovery of children in Newtown, CT using MNRI reflex integration. *Journal of Trauma Stress Disorders Treatment*, 6(1), 1–12.

The experience of survival of traumatic events—natural disasters or human-caused catastrophes; physical, emotional, and sexual abuse; and violence, mass shootings, terrorism, and wars—can be anchored to memories and cause negative projection, fear, and worry. However, some of the current primary treatments are not adequate for many individuals, particularly children, since they do not address the neurosensorimotor needs: "Neuro," which corresponds to the central nervous system and neural pathways taking in and sending out information from and to parts of the body; "sensori," which represents the sensory system; and "motor," which consists of the motor response system.

Masgutova Neurosensorimotor Reflex Integration (MNRI), created by Svetlana Masgutova, PhD, is a hands-on treatment similar to physical or massage therapy, in which the practitioner assists the body through physical patterns befitting brain function and recovery from PTSD. After the Sandy Hook Elementary School tragedy in 2012, the use of MNRI was studied for use with school survivors against a control group with no history of traumatic stress to determine overall stress levels, emotional and behavioral regulation, and cognitive function.

The study found that timing of the treatment was very important. About one-third of children who received their first MNRI treatment three months or more after the shooting already displayed PTSD symptoms: dilated pupils, breath holding, poor eye tracking, overactive sympathetic nervous system response, sweaty palms, all-over perspiration, and startling or tremors. They also reported muscle tension, poor focus at school, distracting memories, desire to escape social interactions, insomnia, and frequent crying or withheld tears. Some were already being medicated for more serious emotional issues. Children who received MNRI treatment before three months had passed showed less overall hypersensitivity in their protective reflexes and fear, greater presence, clearer reasoning communications, and more normal play and laughter.

MNRI led to significant positive changes in the children's reflex patterns along with improved school skills and daily performance in other areas. This study highlighted the importance of and urgent need for professional facilitation of reflex integration for anyone at risk for chronic trauma or PTSD. Children who experienced MNRI within three months of the event showed a faster return to functional or normal levels of reflex pattern expression, more normal symptoms.

> **TAKEAWAYS: This study demonstrated not only how some of these newer forms of trauma-specific therapies can help both children and adults with PTSD, but also how important it is to be treated in the early stages of acute stress. When treated within three months of the traumatic event, there is a chance the trauma has not evolved into PTSD. Also, earlier treatment leads to more rapid improvements.**

L. Natural Disasters and Mental Health: Lessons Learned in Puerto Rico

Marques-Reyes, D. J. (2018, April 22). Natural disasters and mental health: Lessons learned in Puerto Rico. *Georgetown Journal of International Affairs.* Retrieved from www.georgetownjournalofinternationalaffairs.org/online-edition/2018/4/22/natural-disasters-and-mental-health-lessons-learned-in-puerto-rico

In his article, Marques-Reyes addressed the impact of Hurricane Maria, the strongest recorded storm to ever hit the island. Maria was the third costliest tropical cyclone in American history. Thousands of the 3.4 million citizens needed to seek shelter away from their homes, including the mainland. Marques-Reyes wrote "the U.S. government's double standard in handling relief efforts on the mainland versus those on the island exposed Puerto Rico's status as a colony." The residents have been and still are left at the "mercy of a government that lacks meaningful representation and voting power in Congress to approve the necessary aid."

Due to the hurricane, Puerto Ricans faced significant road damage as well as a shortage of drinking water, electricity, cellular networks and medical care for an unnecessary length of time. The island also recorded very high mortality rates. The situation demonstrated the critical need to develop a more thorough preparedness strategy for mental healthcare for future storms. Every year, the Caribbean will most likely be hit by violent storms. When Marquez-Reyes wrote this article in 2017, he stated

> Currently, warning signs of a full-fledged mental health crisis exist, with many people exhibiting post-traumatic stress symptoms. The ongoing crisis, not visible in a wound or a downed power line, has placed significant strain on citizens' mental health.

After a natural disaster, many people experience such symptoms as fear, anxiety, sadness, and shock. If such symptoms continue for weeks or months, the person may have a more serious mental health issue. While many survivors do demonstrate resilience, research shows how psychological issues can arise years later. The amount of time someone is exposed to the trauma can be a critical factor in PTSD. Many Puerto Ricans were challenged with months of suffering. For days after the storm, responders could not reach suicidal patients on the telephone coaching crisis line.

The Puerto Rican response team, which has primarily consisted of FEMA and the Red Cross, needs to be expanded to include public and mental health agencies, schools, local government, social service agencies, businesses, and the media. Disaster response plans must consist of resources typically intended to help women and families experiencing domestic violence, depression, and PTSD. Communities also need to reconnect disaster survivors as quickly as possible to friends, family, and temporary housing locations.

The author's team, consisting of clinical psychology doctoral students from Albizu University, the army special forces, and Facebook personnel, posted message boards at local gas stations. Using antennas installed in the mountains, the team members gave families access to wireless internet so they could let loved ones know they were alive and well. Other agencies need to implement such simple steps to reduce mental health trauma.

Many businesses, as well as homes, did not have proper crisis plans. They also must have a strategy to obtain the resources needed to restore previous conditions. "Thus, mental health clinics and agencies require more than just emergency protocols. A continuity plan detailing what to do or where to go if communication or power goes down can be delivered through special programming and other communication interventions," wrote Marques-Reyes.

Before the storm, the Albizu University, which treats individuals with borderline personality disorder and crisis and suicidal characteristics, emphasized skills required for post-hurricane reality. However, no one expected the hurricane's initial impact would last so long. The staff prepared patients to expect outages for a week, rather than the prolonged six months experienced by many. Several of those treated faced crises without the support of their therapists, medication, telephone coaching, or available mental health clinics. This disaster emphasized how all mental health clinics need long-term continuity plans.

As is usually the case in major storms, rural areas experienced even greater logistical issues in receiving supplies and psychological first aid. When infrastructures will be greatly limited for a lengthy amount of time, it is essential to let people know what actions to take and where to go for support. The following suggestions were made in this article for a "business continuity" plan for future crises:

1. Establish different options that can be taken to restore hospital operations to a minimum acceptable level, with a priority on the data obtained from Hurricane María assessments. Plans must account for damage to facilities or medical technology and the possible failure of resource delivery.
2. Design shelters, which are often public schools, to also act as health centers. Pre-assigned mental health workers, volunteer physicians, and professionals from health agencies should be stationed at each location.
3. Execute secondary preventive PTSD assessments with those individuals who have the longest exposure to suffering and displacement.
4. Set up regional mental health clinics in all areas exposed to the worst conditions, such as flooding, lack of electricity, and no running water, for four or more consecutive months.
5. Review all community emergency strategies to ensure they include immediate and ongoing recovery plans that agencies can activate before the disaster occurs. PTSD assessments of school children should start as soon as possible.
6. Community leaders should meet two days after the disaster in a predetermined safe location after determining the people most in need. Officials will then be able to quickly and more effectively report issues and direct emergency services.

7. Establish education programs on sustainable energy, such as solar and water filtration systems, in areas where power restoration is most challenging.
8. Strengthen the relationship, communication, and coordination between the community's Office for Emergency Management and FEMA.
9. Ensure an emergency management plan exists, taking into consideration the experience from Hurricane María.

Poverty and social inequality existed before María, but this disaster has exacerbated them. To reduce these vulnerabilities, Puerto Rico should develop its social capital and foster unity between social classes in the face of disaster. These steps will create a more resilient nation and help lessen vulnerability in the potential development of a mental health crisis.

TAKEAWAYS: Hurricane Maria's impact on the island's residents clearly demonstrates the importance of this manual's four principles: Effective communication and accurate information for all residents, especially in times of most danger; the goal of establishing a collaborative plan to prepare for mental health interventions after a disaster; the importance of assessing and determining the needs of those at greatest risk; and the necessity of trauma-informed care for those who are most impacted. As both natural and human-caused catastrophes become more severe and common, such needs will be even more essential for the wellbeing of those affected by an event. The concern is that, even though such suggestions are made after each major storm, they are either overlooked or only given lip service.

M. Not-So-Happy Anniversaries (Columbine)

Paula, R. (2019, January 1). *Not-so-happy anniversaries*. Retrieved from http:// paula-reed.com/blog/
Since April 20, 1999, the survivors of Columbine High School and the entire community of Littleton, Colorado, have grappled with the impact of the shooting by two students that killed 13 and wounded over 20 others, as well as the perpetrators. In January 2019, the Marjory Stoneman Douglas High School in Parkland, Florida, invited Paula Reed, a Columbine teacher who survived the tragedy, to speak about the fears of facing the first anniversary of a school shooting. Reed was asked, "When did you feel like your old self again?"

She responded, "You don't and can't get your old self back. Accept that it will be a new norm." She shared how the Columbine school board has tried different ways of remembering the anniversaries of the shooting including school closing, holding a teacher workshop, and continuing business as usual without any commemoration. "The important thing," Paula commented, "is to get the staff's input before making those decisions." The following are more comments from her blog:

Having visited and bonded with survivors at Marshall County High School in Kentucky and Marjory Stoneman Douglas, I am seeing more and more posts about the upcoming first anniversaries of their school shootings. I see a marked difference between posts of people planning public acknowledgment and those of survivors. The planners talk about healing. The survivors talk about the daily effort of surviving. It's weird to be looking at it all from this vantage point—from being the somewhat objective "helper" and the utterly subjective "fellow survivor."

Everyone is trying so hard to use this marker as a way to contain what happened and its aftermath. Those are two different things, the event and its aftermath. The event is already pinned into place. It has an anniversary. That day comes and goes year after year.

The aftermath is amorphous. There are triggers leading up, and it is not over when it's over. It doesn't fit into a day. At least, not for a long, long time.

I can give hope, but I have little to offer in the way of comfort right now. That first year was just so, so hard. I don't know of any way to change that. I ache, literally ache, for these good people.

TAKEAWAYS: Lessons are continually learned from disasters, especially since so few articles have been written by the survivors and first responders. Columbine, Marshall County High School, and Marjory Stoneman High School, along with other communities facing disaster anniversaries, continue to question how to handle the long-term effects. SAMHSA noted anniversaries are a time to 1) acknowledge, normalize, and respond to painful memories and triggers; 2) recognize and remember losses associated with the disaster; 3) stop and assess accomplishments; 4) recognize stakeholders who support the recovery process; and 5) promote resiliency and healing. However, it is essential to know the community, how it is healing, and how it will react to any planned event. The anniversary can enhance resiliency, but it can also renew feelings of grief, anxiety, and sadness, as well as trigger emotional distress.

Reader's Notes

10

Road Map

Chapter 10 Preview
A. Collaboration Pre-Disaster Planning
B. Disaster Response
C. Post-Disaster
D. Long-Term Activities

(For details and more information, refer to Chapter 3)

A. Collaboration Pre-Disaster Planning

1. Name initial convener(s) of the disaster mental health action plan;
2. Determine how many and which individuals for core group;
3. Make a list of collaboration members representing diversity of community;
4. Meet with the area emergency management director about existing medical plan;
5. Name collaboration facilitator;
6. Hold orientation/kickoff meeting;
7. Establish MOA and legal considerations;
8. Define vision and mission, structural approach, and ethical considerations;
9. Finalize all members' roles and responsibilities on collaboration and/or at disaster site;
10. Determine mental health community assessment approach;
11. Research disaster types and potential of occurring;
12. Develop a list of trained CCP/PFA volunteers;
13. Make a list of local licensed trauma-informed therapists;
14. Establish relationships with government and nonprofit disaster mental health responders for backup CCP/PFA volunteers;
16. Develop communication plan for all disaster stages; and
17. Begin community education process to build resiliency.

B. Disaster Response

1. Mobilize and deploy all leaders and coordinators;
2. Initiate phone chain through the call center and contact CCP/PFA volunteers and trauma-informed therapists for the psychological services center;
3. Set up shelter locations if needed;
4. Register all volunteers and trauma-informed therapists at the volunteer center;
5. Set up free psychological services center(s); and
6. Implement communication plan.

C. Post-Disaster

1. Continue communication, shelter operations, and free psychological services as needed;
2. Reassess action plan and make necessary changes;

3. Apply for funding for additional mental health services;
4. Promote importance of seeking mental health support, particularly with at-risk groups and first responders;
5. Sponsor appreciation event for volunteers and first responders; and
6. Establish community foundation for incoming funds.

D. Long-Term Activities

1. Update action plan on regular basis, as well as contact names and phone numbers;
2. Continue to train volunteers and hold exercises;
3. Plan regular resiliency activities;
4. Continue to share latest information on trauma-informed, brain-based treatments among mental health practitioners;
5. Consider developing a communitywide wellness or resiliency center; and
6. Sponsor wellness workshops to address compassion fatigue for volunteers, first responders, and mental health professionals.

Reader's Notes

11

Conclusion

While this manual was close to final submission for publishing, the Arkansas floods, called "horrible scenes," worsened as rains continued to fall, with the threat of Tropical Storm Barry bringing more heavy precipitation over the next several days. Exhausted Oklahoma residents cleaned out their muddied homes as the Arkansas River kept rising hundreds of miles downstream. Just a week before, 53 tornadoes twirled and touched down in eight states from Idaho to Colorado, along with hail the size of tennis balls. Areas of North Carolina, swamped by Hurricane Florence a year earlier, were experiencing a drought, with precipitation eight inches below normal.

As expected, the storms are taking their mental health toll. Looking back on 2017, the University of Texas Health Science Center at Houston School of Public Health (Linder, 2018) reported that over half the residents of Harris County Texas said they were still struggling to recover four months after Hurricane Harvey soaked the Houston area and displaced one-third of the population. The national rate of serious psychological distress (SPD) is 14%. Following Harvey, 18% of Harris County residents showed signs of SPD. With people who had serious damage to their vehicles, the number rose to 37%; among those with serious home damage, the number spiked to 48%. In contrast, a 2010 survey of the Houston area found 8% of residents met the scientific criteria for SPD.

The Nebraska Farmers Union is very concerned about its members' mental health, according to its president, John Hansen (Simpson, 2019), and has been regularly publicizing a hotline number for those who need help. Because of their economic ups and downs, farmers typically have had a higher incidence of mental health distress and suicide. On a more positive note, farmers are less hesitant about seeking help. Increasing awareness of mental health and emotional wellbeing in the media has helped reduce the stigma. Nebraskan mental health workers likewise reported that the number of people needing help since the flooding has grown exponentially (Young, 2019).

The following two mental health organizations have demonstrated many of the principles noted in this book: Trillium Health Resources and Colorado Crisis Education and Response Network (CoCERN). Trillium is a Local Management Entity-Managed Care Organization (LME/NCO) that manages mental health, substance use, and intellectual/developmental disability services in eastern North Carolina. Trillium does not provide direct care but partners with agencies and licensed therapists to off er services to people in or near their own communities.

CASE STUDY: Trillium Health Services in North Carolina

The North Carolina region has been bombarded by hurricanes for decades. Cindy Ehlers, MS, LPC, born and raised in North Carolina, is executive vice president of clinical operations at Trillium Health Resources, where she has worked for 25 years. Ehlers said she has thus far personally experienced 75 hurricanes during her life; her 75-year-old mother has not forgotten Hurricane Hazel that hit in 1954; the death toll was somewhere between 400 and 1,000 in the U.S. and Canada. Ehlers has too often seen the physical and psychological devastation caused by storms, especially the 2018 Hurricanes Florence and Michael. Over the years, Ehlers and her team have gone well beyond responding to post-disaster mental health needs. They have also emphasized prevention and continuous improvement efforts.

A few days before Hurricane Florence, they contacted their 4,500-plus patients to ensure they had an evacuation plan and necessary medication and personal health items. Ehlers's team then helped anyone who had not yet met these needs. During the ten days of the storm, they took over 900 calls on their crisis hotline. Many of these people had been evacuated to shelters and were experiencing anxiety and panic attacks; some had suicidal thoughts. From 2018 to the beginning of the hurricane season in 2019, this same team knocked on the doors of over 250,000 residents in eastern North Carolina to see if the residents needed any support, were educated about PTSD, and linked to any services and resources needed to get back on their feet.

Ehlers has stories that are difficult to hear, but all too real. She may be a vice president, but she has continued to help with the crisis hotline. At the height of Hurricane Florence, she took a call about two men, both autistic and nonverbal, who had been evacuated by boat from their house to a shelter. One of them was also a fragile diabetic. Their legal guardian was incapacitated and taken to the hospital just days before the storm, and only a family friend was there to look after them. No one at the shelter was prepared to meet their personal needs. Ehlers worked from her remote evacuation location in Richmond, Virginia, to help relocate these young men to a nearby group home with a nursing staff. She talked by phone to providers in North Carolina to make sure their needs were met. Ehlers and other mental health providers—from Puerto Rico, for example—have related very disturbing stories about people who could not leave their homes because of an infirm family member. When the power went off, some of these ailing people died without technical support, such as oxygen machines. In some cases, these homes were not evacuated for a week or more.

Ehlers said she appreciated the support of the Red Cross, FEMA, and other national concerns during the storm, yet she stressed how her local knowledge is crucial for the wellbeing of the survivors. She and her team have become very familiar with the geographical area—a mix of cities, towns, and very rural locations—and the particular needs of the most at-risk individuals. Trillium has the ability to quickly answer any questions that arise on the location of victims, shelters, and available mental health providers. Also, several times in the past, the roads have quickly become impassable, and no one but local support teams can get to those in need. Then, survivors have to rely solely on local volunteers. Ehlers humbly said of her role, "This is where I belong. I am a public servant doing what I can to help."

CASE STUDY: Colorado Crisis Education and Response Network (CoCERN)

CoCERN is a newly created multi-agency, inclusive, and organized collaborative network for behavioral health disaster response. Over the years, Colorado has faced many different forms of natural and human-caused disasters, such as several mass shootings, wildfires, infectious disease, avalanches, and floods. Colorado ranks eighth in the size of American states, with only about six million people; Denver is the largest city with 700,000 people. With a home-rule status, Colorado has a state-supervised and county-administered human services system. County departments are the main providers of direct services to the state's families, children, and adults. From a mental health standpoint, the state has significantly fewer than the number of psychiatric beds needed.

The development of a collaborative such as CoCERN is very practical given these mental health constraints. Curt Drennen, PsyD, RN, at the Colorado

Department of Public Health and Environment/Emergency Preparedness and Response, said this collaboration was formed to provide efficient and effective services to survivors, responders, responder families, and the public after any large-scale disastrous event. Co-CERN's mission rests on the following characteristics:

1. Trust is required for effective partnerships. All CoCERN partner agencies are to act with a trust in the whole and to support each other in their primary missions;

2. Collaboration is necessary for the ongoing collaboration of individuals from different organizations and agencies and must be part of all levels of planning and response processes;

3. Cooperation is a core responsibility of all partnering organizations and must exist at all levels of planning and response;

4. Coordination ensures that CoCERN, which is a body functioning with multiple parts, works together respectfully before, during, and after a response effort.

5. Strong, clear communication is a necessity for a strong disaster response; and

6. Inclusion is critical because CoCERN strives to meet the needs of all Colorado citizens during crisis and recovery. Thus CoCERN works with all survivors, regardless of national origin, political affiliation, sexual orientation, and religious/faith-based background. It will reach out to any and all in need and work deliberately to prevent any inappropriate marketing or proselytizing during a disaster response.

CoCERN may be activated for behavioral health response if the local disaster resources are depleted or overwhelmed. When requested, the partners provide support and services to the lead local responding health agency or organization, survivors, responders and/or their families, and the public after any large-scale event. Support includes mental health services to survivors and/or responders. The collaborative is governed by a council comprising individuals from area agencies and organizations, who have agreed to this responsibility and been given the authority by their agencies. Some of the partners include the Colorado Department of Human Services, the Colorado Department of Public Health and Environment, the American Red Cross, Colorado Victim Assistance, and the Salvation Army, in addition to several mental health centers and clinics.

This strict agreement by CoCERN members to adhere to their roles and responsibilities is notable. Not only did these organizations collaborate to develop a disaster mental health plan, but they also took the additional step of being responsible for its implementation. After the disaster, the members assess results and determine the best ways to make necessary improvements. Included in CoCERN's "best lessons" are:

Be there from the beginning, and let others know you will be there in the end. You know the community best and can bring continuity to the disaster response/recovery;

It takes an entire community for disaster response. Participation in a local healthcare coalition and other pre-disaster planning/partnerships supports awareness of community and emergency partners who may benefit each other not just during disasters, but also day to day;

Behavioral health relationships with emergency and recovery managers and participation in emergency operation centers help ensure behavioral health is integrated early and throughout community response and recovery;

It is one thing to have a plan or a policy about what happens during a disaster, but true preparedness happens only when you train, exercise, and revise those plans and take time to build relationships;

Before responding, your team needs to know how members will communicate with their agencies during a disaster;

When disaster response is a volunteer capacity drawing on agency staff, it is good to have participation in the disaster response team throughout the agency so no one team, service, or program feels the impact of off-site work; and

It is better to respond than not respond at all because the community knows you will be there.

Drennen said CoCERN members willingly offer resources and support to others who are facing similar challenges. There is no need to reinvent the wheel, but rather to make adjustments to suit each collaboration's community needs. Drennen has stark memories of the Columbine High School shooting and said that, compared to the response to that event and the 2002 Hayman forest fire, the state has come a long way in having a major impact on mental health stigma in its communities.

INTERVIEW: Professionals United for Parkland (PU4P)

Robert W. Schmidt, co-author of this manual, had the opportunity to visit the Marjory Stoneman Douglas High School in Parkland, Florida, for a staff work day. He taught the staff how to use EFT/tapping for stress management. He also interviewed Luna Medina-Wolf, LMHC, CRC, MCAP, and president of Professionals United for Parkland (PU4P), a group that was started after the tragedy occurred. This organization offers another example of how communities faced with new challenges after a disaster can create an organization to support mental health.

SCHMIDT: When did PU4P first get started?

MEDINA-WOLF: Initially it was a Facebook group created by Melissa based on the lists Les and I created. Then a group of professionals met on 2/18/18 to discuss how we can help the community. We started the process to become a nonprofit in March 2018, a little more than a month after the Marjory Stoneman Douglas tragedy in Parkland, Florida. 9/14/18 was our official nonprofit status.

SCHMIDT: So PU4P is a 501(c)(3)?

MEDINA-WOLF: Yes, that makes it much easier for us to collect donations.

SCHMIDT: I met some of the officers when I was in Parkland in January. Could you tell me the names of all the founding members?

MEDINA-WOLF: The people who got it going were Melissa Buffington, Les Gordon, Judith Aronson-Ramos, Shane Friedman, Lisa Zucker, and me.

SCHMIDT: What is the mission of PU4P?

MEDINA-WOLF: Here's a copy of our mission statement. You will find it on our website:

Professionals United for Parkland was created to identify and meet the short- and long-term needs related to mental health/wellbeing of the south Florida community in the aftermath of the Marjory Stoneman Douglas tragedy through evidence-based services including: education for the general community and professionals, clinical training, clinical services, support for clinicians, and more. We work alongside other local organizations and groups to ensure that we identify gaps in current services and that the needs of our community are being adequately addressed. We are entirely nonpolitical.

SCHMIDT: Tell me about some of PU4P's activities.

MEDINA-WOLF: PU4P provides a directory of accessible trauma-informed therapists. We facilitate the creation and promotion of trauma and grief clinical
training. We assess the mental health needs of the community and provide
support in the form of training, consultation, group therapy, and a directory
for referrals.

SCHMIDT: Are all the members alumni of Florida Atlantic University? Are they all
counselors?

MEDINA-WOLF: No, not at all. We have people from all over the community from
all occupations.

SCHMIDT: What does PU4P do to raise money?

MEDINA-WOLF: Mostly social media. We are currently planning a 5K run.

SCHMIDT: What has changed in PU4P since you began?

MEDINA-WOLF: Initially, we had many volunteers who offered their counseling
services pro bono. We considered applying for grants, but determined it
was not feasible. That's when we created the list of trauma-informed therapists. We made a requirement for therapists who wanted to be on the
list that they see at least two families pro bono a year. Now we are more
focused on training and education, along with finalizing vetting the therapists on the list.

SCHMIDT: How many therapists are on the list?

MEDINA-WOLF: At first, there were about 300, but it has dropped to only 25.
However, we just began the re-vetting process a few months ago. I suspect
some of our members wonder if there may not be a need anymore.

SCHMIDT: Are you saying people don't need counseling anymore?

MEDINA-WOLF: Absolutely not! People still need counseling and will likely continue needing counseling for a long time. Thankfully, after the two deaths
by suicide, the town reacted by creating "Eagle's Haven." It's a wellness center funded by Children Services Counsel (CSC) and operated by an agency
called JAFCO.

SCHMIDT: Who staffs the center, and what do they offer?

MEDINA-WOLF: They are all licensed professionals who often refer from the PU4P
therapist lists and other community agencies. They offer activities like yoga,
music therapy, art therapy, kickboxing, and tai chi. You see, the town has
increased funding for mental health services, and CSC is applying for a
VOCA (Victims of Crime Act) grant for these services.

SCHMIDT: Do you have any suggestions for those who want to start an organization in their community like PU4P?

MEDINA-WOLF: They should connect with the community agencies early on rather than compete with other groups. We are doing it now, and people are excited and want to be involved and connected. I would suggest they look for people who are experienced in marketing an organization, someone with community outreach or legal experience. It's also helpful to connect with political leaders.

SCHMIDT: You just described what we covered in our book: The need for collaboration early on. Thank you so much for your time and for all the good things you are doing. (See www.PU4P for more information.)

One of the aims of this manual is to encourage communities to place an emphasis on disaster mental health prevention rather than reaction. Granted, the case studies and lessons learned in this manual are primarily about communities not developing a plan until disaster came their way. However, the individuals involved in these catastrophes agreed that strategically responding to a crisis while it is occurring is much more effective than doing so "after the fact." Many unnecessary mistakes are made when decisions are made on the fly, which can have a detrimental impact on those involved.

Effective disaster mental health preparedness, response, and recovery depend on collaboration among many levels of relationships. Agencies, organizations, neighborhood groups and public human service systems need to join their efforts to plan critically and strategically. This relationship building also includes collaboration across disciplines and sectors in order to impact the socioeconomic, cultural, and political forces shaping the community (Gil-Rivas & Kilmer, 2016). In the best situation, such partnerships will take place before a disaster occurs. They should respond to the disaster's and community's uniqueness and be able to quickly change to fit unexpected challenges (Norris, Stevens, Pfefferbaum, Wyche, & Pfefferbaum, 2008). "Central to this approach is an emphasis on reorganizing communities' strengths and developing empowering collaborations with community groups and organizations, with the goal of increasing community capacity to manage the demands associated with disaster," (Gil-Rivas & Kilmer, 2016).

Collaborative preparedness leads to much better outcomes—in the short- and long-term for everyone involved—by significantly reducing the survivors' high levels of stress and anxiety. It is hoped that being proactive also increases the number of individuals who receive trauma-informed treatment before the onset of PTSD and suicidal thoughts (or, regrettably, actions). The right plan builds resiliency for all community residents who are facing a large number of challenges even without facing a disastrous event. By integrating the four principles of collaboration, communication, assessing vulnerable populations, and trauma-informed treatment, disasters may still have an impact on emotional wellbeing, but survivors can more quickly begin to rebuild their lives.

References

Gil-Rivas, V., & Kilmer, R. P. (2016). Building community capacity and fostering disaster resilience. *Journal of Clinical Psychology*, *72*(12), 1318–1332.

Linder, S. (2018, April 4). Unprecedented psychological distress months after hurricane Harvey: More than half of Harris county residents are still struggling. *Science Daily*. Retrieved from www.sciencedaily.com/releases/2018/04/180404143415.htm

Norris, F. H., Stevens, S. P., Pfefferbaum, B., Wyche, K. F., & Pfefferbaum, R. L. (2008). Community resilience as a metaphor, theory, set of capacities, and strategy for disaster readiness. *American Journal of Community Psychology*, *41*(1–2), 127–150.

Simpson, A. (2019, April 25). Farmers wash up 'in a Fragile Place' after historic Midwest floods. *Pew Trust*. Retrieved from www.pewtrusts.org/en/research-and-analysis/blogs/stateline/2019/04/25/farmers-wash-up-in-a-fragile-place-after-historic-midwest-floods

Young, J. (2019, March 27). Local mental health providers say need is great for care among Nebraska flood victims. *Lincoln Journal Star*. Retrieved from https://rapidcityjournal.com/news/local/mental-health-providers-say-need-is-great-for-care-among/article_1c1989ec-fe97-5de6-983e-cc260b86a44b.html#1

Reader's Notes

Appendix

General Resources

Community Mental Health Center Model Disaster Response Plan of New
Hampshire
https://webcache.googleusercontent.com/search?q=cache:kzXNQFzvNJ0J:www.
k-state.edu/kahbh/images/CMHC%2520model%2520disaster%2520response%
2520plan%2520Template%25201.doc+&cd=25&hl=en&ct=clnk&gl=us

Crisis Counseling and Assistance Training Program (CCP): www.samhsa.gov/
sites/default/files/images/fema-ccp-guidance.pdf

Disaster Behavioral Health: Resources at Your Fingertips
https://files.asprtracie.hhs.gov/documents/aspr-tracie-dbh-resources-at-your-fin
gertips.pdf

Disaster Literature
https://disasterinfo.nlm.nih.gov/search/?q=children+OR+child+OR+pediatric+
OR+infant+OR+newborn+OR+neonatal+OR+baby+OR+teen+OR+adolescent

Disaster Mental Health: A Critical Response
www.urmc.rochester.edu/MediaLibraries/URMCMedia/flrtc/preparedness-res
ponse-tools/documents/H_DMH_Part_Manual.pdf

Disaster Mental Health Preparedness in the Community: A Systematic Review
Study www.ncbi.nlm.nih.gov/pmc/articles/PMC5489140/

Disaster Mental Health Resources
www.phe.gov/emergency/events/sandy/Pages/mental-health.aspx

Disaster Planning Handbook for Behavioral Health Treatment Programs
https://store.samhsa.gov/system/files/sma13-4779.pdf

Disaster Relief and Recovery Services | American Red Cross
www.redcross.org/get-help/disaster-relief-and-recovery-services.html

Disaster Relief Services | Disaster Assistance | Red Cross
www.redcross.org/about-us/our-work/disaster-relief.html

Hurricane Relief | Tropical Storm Relief | Red Cross
www.redcross.org/about-us/our-work/disaster-relief/hurricane-relief.html

New Jersey Department of Human Services: Introduction to Disaster Mental Health and Crisis Counseling
www.state.nj.us/humanservices/dmhas/home/disaster/credentialing/DRCC_Training_Materials/Intro_Disaster_MH_Crisis_Counseling.pdf

Meditation Book

◆ Harris, Frank. (2017) *Meditation for Fidgety Skeptics*. New York: Spiegel and Grau.

Meditation: Free Websites

◆ Mindful Meditations. www.mindful.org/audio-resources-for-mindfulness-meditation/
◆ Tara Broch: Guided Meditations. www.tarabrach.com/guided-meditations/
◆ Guided Meditations: Chopra Center. *https://chopra.com/articles/guided-meditations*
◆ UCLA Guided Meditations. *www.uclahealth.org/marc/mindful-meditations*

Mental/Behavioral Health (Non-responders)

https://asprtracie.hhs.gov/technical-resources/68/mental-behavioral-health-non-responders/60

MNRI. Musgatova Neuro-Reflex Integration National Center
6275 Hazeltine National Dr., Orlando, FL 32822
https://masgutovamethod.com/

Multi-State Disaster Behavioral Health Consortium
www.nasmhpd.org/content/multi-state-disaster-behavioral-health-consortium

Nebraska Behavioral Health All-Hazards Disaster Response
www.disastermh.nebraska.edu/files/2018/stateplan/03-7-2018%20DBH%20State%20Plan%202017%20Plan%20Narrative.pdf

Newtown Sandy Hook Community Foundation (NSHCF). www.nshcf.org/

Psychological First Aid Guidebook: The PFA Guide for Field Workers to learn more about PFA at: www.who.int/mental_health/publications/guide_field_workers/en/

Recovering Financially | Disaster Relief | Red Cross
www.redcross.org/get-help/disaster-relief-and-recovery-

Resiliency Center of Newtown (RCN). https://resiliencycenterofnewtown.org/
Therapy Dogs Website: www.therapydogs.com

Trauma Specialists

- ♦ Gary Craig. Creator of EFT/tapping. www.emofree.com
- ♦ David Grand, PhD. Creator of Brainspotting. www.brainspotting.com
- ♦ Lori Leyden, PhD, MBA. International Trauma Specialist. www.createglobalhealing.org
- ♦ Bruce Perry, MD PhD. Child Trauma Academy. https://childtrauma.org/
- ♦ Deborah Del Vecchio-Scully, LPC. Trauma Specialist
- ♦ Francine Shapiro, PhD. Creator of EMDR. EMDR Institute. www.emdr.com/francine-shapiro-ph-d/
- ♦ Bessel Van der Kolk, MD. Neuroscience of Trauma. https://besselvanderkolk.net/
- ♦ The Trauma Center at Justice Resource Institute. www.traumacenter.org/

Index

Note: Numbers in *italics* indicate a figure

For Product Safety Concerns and Information please contact our EU
representative GPSR@taylorandfrancis.com
Taylor & Francis Verlag GmbH, Kaufingerstraße 24, 80331 München, Germany

www.ingramcontent.com/pod-product-compliance
Lightning Source LLC
Chambersburg PA
CBHW080234270326
41926CB00020B/4227